CANADIAN SOCIETY:

Pluralism, Change, and Conflict

edited by

RICHARD J. OSSENBERG

University of Calgary
Calgary, Alberta

P

PRENTICE-HALL ✦ OF CANADA LTD.

Scarborough h Ontario

PRENTICE-HALL, INC., ENGLEWOOD CLIFFS, NEW JERSEY
PRENTICE-HALL INTERNATIONAL, INC., LONDON
PRENTICE-HALL OF AUSTRALIA, PTY., LTD., SYDNEY
PRENTICE-HALL OF INDIA, PVT., LTD., NEW DELHI
PRENTICE-HALL OF JAPAN, INC., TOKYO

Library of Congress Catalog Card No. 76-134454
0-13-113282-2 (pa.)/
0-13-113290-3 (cl.)/
1 2 3 4 5 75 74 73 72 71

PRINTED IN CANADA

Contents

Preface

This volume grew out of the 1967 Summer Institute on Canadian Society held at the University of Calgary in Calgary, Alberta, Canada. The Institute, planned and hosted by the Department of Sociology and Anthropology and co-sponsored by the Division of Continuing Education, brought to Calgary a number of guest lecturers who had distinguished themselves through their studies of various aspects of Canadian society.[1]

The main purpose of the Institute was to introduce to both the academic and wider communities the ideas held by the visiting lecturers about the fundamental social structure, evolution, and social problems of Canada at a strategic time in her development — the Centennial of Confederation.

All of the authors in this volume participated in the Institute and their papers are based largely on the lectures they presented. While differing in focus, the articles have a number of common approaches. First, the authors have approached their subjects from a *macroanalytical* perspective or, as one of them phrases it, the "big picture" point of view, which avoids the trees that so often obscure the forest. In this respect, detailed data are treated only in the context of their theoretical and heuristic relevance. Second, the authors have provided historical material relevant to their subjects, thus offering evolutionary and dynamic dimensions which are often lacking in social science documents. It is my conviction that social analysis without consideration of historical factors is barren of seminal properties. Ahistorical studies can only capture a momentary and perhaps distorted fragment of social causality. Third, wherever possible, the authors have introduced comparative materials in the belief that a society cannot be properly understood unless its similarities to and differences from other societies are considered. It is my hope that a meaningful definition of Canada has come closer to our grasp because of the comparative emphasis found in this volume. Finally, the authors share a tolerance for an open-ended theoretical and methodological approach to studies in the social sciences; understanding can be achieved from many different sources and through many different avenues. There are no rigid and unchanging canons in the social sciences; nor indeed are there

---

[1] In addition to the contributors to this volume, the visiting lecturers included Bernard Blishen, George Grant, Edward Gross, Harry Hawthorn, Frank Jones, Mason Wade, and J. F. C. Wright.

in any scientific discipline because the essence of the scientific enterprise is discovery and innovation.

Some of the authors, including the editor, take strong positions in their treatment and interpretation of their subjects which may alarm adherents to the myth of "value-free" social science. Many of the great problems and injustices in Canada are boldly labelled. They are not merely described as "the nature of things" as they might be by "value-free" analysts who, by so doing, may actually be manifesting a subjective endorsement of the status quo. However, others in this volume represent the more classical stance of "neutrality" and thus help to provide the fuller range of theoretical positions which was one of my primary goals.

This volume is not a comprehensive treatment of Canadian society as a whole; instead, selected aspects of Canadian society are examined in their broad structural and historical dimensions with some flavour of regional differences. There is more than the usual emphasis given to Canada's minorities, especially French Canadians and Native Peoples who are often treated as incidental in books and papers dealing with the nature of Canadian society. The "hinterland" of Canada is treated as being of the same importance as the "metropolis", reflecting the view of the editor and some of the other authors that Canada, in contrast to other industrial societies, contains a strategic and pervasive duality between "metropolis" and "hinterland" and that unduly great emphasis given to urban-industrial topics would miss, by a wide margin, the very essence of Canadian society.

The articles all deal, in some way, with Canada's social class structure and ethnic group relations. The authors, in various ways, underline the *pluralism* of Canada where clear distinctions between social class and ethnic groups have been traditionally encouraged — in contradistinction to the assimilationist *ideal,* most fully expressed in the United States. Some of the negative aspects of Canada's pluralism are discussed, especially the inevitable conflicts stemming from the maintenance of group distinctions during a time of rapid social change and widespread uncertainty. On the other hand, the potential of Canada's pluralistic social diversity in stimulating fresh responses to urgent problems of change and development is also intimated.

For the completion of this volume, I am indebted to many individuals and organizations. The idea of a summer session consisting of distinguished visiting lecturers, which was to become the Summer Institute on Canadian Society, originated with Clement D. Blakeslee, formerly of the Department of Sociology and Anthropology, University of Calgary. Some of my own ideas about Canadian society, as well as societies generally, were influenced through the many exciting and stimulating discussions I had with Professor Blakeslee. Dr. Donald L. Mills, formerly Chairman of Sociology and Anthropology, University of Calgary and presently Professor there, activated discussions about the Institute and called upon me to plan and coordinate the project. His assistance and encouragement helped to lighten a task which was exciting but sometimes burdensome.

I wish to also acknowledge the assistance and cooperation of the Division of Continuing Education, University of Calgary, especially its Director, Dr. Fred Terentiuk, and Administrative Assistant, Mr. Morris

Baskett. Both provided financial, administrative, and moral support for the Institute. I am also grateful to the University of Calgary for a grant to assist completion of the project and I thank Dr. Walter B. Trost, former Vice-President, for his assistance in securing financial support.

Thanks are due to Mr. Gerrard Halpin, Vice-President, and Mr. John White, Associate Editor, both of Prentice-Hall of Canada, for material support and considerable sympathy in dealing with a sometimes obstinate editor. Acknowledgment should also be extended to Mrs. Sarah Swartz for her excellent editorial and production work.

The authors who have contributed to this volume have given me both encouragement and immense gratification. Their sympathetic and generous responses to my suggestions for themes and editorial minutae surpassed my expectations. I am delighted and proud to have been associated with them in this cooperative venture.

A special acknowledgment is due to Dr. A. K. Davis, Department of Sociology, University of Alberta, Edmonton. Dr. Davis assisted me in the editing of the volume and his suggestions and encouragement were invaluable. His contribution to the volume warranted a co-editorship, but he resisted my persistent attempts to corral him into that role.

R.J.O.

Contributors

PETER CARSTENS

Peter Carstens is Professor of Anthropology at the University of Toronto.

Before joining the Faculty of that University, he was lecturer in Social Anthropology in the School of African Studies at the University of Cape Town from 1956-64. During the academic year 1964-65, he was visiting Associate Professor at the University of North Carolina, Chapel Hill.

Dr. Carstens was educated at Rhodes University and the University of Cape Town and holds degrees in both Sociology and Social Anthropology. While on sabbatical leave from South Africa (1962-63), Dr. Carstens carried out fieldwork among several Canadian Indian groups in British Columbia. This research was supported by a Koerner Foundation Fellowship from the University of British Columbia. In South Africa, he carried out extensive research in the Coloured Reserves of the Cape Province and Southwest Africa.

Dr. Carstens is the author of *The Social Structure of a Cape Coloured Reserve: A Study of Racial Integration and Segregation in South Africa* (1966).

S. D. CLARK

S. D. Clark is Professor in the Department of Sociology, University of Toronto, a department which he founded and chaired for many years.

Born in Saskatchewan, Dr. Clark is a graduate of the University of Saskatchewan where he also began his graduate work, followed by advanced studies at the University of Toronto, London School of Economics, and McGill University. He received his Ph.D. from the University of Toronto.

In 1960, Dr. Clark was awarded the Tyrell Medal by the Royal Society of Canada and he is a Fellow of that Society. In 1960-61, he was Visiting Professor of Sociology, University of California, Berkeley. Dr. Clark is a Council Member of the International Sociological Society and Honorary President of the Canadian Sociology and Anthropology Association.

Dr. Clark's publications are numerous and comprehensive in scope. Among his notable contributions to the social history of Canada are *The Social Development of Canada* (1942) and *Movements of Political Protest in Canada: 1640-1840* (1959). His parallel interest in the contemporary community is reflected in books such as *The Developing Canadian Community* (1962, 1968), and *The Suburban Community* (1966). His chapter in this volume is reflective of his continuous interest in the sociological context of economic and political pressure groups, initiated by his study, *The Canadian Manufacturers Association: A Study in Collective Bargaining and Political Pressure* (1939).

ARTHUR K. DAVIS

Arthur K. Davis grew up in northern New England, and received his three degrees from Harvard, where he studied under Talcott Parsons and the late P. A. Sorokin. He taught sociology and related social sciences at Harvard, Union College, Columbia University, University of Pennsylvania, and University of Vermont. In 1958, he moved to Saskatchewan, where for six years he headed the research wing of the Centre for Community Studies in Saskatoon. He became Professor of Sociology and Anthropology at the University of Calgary in 1964, and since 1968 has been Professor of Sociology at the University of Alberta.

His interest in developing a metropolis-versus-hinterland perspective for Canadian society stems in large part from the influence of such Canadian economic historians as Innis and Fowke; from the neo-Marxian American political economists Paul Sweezy, Paul Baran and Andre Frank; and the historian William A. Williams. Now a naturalized Canadian, he attributes the jelling of his present views to his experiences on the Canadian prairies during the last dozen years.

Professor Davis has published papers on such varied topics as social theory, Thorstein Veblen, urban Indians in western Canada and modern Chinese history.

FREDERICK ELKIN

Frederick Elkin is Professor of Sociology at York University, Toronto.

He was born in the United States and received his B.A., M.A., and Ph.D. at the University of Chicago. He has taught at the University of Missouri (1951-52), McGill University (1952-62), Université de Montréal (1962-64) and York. He has served as Chairman of the Department of Sociology at York (1964-69) and as Acting Dean of Graduate Studies (1968-69). He has had research positions at the Motion Picture Association of America, National Opinion Research Center, and Defence Research Board of Canada, and has served as research consultant for the Vanier Institute of the Family, and Boys Village.

His publications include *Child and Society* (1960), *The Family in Canada* (1964), and numerous chapters in books and articles in learned journals. His major areas of interest include mass media, social psychology, and the family.

OSWALD HALL

Oswald Hall, born in Prince Albert, Saskatchewan, is Professor of Sociology at the University of Toronto.

Prior to joining the University of Toronto in 1956, Dr. Hall taught at several universities in both Canada and the United States, including McGill University, Brown University, Tulane University, and the University of Chicago.

Following the completion of his B.A. degree at Queen's University in 1935, Dr. Hall continued his studies and was awarded an M.A. at McGill University in 1937, and completed his Ph.D. at the University of Chicago in 1944.

Dr. Hall's extensive research and publications in the area of occupations and professions have related to his wide experience in posts connected with both universities and Canadian government organizations, including his position as Research Supervisor of the Royal Commission on Bilingualism and Biculturalism, 1964-66.

JAMES N. McCRORIE

James N. McCrorie is a native of Montreal and a graduate of McGill University. After receiving his B.A., he was awarded for two years the Saskatchewan Field Fellowship offered by the Centre for Community Studies in Saskatoon. During these two years in the early 1960's, he immersed himself in a study of the history and present status of the Saskatchewan farmers' movement. This became his Ph.D. dissertation at the University of Illinois, and also led to a publication, *In Union is Strength* (1965).

For two years, Dr. McCrorie was Director of Research and Education for the Saskatchewan Farmers' Union, Saskatchewan. In 1966, he joined the Sociology Department of the University of Saskatchewan, Regina Campus. After an intervening year at The University of Calgary, he returned in 1969 to head the Sociology Department at Regina.

He maintains close contact with various farm, labour and other interest groups on the Saskatchewan scene.

JAMES MACDONALD MINIFIE

James M. Minifie was born in Burton, Staffs., England and educated at Lichfield Grammar School until he emigrated to Canada in 1912. His family settled on a homestead near Vanguard, Saskatchewan, and he continued his schooling at Malvern Link School until joining the Canadian Army in March, 1916. After World War I, Mr. Minifie attended Regina College and the University of Saskatchewan. He is the holder of an O.B.E., B.A., and LL.D.

A Rhodes Scholar, he read English at Oriel College, Oxford, before attending the Sorbonne. He joined the New York Herald Tribune in 1929, served in its Paris bureau, and covered the Spanish Civil War. He was head of the paper's Rome bureau from 1937 to 1940. While serving in the London bureau, he was injured in the blitz during the early years of World War II. He covered the White House from 1941 to 1943 when he joined the Office of Strategic Services. In May 1953, he became Washington Correspondent of the Canadian Broadcasting Corporation.

Mr. Minifie is author of *Peacemaker or Powder-Monkey?* (1960), *Open at the Top* (1964), and *Who's Your Fat Friend?* (1967). Acting now as radio conslutant and contributor for the C.B.C., he is currently working on *Homesteader,* an autobiographic record of prairie pioneering years ago, before the days of instant mass media.

RICHARD J. OSSENBERG

Richard J. Ossenberg is Associate Professor of Sociology at the University of Calgary.

Born in Buffalo, New York, Dr. Ossenberg first migrated to Canada in 1961 and became a Canadian citizen in 1969. He received his B.S. and M.A. from the University of Buffalo, and was awarded his Ph.D. by the State University of New York at Buffalo in 1966.

Following exploratory research on French-English relations in Montreal, Dr. Ossenberg taught at York University, Toronto, and conducted research relating to community action programs in New Haven, Connecticut. He moved to Calgary in 1965.

Dr. Ossenberg is past Program Director of the Canadian Sociology and Anthropology Association, and President of the Western Association of Sociology and Anthropology. His major research concern is the development of a general sociology of Canada. His studies have included a social reconstruction of the history of French-English relations, "The Conquest Revisited: Another Look at Canadian Dualism," in *The Canadian Review of Sociology and Anthropology* (1967), and research on poverty in Calgary for the Government of Alberta, *Community Opportunity Assessment: Calgary Study* (1967).

FRANK G. VALLEE

Frank G. Vallee is Professor and former Chairman, Department of Sociology and Anthropology, Carleton University, Ottawa. He received his B.A. degree from McGill University and his Ph.D. at London, 1955.

Dr. Vallee's research over the past several years has been primarily concerned with the problems and dynamics of ethnic group relations in Canada, especially the Indians and Eskimos, and the situation of the French Canadians outside of the Province of Quebec. *Kabloona and Eskimo in the Central Keewatin* (1967) is one volume among several publications by Dr. Vallee, based on his extensive research.

Dr. Vallee has served as an appointed member of the Northwest Territories Legislative Council (1964-67) and as consultant to several government agencies. Currently on sabbatical leave in Hawaii, Dr. Vallee is continuing his studies of comparative ethnic relations.

The
Canadian
Dialectic:

Hinterland Versus Metropolis

1

EDITOR'S INTRODUCTION

Sociology, similar to all other academic disciplines, abounds in fads and fallacies, many of which are accepted as "reality". The process of becoming a member of any profession, academic or otherwise, referred to as "secondary socialization", generally calls for a constriction of the initiate's ideas in order to conform to the well-defined and encapsulated set of expectations which provides each profession with its distinctive but narrow boundaries. This process invariably results in "closure"; ideas which do not fall within the limited range deemed as "relevant" are automatically discarded or treated with less than passionate enthusiasm. Sociology, which has pretended to transcend this process by being a "generalizing" science is, unfortunately, a good example of this fault. A basic understanding of social behaviour has not been achieved; the ability to predict, even over the short run, is virtually non-existent. As Gross has stated, "Our darkness appears to stem less from the shortage of time or talent than from the prevalent run of intellectual folkways, beliefs that set the course of academic thinking and tend, in some instances, to shut out the ill born and the institutionally unsponsored."[1]

As pointed out by Davis in the following article, an understanding of the nature of Canadian society has been severely hampered because of the "vested interests" of social scientists who, in more or less accepting the functionalist frame of reference in the analysis of social behaviour, have conformed to a professional expectation particularly widespread among sociologists which may have only limited relevance to reality. Functionalism, which is the most commonly accepted conceptual framework among social scientists, either explicitly or implicitly accepts the premise that all "normal" states of societies are characterized by "equilibrium", the general sharing of similar values and norms, and the universal transcendence of the group over the individual; pervasive and inherent social conflict is either ignored or considered to be abnormal.

But as Davis clearly shows, the social evolution of both Canada and the United States can be seen as a series of pivotal turning points brought about by social conflicts between different economic and cultural interest groups, especially between competing elites, as in the case of the American northern and southern capitalist groups which precipitated the Civil War, or between metropolis and hinterland as expressed in the Canadian conflicts between prairie populism and the eastern financial establishment.

[1] Llewellyn Z. Gross, ed., *Symposium on Sociological Theory* (New York: Harper and Row, 1959), p. 1.

3

Davis discusses numerous other conflicts between different groups in both Canada and the United States in an attempt to show the direct relevance of a "dialectic" or conflict model in the interpretation of Canadian society. One of the most significant differences between both countries, as Davis suggests, is the continuation of basic and pervasive social conflict, expressed in political ideologies, in Canada, compared to the decrease in oppositional ideologies in the United States. Thus, Quebec separatism, with a generally socialistic basis, and prairie populism, expressed in the popular support of the C.C.F. in Saskatchewan, as well as the National New Democrtic Party, are viable oppositional forces. In a sense, conflict in Canada, largely reflecting the nature of Canadian pluralism, has become institutionalized or "built into" the system. In the United States, on the other hand, the "oversuccess" of capitalism, as discussed by Davis, has resulted in massive absorption of political and economic interest groups which had or would have developed anti-establishment ideologies. In sociological parlance, potentially oppositional economic or ethnic groups, with a few notable exceptions, have become assimilated or acculturated. It may be more realistic, however, to consider the process as one of co-optation or manipulation, but these terms have not been admitted to the sacred but distorted realm of sociological jargon.

The importance of analyzing Canadian society in terms of her intimate historical and contemporary links with the United States is also stressed by Davis. The fact of massive American economic penetration into and control over Canadian industry is now commonly known but the implications of this penetration have not been fully analyzed. Almost all Canadian institutions, ranging from the economy to the family and religion, have been affected in some way by the American presence. The basic profile of the social class system in Canada is a mirror image of that of the United States, but for variations in ethnic composition of the various classes and perceptions of the meaning of social class.

Reaction and opposition to the American influence have also been important factors in the development of Canadian society. The development of the Canadian West with its accompanying surge for Canadian sovereignty was vital in establishing both geographical and social boundaries to Canada. These and other forms of reaction are discussed by Davis. During the earlier development of Canada, the American influence was also considerable although the reaction to it was far more complex. The American revolution and the numerous invasions of Canada around that time brought a complexity of reactions. The lower class French Canadians welcomed these incursions as a means for emancipation from both the English and French colonial elite, while members of the latter group opposed it in order to retain their power and block the developing aspirations of the French Canadian masses.[2]

[2] R. J. Ossenberg, "The Conquest Revisited; Another Look at Canadian Dualism", *Canadian Review of Sociology and Anthropology*, IV, No. 4 (November, 1967), pp. 201-218.

Davis's suggestion that the socialization of Canada is a necessary step to independence may cause some consternation to "apolitical" social scientists who believe in the fictitious "value free" or "neutral" view of society and who thereby perhaps unwittingly simply reflect their own endorsement of the ideology of social darwinism as first expounded by Herbert Spencer, a minority point of view in consideration of the history of ideas which led to the development of modern social science and certainly not one to be confused with progress.

But regardless of the images of society held by the reader, Davis's suggestion has considerable merit. No social scientist would deny the important role of the economic system in affecting social behaviour, although they may assign different weights to it. Structural similarities at the economic level tend to "level" the social differences that may have existed between two countries such as the United States and Canada. And political systems, being largely dependent upon economic systems, would tend to increasingly converge between the two countries. Therefore, a drastic departure from the American economic model, whether it be in the form that Davis suggests or otherwise, appears to be a necessary first step toward the future evolution of a distinctive and independent Canadian society.

Davis rightly underlines the importance of the conflict between separatist elements in Quebec and the rest of Canada but perhaps exaggerates the potential for Quebec separation. As I have attempted to demonstrate elsewhere in this volume, the internal conflicts within the French Canadian population have plagued the development of a viable French Canadian identity which would be a necessary first step to popular support for separation in Quebec province.

The following article presents the basis and rationale for a new conceptual approach to the analysis of Canadian society. Drastic new approaches to the study of Canada and other societies are called for, and what is especially urgent is an increased recognition of ideas and methodologies which are presently outside the narrow confines of an ideologically and conceptually impoverished social science.[3]

[3] Llewellyn Z. Gross, "Preface to a Metatheoretical Framework of Sociology", *American Journal of Sociology*, LXVII, No. 2 (September, 1961), pp. 125-143.

1

Canadian Society and History as Hinterland Versus Metropolis

ARTHUR K. DAVIS

THRUST AND DRIFT IN CANADIAN HISTORY: LOOKING BACK FROM 1967

The Centennial of 1967, on the surface, was a year of effervescence and affirmation for Canada. This was especially true in English Canada. But two of the most significant events of that year occurred in Quebec. One was the fabulous Expo 67 at Montreal. Here were the pavilions of the ascending metropolitan Great Powers, the Soviet Union and the United States; and those of such descending metropolitan empires as Great Britain and France. And here also were the exhibition buildings of hinterland communities — some of them on the upswing — like Cuba, Czechoslovakia, Mexico, the Arab Nations, Africa Place, Quebec, and the Indians of Canada. The metropoles of the world confronted the hinterlands of the world at Expo 67, and all made their declarations.

The second of the two significant events was the thunderous shout of Charles De Gaulle, President of France, somewhere in Quebec along the lower St. Lawrence River: "Vive le Québec libre." This slogan rattled the tea cups in Ottawa; indeed, it evoked screams of rage — a sign of insecurity on the part of the screamers, no doubt. One interpretation of the incident is that it may owe something to the sense of frivolity on the part of some of the University of Montreal students who helped to arrange the General's tour. Yet it can also be argued that De Gaulle's real target was the rival imperium at Washington, rather than Washington's Ottawa satellite. This points up a central concern of this article: the history, present stance, and future of the North American hinterlands vis-à-vis the United States empire. The South American hinterlands, beginning with Mexico, can be examined in a similar manner.[1] But these answers must wait.

Four themes emerge from our review of Canadian history since Confederation. One is the development of the western wheat economy,

[1] Visits to Mexico and to India in 1969 by the present writer persuaded him that the concept of North American society should be broadened to include Mexico as well as Canada, and that even such a vast canvas as the New World American empire may be too small in an economic and political sense, if we want to understand the modern world. Conspicuous in both Mexico City and New Delhi were neon signs, branch plants, and subsidiaries of American multinational corporations.

6

stemming from the "National Policy" that shaped up from Confederation. The second is the continuity of the French community in Quebec, despite — and even because of — its subordination to English Canada ever since the conquest of 1760. The third is the key importance of foreign imperialism throughout the entire development of Canadian society — mostly British but more recently American. The fourth is urbanization and the rise of urban industries in a capitalist context. The urban population of Canada first exceeded the rural population during the 1920's, and by 1966, about three Canadians out of four lived in urban centres. All these themes seem to be best viewed in terms of a metropolis-versus-hinterland frame of reference.

Looking back in 1967 over the English Canadian historical record, the milestones of change during the past two or three centuries were there for all to see and read. From a straggling line of colonial settlements along the St. Lawrence valley and the maritime region, a new nation — or perhaps a collection of regional communities — had emerged, built on fur-trading posts, fishing outports, timber exports, wheat exports, and oil and gas exports.[2] The pattern of export staples is still important, but manufacturing surpassed primary industries (agriculture, fisheries, forestry, mining) in the 1920's, and has continued to forge ahead.[3]

[2] The "staples theory of Canadian economic development" deserves our special attention. Cf. H.A. Innis, *The Fur Trade in Canada* (Toronto: University of Toronto Press, 1956); H.A. Innis, ed., *Essays in Canadian Economic History* (Toronto: University of Toronto Press, 1956); W. Easterbrook and H. Aitken, *Canadian Economic History* (Toronto: Macmillan, 1958); Deutsch, et al, *The Canadian Economy* (Toronto: Macmillan, 1962); W. Easterbrook and M. Watkins, *Approaches to Canadian Economic History* (Toronto: McClelland and Stewart, 1967).

[3] The contribution of manufacturers to gross national product was 105 per cent of all four primary industries for 1926-29; it was 205 per cent for 1953-56. Within the primary sector, mining (including oil) had risen to constitute about one-third of all primary production by the mid-1950's. See R. Leach, ed., *Contemporary Canada* (Toronto: University of Toronto Press, 1968), Chap. iv, esp. p. 84; figures cited from M. Urquhart and K. Buckley, *Historical Statistics of Canada* (Toronto: Unievrsity of Toronto Press, 1956), pp. 133, 141.

Other parameters substantiate the rising importance of manufacturing and the service industries relative to primary industries. The following is the per cent distribution of the employed labour force for 1946 and 1967.

	1946	1967
Agriculture and other primary industries	29.4%	10.6%
Manufacturing	26.0	23.8
Service (incl. public admin. & defense)	16.8	29.5
Trade	12.3	16.6
Transportation, Utilities	8.1	8.9
Construction	4.8	6.4
Financial, Insurance, Real Estate	2.7	4.2
TOTAL	100.1	100.0

Further, the net income of farm operators from farm production in 1966 was 5.1 per cent of net national income at factor cost — although farmers made up 7.6 per cent of the 1966 labour force. (*Canada Year Book*, 1968, pp. 759 and 1064).

From the standpoint of English Canada in 1967, the century of Confederation had been a pronounced success. The national policy of western settlement as a new "investment frontier" for Ontario and Montreal business and financial interests — a competitive Canadian reaction to the immense American industrial and agrarian expansion after the mid-nineteenth century — had achieved a great deal, not all of it intended. By 1885, the heavily subsidized all-Canadian railroad link between the maritimes and the Pacific had been forged, despite the thousand-mile barrier of rocky bushland north of the Great Lakes and in spite of the 600 miles of far-western mountain ranges. To make way for agricultural settlement on the prairies, the Indians had been shunted aside onto isolated reservations, and the rebellious Métis had been defeated at Batoche, Saskatchewan. The ill-advised hanging of the Métis leader Louis Riel at Regina in 1885 doubtlessly reinforced the resentment as well as the sense of subordination of both the French and the Indian underclass communities to the Anglo metropolitan elites of Toronto and Montreal.[4]

Another key aspect of the national policy — too little recognized — was the federal program of agricultural research to adapt techniques imported from the humid East to the semi-arid conditions of the western high plains.[5] Above all, low-cost land settlement policies in the western reaches were backed by strong government and business encouragement of massive immigration from Europe, Eastern Canada, and the United States. The Canadian achievement, seen in historical perspective, is truly of epic proportions. For eastern manufacturing interests, the high-tariff policy instituted in the 1870's was of prime importance.

By 1930, however, the wheat economy was over-established in the prairie provinces; the exodus of farmers from the Palliser dry triangle in southwestern Saskatchewan and southeastern Alberta to the forested fringe north of Prince Albert, Saskatchewan, and to the Peace River country in Alberta had begun during the 1920's. Indeed, although the number of farms in Saskatchewan reached a peak in 1936 and thereafter declined, the percentage of farms having 200 acres or less began declining

---

[4] Even so, pacification of the Indians was accomplished in Canada with much less violence than in the United States. We say this in full awareness of the near-deliberate extermination of the Beothuk-speaking Indians in Newfoundland by 1820. See D. Jenness, *Indians of Canada* (4th ed.) (Ottawa: National Museum of Canada, 1958), p. 266.

[5] The first of the Dominion Experimental Farms on the prairies was established in 1886. Over the next two or three generations, these research stations resolved a series of key problems, culminating perhaps in the salvaging of the semi-arid Palliser triangle in southeastern Alberta and southwestern Saskatchewan during the 1930's. James Gray writes: "The conquest of the desert in the Palliser triangle is the greatest success story since the completion of the Canadian Pacific Railway . . . Canada could not have existed without the settling and farming of the Palliser triangle . . . Canada could not have survived, economically or politically if the vast area had been permitted to go back to wheat-covered wasteland and short grass cattle range." *Men Against the Desert* (Saskatoon: Modern Press, 1967).

in 1901 and continued to decline thereafter except for a slight increase during the depressed 1930's.[6]

There were other unplanned reactions to the national policy. The western hinterlands, settled by persons many of whom shared the acquisitive motivation of the eastern capitalists, displayed from the turn of the century a chronic and insolent tendency to fight back against the railroads, the elevator companies, the old-line political parties and other eastern-oriented agencies and interests that exploited the western colonials.[7] But with some concessions, the eastern establishments usually prevailed. The West made no headway against the tariff.

In brief, the Canadian national policy for Rupertsland or (from 1870) for Western Canada turned aside, at least for the time, the threat of American political absorption of the western region. For example, the decision to run the Canadian Pacific rail line parallel and close to the American border, straight across the Palliser dry triangle and over the Kicking Horse Pass of the Rockies instead of further north over the more fertile and profitable crescent and the more gradual Yellowhead route, was basically a political rather than an economic decision. The national policy came along in the second half of the nineteenth century just in time to nourish enough Canadian nationalism and Canadian socio-economic power to stave off the burgeoning American western and industrial expansion — a defensive role played earlier in the nineteenth century by British imperial might. After the mid-nineteenth century, however, Great Britain became increasingly pre-occupied by challenges from other rising metropolitan empires — European, Japanese, and ultimately American. In the twentieth century, Britain was so decisively drained and undercut by two world wars, by the surging communist revolutions in eastern Europe and China, and by the successful nationalist drive for independence in India, that she sank to the status of an American satellite. Canada, accordingly, had to face up to the American colossus without outside aid, and without adequate internal development of national self-consciousness and self-confidence.

If the national policy, developed in Canada mainly during the third quarter of the nineteenth century, had its most obvious successes in western development during the century of Confederation ending in 1967, no less significant — and perhaps more so, in the long run — was its impact on Quebec after the turn of the twentieth century. The rising importance of urbanization, manufactures, and the service industries (including public administration and defence) in Canada has been previously indicated. These have steadily surpassed primary industries; small towns and country life have consequently been subjected to increasingly frustrating, backward

---

[6] Census of Canada. Cited in Saskatchewan Royal Commission on Agriculture and Rural Life, Report No. 7, *Movement of Farm People* (Regina: Queen's Printer, 1956), p. 86.

[7] See J.N. McCrorie, *In Union Is Strength* (Saskatoon: Saskatchewan Farmers Union, 1964); J. Irving, *The Social Credit Movement in Alberta* (Toronto: University of Toronto Press, 1959), and sources therein cited.

conditions — with diminishing chances of catching up — barring drastic institutional changes in Canadian society.[8]

Yet Quebec, like the western prairies, presented itself to the Anglo-Canadian business and political establishments as a promising hinterland for economic and political exploitation.[9] Quebec was rural, Catholic, politically stable, guided by conservative and anti-labor ecclesiastical and provincial regimes, and afflicted with a large surplus rural population — only part of which could be drained off to the factory towns of Ontario and New England. Consequently, the pattern of Anglo management and French-Canadian labour soon became established in Quebec industries, and still continues. Industrialization proceeded apace. The local French municipal and provincial political and professional elites were not seriously threatened by these developments. They simply did business with Anglo entrepreneurs as middlemen; and as time went by, the entrepreneurs became Americans. The Duplessis regime in Quebec (1940's and 1950's) sold economic concessions, like good middlemen, to the Anglo-American exploiters.

The retaliative reaction of the prairie hinterlands, as manifested most overtly but by no means exclusively in the populist movements of the Saskatchewan Co-operative Commonwealth Federation (CCF, 1930's ff.) and Alberta's Social Credit (1930's ff.), has emerged with compound force in Quebec during the 1960's. Perhaps the first manifestation was the Creditiste movement of Raoul Caouette, based on the small-producer, petit-bourgeois entrepreneurs and farmers of northern Quebec and to a degree on the urban working class. The second and probably more decisive manifestation is *Le Parti Quebecois* led by René Lévesque, aiming at complete independence for Quebec. Today it is Lévesque who is surely the real "leader of the opposition" in Canada.

Looking back in 1967, therefore, there was — for English Canada — a centennial record of epic achievement, at least in the short-run. Cities, farms, railroad lines, airlines, universities — in a word, an advanced civilization — had been built against immense odds of geography and climate. More important, all this had been done on the dangerous edge of American expansion. But for Quebec, the same could not be said. French Canada remained economically, politically, and psychologically inferior to Anglo Canada. And the Quebec question lent much ambiguity to the Canadian self-image in that summer of 1967. Many people spoke rhetorically and wishfully of "national unity", but few tried to spell it out.

Looking ahead, therefore, the grounds for Canadian optimism and self-congratulation in 1967 seemed dubious and shadowy. Despite the great national development achieved during the preceding century, there was no clear and common purpose or direction for the Canadian people

---

[8] "Drastic" here means such institutional changes as a guaranteed annual income issued without regard to work or residence or a policy of central planning for, and massive investment in, economically depressed communities and/or regions.

[9] Hubert Guindon, "Two Cultures", in *Contemporary Canada,* ed. R. Leach (Toronto: University of Toronto Press, 1968), Chap. ii; also M. Chapin, *Quebec Now* (New York: Oxford Press, 1955), Chap. iii in particular.

in 1967. The old national policy had obviously run out of gas years ago. Nothing had emerged to replace it. Indeed, as Peter Newman put it:

> It was a time of distemper . . . a time when many Canadians were left with the feeling that much of what was happening had no meaning . . . We were only dimly aware that we were enduring the pains of passage from the safety of the past to we knew not what. The politics of the period (1963-68) was essentially a politics of transition.[10]

It seemed to be an era of issues rather than of resolutions — of questions rather than answers. How could Canadian political independence survive in the face of the soft undermining lure of the on-going American economic and communications take-over? What about those still festering injustices long ago inflicted upon Canada's native Indians and Eskimos? What about the perennial and well documented grievances of various agrarian, urban and regional underclasses? Perhaps the most potent — and in our view the most hopeful — of the unresolved issues was the smouldering ferment of independence in Quebec. In brief, it appeared in 1967 that the challenges ahead could easily outweight the accomplishments of the past.

Two minor indicators may be cited here to point up the irresolutions of our time. One was the series of five graduate seminars on Canadian society given during the Calgary summer session of 1967. This program brought nearly a score of leading academics and writers to the foothills campus for short visits at different times. The essays in this volume though incomplete, convey a fair cross-section of the ideas and insights that glinted in the bright western sunlight of that landmark summer. Yet many questions went unanswered. Doubts remained. No concensus on the nature or course of Canadian society emerged.

The other indicator of the unfocused and uncertain nature of the national self-image was the present writer's auto trip from Calgary to Montreal in early June, 1967, for a visit to Expo 67. Speeding eastward over the endless prairies along the Trans-Canada Highway, we passed hikers with packs and signs on their back reading: "Expo 67. No Rides Please." Somewhere north of Lake Superior, we passed a train of mule wagons marked Expo 67. Newspapers we read on the way carried stories about canoes heading for Expo from the edge of the Rocky Mountains. But the most impressive of all these happenings were the dozens of yellow school buses we passed. They were loaded with school kids headed for Expo. On the sides of those buses were big banners stating their origin and destination — Expo. Some, like ourselves, had started from the far West. Everyone was headed for Expo. By the time we reached Expo, something had happened to us. Expo was a transcending experience. And I think something happened to Canada during that centennial summer of 1967, just because of Expo. Like the primitive, rock-bottom Australian corroboree, Expo was in some part a national and multi-national and international affirmation.

But an affirmation of what no one could say.

---

[10] *The Distemper of Our Times* (Toronto: McCelland and Stewart, 1968), p. xii.

NOTES ON METHOD

Why have academic sociologists, both Canadian and American, found it so difficult to produce and convey a live and realistic conception of Canadian society? This question warrants further discussion. In our view, it is impossible to conceptualize a holistic view of Canadian society apart from American society. This means that the minimal frame of reference for Canada is North American society. Such a perspective has been well established in the works of such Canadian economic historians as Innis, Fowke, Aitken, and others.[11] Even North America as a frame of reference is not enough. The perspective must ultimately include Latin America and all the other satellite hinterlands of the American metropolis that are scattered around the world.

Most Canadian and American-trained Anglophone sociologists do not understand either Canadian or American society mainly because they have been trained in the prevailing static, abstract, ideal-typical, structural-functional, ahistorical tradition. Structural-functionalism affords important insights, both segmental and holistic, but it lacks a time dimension and must therefore be supplemented by a historical perspective. Further, this historical dimension must include a dialectical aspect: the viewing of the evolution of a society as a series of oppositions.

The premise of thesis-antithesis-synthesis may at some times and in some places be relevant and applicable. But for the historical review of Canadian and North American society presently in hand, we prefer a metropolis-hinterland perspective. Metropolis continuously dominates and exploits hinterland whether in regional, national, class, or ethnic terms. But the forms and terms of domination change as a result of confrontations. Spontaneous and massive social movements in regional hinterlands or urban underclasses may force their way toward an improved status for the colonials within the going system. On the other hand, metropolis-hinterland conflict may be latent for long stretches of time rather than overt. It may be outweighed by conditions of prosperity or by temporary alliances in the face of larger confrontations.

Hinterland means, in the first instance, relatively underdeveloped or colonial areas which export for the most part semi-processed extractive materials — including people who migrate from the country to the city for better educational and work opportunities. Hinterland may also usefully denote urban under-classes as well as rural peasantries and rural proletariats. *Metropolis* signifies the centres of economic and political control located in the larger cities. Further, the term may denote urban upper-class elites, or regional and national power structures of one sort or another.

Moreover, we must recognize hierarchies of metropolis-hinterland relationships. As northern Saskatchewan in certain respects may be seen as an economic and political hinterland of southern Saskatchewan, so Saskatchewan, itself, is in large part a hinterland of eastern Canada; and Canada, of the United States. Needless to say, the United States likewise

---

[11] See H. Aitken, J. Deutsch, W. Mackintosh, et al, *The American Economic Impact on Canada* (London: Cambridge University Press, 1959).

includes a complex network of hinterland or under-class groups, regions, marginal colonials, and so on.

The symbiotic *metropolis-hinterland* model assumes (1) conflict of interests between metropolis and hinterland; and (2) a tendency on the part of hinterland groups and interests to fight back eventually against their metropolitan exploiters in order to gain a larger place in the regional or national or international sun. In fact, we really need to think of inherent "surges and down-swings" of specific metropolitan-hinterland conflicts – to borrow J. M. McCrorie's terminology.[12]

The metropolitan-hinterland perspective is obviously a variation of the dialectical approach stemming from the Marxian tradition of social thought. The dialectical premise is that major long-run changes in the socio-economic structure of a society result from oppositions. In the limiting case of major revolutions, as analyzed by the historian Crane Brinton,[13] a collision of incompatible interests eventually produces a new institutional pattern which is not wholly like either of the original opposing complexes, but which includes significant elements from each – doubtless in unequal proportions – the mix depending on the particular case.

Brinton's dialectical approach to four major revolutions probably owes more to Marx than to Pareto, his official mentor. It would apply also to the mid-nineteenth century American Civil War, which finalized the transfer of economic and political power from the southern plantation capitalists to the northern industrial capitalists allied with the western agrarians. But for Canada, where political change has been less extreme at least since 1760, and also for American society since 1865, a modified dialectical model seems more appropriate. The metropolis-hinterland perspective lends itself to a wide variety of conflicting situations, both latent and overt. It also lends itself to the analysis of cases wherein hinterland successfully wins successive concessions from metropolis, particularly under conditions of increasing affluence or under conditions where the concessions to hinterland interests can be compensated by greater exactions or revenues from new or other external hinterlands.

In a nutshell, for analyzing such cases of modern development as Canadian western settlement, Quebec-in-Canada, Canada-in-North America, and United States-in-the-world during the last century of Canadian history, as well as American domestic evolution, a comparatively short-run metropolis-hinterland variation of the long-run dialectic seems preferable. We need a frame of reference somewhere between the timeless, static and usually non-holistic structural-functional model on the one hand, and the holistic, dynamic, long-run limiting case of the Marxian dialect on the other hand. It should be essentially dialectical, holistic, and historical, but capable of illuminating those regional and national confrontations which do not evolve

---

[12] McCrorie, *In Union Is Strength*, 1965.
[13] *Anatomy of Revolution* (Englewood Cliffs, N.J.: Prentice-Hall, 1952). This work analyzes four modern revolutions: the English Revolution of the mid-seventeenth century; the American Revolution of 1776; the French Revolution of 1789; and the Russian Revolution of 1917. Brinton would have done better to include in his four cases the second American revolution (1861) rather than the first (1776).

into full-fledged structural revolutions. Instead, these colonials seek to improve their status within a modified existing order rather than in a drastically and perhaps violently re-structured system. However modified, the metropolis-hinterland hierarchical and exploitive pattern remains. This might not necessarily be true for a full-fledged thesis-antithesis-synthesis sequence.

For example, as historian W.A. Williams has shown, in 1900 the American population was still rural by a three-to-two ratio. (In 1870 the ratio had been three-to-one.) It was the agrarian majority (including flour millers, meat processors, and farm machinery manufacturers) that first opted in the 1870's for market expansionism abroad, in order to help sell agricultural surpluses. They saw themselves as domestic colonials of the northeastern United States metropolis; only in the 1890's did those northeastern industrial leaders adopt a similar attitude toward economic expansion abroad, as the price of avoiding even more radical agrarian and western populist movements.[14] In this way, the American colonials improved their position within the system that was exploiting them, not by decisively altering the sysem, but by shunting part of the exploitation stress abroad — by intensifying the American thrust toward foreign imperialism.

Another example is the radical American labour unionism of the 1870's to the early 1900's which evolved into "business unionism" by the 1920's. The skilled craft unions, and later the big industrial unions in the 1930's, forced their way to a better place at the head table of the American establishment. But the "victory" turned organized labour into one of the strongest supporters of reactionary and aggressive American foreign imperialism after World War II.[15]

A parallel case of regional mass movements making their way into the national establishment is documented in J.N. McCrorie's history of the Saskatchewan farmer's movement since 1900.[16] Another Canadian example is the slow drift of the Canadian economy vis-à-vis the United States during the last generation from a competitive to a branch-plant status.[17]

---

[14] W.A. Williams, *The Roots of the Modern American Empire* (New York: Random House, 1969).

[15] See Bert Cochran, *American in Mid-Passage* (New York: Monthly Review Press, 1958), pp. 29-30: "American labour history has been one of the most violent of the whole world. Goaded beyond endurance, workers would rise up every fifteen to twenty years. But the system was never in danger. The variegated composition of the American people ensured that the uprising affected but a segment of the nation. The growth of the middle classes stunted the numerous labor parties that repeatedly dotted the landscape. The extreme expansion of American capitalism, thwarted by no fedualistic obstructions, and with a virgin continent to ravage, permitted the doling out of material privileges. The mass movement, in defeat or victory, would inevitably lapse into acquiescence." See also C. and M. Beard, "The Labour Movement", in *The Rise of American Civilization* (New York: Macmillan, 1930), Chap. xxi.

[16] McCrorie, *In Union is Strength*, 1965.

[17] George Grant, *Lament for a Nation* (Toronto: McClelland and Stewart, 1965); M. Watkins, et al, *Foreign Ownership and the Structure of Canadian Industry* (Ottawa: Privy Council Office, 1968).

Throughout all these changes, however, metropolis-hinterland patterns appear to persist, whatever the alterations in the degree, scope, intensity, and terms of the stressful relationship. Thus, in drifting into the American empire, Canada has acquired a share or stake in the American metropolitan domination of Latin America, Vietnam, and other such hinterlands. For instance, Canadian industries produce armament materials for sale to the United States and use in Vietnam.

The aridity of the prevailing structural-functional interpretations of Canadian society is easily illustrated. They are authored by sociologists born and/or trained for the most part in the United States. Their views run approximately as follows. Canadian values stand somewhere between those of the United States and Great Britain: "We are not American, and we are not British." Ordinarily, such an argument ends with a perfunctory nod to the presence in Canada of a French-speaking minority. A typical example is the late K. Naegele's "Canadian Society: Some Reflections" and "Further Reflections".[18] Because thousands of Canadian university sociology students have been nourished on this volume of readings during the past decade (the first edition was published in 1961), the message of this package deserves our careful attention. In essence, the abstractions of the German sociologist Max Weber are the model for Naegele's essay. That Weber's life ended in 1920, and that he wrote nothing about Canada seems not to have worried his North American disciples one whit. Two generations later, they can come up with nothing better than a watered-down application of Weber's sociological analysis.[19]

True, the latest (1968) edition of *Canadian Society* wisely retitles Naegele's opening essay as "Modern National Societies", but with no gain in insight into the Canadian situation. In place of Naegele's "Further Reflections", there appears a much more informative paper by Vallee and Whyte. After summarizing a number of key population, economic and social trends, Vallee and Whyte remark upon the difficulty, the scarcity, and (we might add) the relative barrenness of efforts by Anglo-Canadian sociologists to see Canadian society as a whole. In our opinion, the real obstacle to a holistic view of Canada is the inherently static and piecemeal structural-functional approach from which Vallee and Whyte do not entirely escape.

Further to the present argument, static and abstract structural-functional exercise is displayed by S. Lipset in another widely used Canadian university sociology textbook.[20] Lipset is the author of a significant albeit

[18] B. Blishen, Jones, Naegele, and Porter, *Canadian Society: Sociological Perspectives* (2nd ed.) (Toronto: Macmillan, 1964), pp. 1-19, 497-522.

[19] They do not even do justice to Max Weber, who was not merely a sociologist, but also a first-class economic historian. The North American disciples of Weber have latched onto Weber's timeless abstractions while ignoring for the most part his deep-rooted historical context. Here we refer, of course, to T. Parsons and his followers.

[20] W. Mann, ed., *Canada: A Sociological Profile* (Toronto: Copp Clark, 1968), pp. 488-498. The Lipset paper originally appeared in the *Canadian Review of Sociology and Anthropology,* November 1964.

mistitled book on the Saskatchewan Co-operative Commonwealth Federation.[21] But in his 1964 paper, he merely applies the well-know Parsonian
pattern-variables to Canadian society. The scheme runs like this. All
societies may be ranged according to Lipset somewhere on the following
continua: (1) achievement-ascription, (2) universalism-particularism,
(3) self-orientation − collectivity-orientation, (4) equalitarian-elitism.
Lipset concludes that the United States shapes up nearer the left-hand edge
of these continua than does Canadian society.[22] He further argues that in
contrast to the United States, Canada has a counter-revolutionary bent.

We believe that both of these claims by Lipset are largely erroneous,
insofar as they are applied to the past century. First, the conception of the
United States as a universalistic, achievement-oriented, equalitarian society
− a conception so deeply rooted in three centuries of ideological expressions
and verbal ritual that a majority of American social scientists automatically
affirm it − needs severe revision. Judged by the evidence of historical fact
rather than by the liberal rhetoric, the United States is a hierarchical, racist
society − contrary to the long-nourished American middle-class, "liberal"
self-image. At least, it makes far more sense to attach the necessary qualifications to the latter statement than to the former. Second, Canada as a
hinterland society vis-à-vis France (until 1759), then Great Britain, and
(in recent decades) the United States should have considerably more
revolutionary potential than the United States simply because of the metropolis-hinterland relation between them, and the greater intensity of internal
metropolis-hinterland confrontations within Canada during recent decades.
Sooner or later, hinterlands fight back against the metropolitan interests
that exploit them.

The Lipset concept of American society and Canadian society based
on diluted Max Weber is so laced with invalid claims and ideological blind
spots that it is a waste of time to refute it. For example: "The existing
Canadian national identity is in large part a reaction against a long-term
supposed threat to its independence and traditions, against absorption into
the America republic."[23] Supposed? The threat was and is real. It has been
amply documented by such writers as Vernon Fowke, Charles Beard,
George Grant, and Melville Watkins. John A. Macdonald, the first Prime
Minister of Canada (1867-73; 1878-91), knew very well that the main
threat to Canada came from the south. Far more important, the threat of
the United States has been a guiding light of Canadian foreign policy until
the recent fad for "continentalism", a euphemism for buying (or selling)
into the American economic empire.

[21] *Agrarian Socialism* (Berkeley: University of California, 1950). Lipset in this
    early volume of the CCF movement collected much information and many
    insights, but he erred fundamentally in mistaking this primarily rural, petty-
    bourgeois populist surge for a transplanted urban socialism. Fortunately, Lip-
    set's blunder is corrected in the new edition of *Agrarian Socialism* (New York:
    Doubleday Anchor, 1968) not by Lipset (his 1950 test is purposely unchanged)
    but by the new non-Lipset material in Part II, especially the essays by anthro-
    pologist John Bennett and economist John Richards. See also A.K. Davis,
    "The Saskatchewan CCF; The Unfinished Battle fo rthe Shire", *Our Gener-
    ation*, VI, No. 4 (1969), 48-62.

[22] See Mann, *Canada: Sociological Profile* for explanation of these concepts.

[23] Mann, *Canada: Sociological Profile*, p. 497.

When Robin Mathews argues that the threat to Canada's identity is a consequence of too many Americans in Canadian universities, he misses a main point.[24] Perhaps a better target would be, not the nationality of professors, but the relative merits and demerits of professorial ideas. Canadian social scientists are by no means exempt from the charge that their emphasis on structural-functional approaches — usually mediocre piecemeal studies of short-run situations and of a very limited number of empirical variable — has obscured their view of the forest because of their focus upon specific trees. Wrote the late C. Wright Mills:

Classic social analysis ... is the concern with historical social structures; ... its problems are of direct relevance to urgent public issues and insistent human troubles. ... [25] Of late the conception of social science I hold has not been ascendant. My conception stands opposed to social science as a set of bureaucratic techniques which inhibit social inquiry by 'methodological' pretensions, which congest such work by obscurantist conceptions, or which trivialize it by concern with minor problems unconnected with publicly relevant issues. ... [26] Neither the life of an individual nor the history of a society can be understood without understanding both. Yet men do not usually define the troubles they endure in terms of historical change and institutional contradiction. ... [27] The sociological imagination enables us to grasp history and biography and the relations between the two within society. That is its task and its promise. To recognize this task and this promise is the mark of the classic social analyst.[28]

It is time to emphasize the historical, holistic and comparative approach of classic social analysis in our studies of Canadian society. In no way would this detract from the significant and indeed indispensable contributions of orthodox structural-functional analysis to an understanding of Canada in the modern world.[29]

---

[24] R. Mathews and J. Steele, *The Struggle for Canadian Universities* (Toronto: New Press, 1969), especially pp. 1-11.

[25] *The Sociological Imagination* (New York: Oxford University Press, 1959), p. 21.

[26] *Ibid.*, p. 20.

[27] *Ibid.*, p. 3.

[28] *Ibid.*, p. 6.

[29] The interesting point is that a great deal of work has already been published along historical and holistic lines in Canada. No student of Canadian society should be ignorant of the previously mentioned "staples theory" of Canadian development. The same may be said of Harold Innis' classic study of *The Fur Trade in Canada* (Toronto: University of Toronto Press, 1956) and his *Essays in Canadian Economic History* (New Haven: Yale University Press, 1930). The series edited by S. D. Clark, *Social Credit in Alberta* (10 vols.) (Toronto: University of Toronto Press, 1950-59), and an earlier series edited by W. Mackintosh and W. Joerg, *Canadian Frontiers of Settlement* (Toronto: Macmillan, 1930's), are likewise indispensable. Yet it must be said that some of the keenest insights into modern Canadian and North American social development are to be found in non-sociologist sources like George Grant, Peter Newman, Pete Seeger, Joni Mitchell, Buffy St. Marie, and so on. The academic sociologist are making very few contributions to national self-understanding.

We can learn certain valuable lessons from orthodox structural-functional analysis. First, social systems change unevenly, but they change as wholes. In the short-run, one sector of the system may lead at one time, another sector at another time. In the long-run, of course, the system as a whole changes in one direction, until confronted by a major opposition. For example, changes in one institutional area may induce changes in another. One effect of the post-World War II extension of education and family allowances in far Northern Saskatchewan was to tie the formerly semi-nomadic Métis and Indian trapping families more closely to village settlements.

In other words, social systems share a property common to systems in general — some degree of interdependence of parts. This also means, in some measure, cohesiveness of the whole, however loose. Hence follows the limited capacity of each component part of the system to continue short-run change that is not paralleled by complementary changes in other components. Thus during the late 1940's and early 1950's, the Saskatchewan CCF Government built a modern elementary school system in the far northern reaches of the province. This well-meaning education effort declined by the middle 1950's, because it was not accompanied by such other changes as greater job opportunities, wider experience, and acceptance by Métis and Indians of modern standards of living or migration to the south.

Finally, while we suggest that major changes in social structure result from oppositions, this does not mean that all structural changes are explainable in this way. At least one other leading mode of structural change must be considered. That is the impersonal, unplanned evolution of large social processes.[30] As illustrations of this category of change, we may point to the cumulative development of science and technology, of voluntary migrations, and the movement in advanced economies toward large-scale corporate organizations in business and the modern State. This type of change seems to consist of the realization of potentialities inherent in a system; of the unfolding of immanent tendencies as facilitated or modified by external, local, or otherwise varying conditions. Max Weber's concept of "rationalization" appears to convey what we mean. Equally relevant is Sorokin's concept of immanent change.

Let us affirm above all, however, that Weberian rationalization, Sorokinian immanence, Marxian dialectical oppositions, and our own metropolis-hinterland modification of the Marxian dialectic (by no means original with us) are not mutually exclusive concepts and processes. Our sense of the present as on-going history may be illuminated by all of these and indeed by other conceptualizations.

CANADIAN SOCIETY IN THE NORTH AMERICAN EPMIRE: LOOKING BACK AND LOOKING AHEAD

Since the seventeenth century, Canadian history has been in large part a reaction to the activities of foreign empires. Until 1760, it was the

---

[30] Unplanned as a whole, that is, however rationally the component actions of the larger process may be planned and carried out.

French impact that was pre-eminent; then came the British impact for over a century and a half. After the first World War, the Americans quickly displaced Britain as the primary influence on Canadian society — a trend that was reinforced by the rapid decline of Britain itself to a satellite status within the American orbit. So far had the American fact developed in Canada by the 1960's that George Grant felt constrained to write his well-known essay on the demise of Canadian nationalism.[31] Yet the American influence on Canada began long before the 1920's. Its origins go back at least to the war of the American colonies of independence, 1776-83. And when we review the origins of the national policy during the third quarter of the nineteenth century, it is not too much to say that Canadian history and socio-economic development during the century of Confederation just ended have been a secondary reaction to the initiative of American events. It has indeed, been a pale reflection of American stratagems and American drift.

The stirrings toward nationalism and independence in Quebec today may, however, open the way to an alternative to "continentalism", which means the continued drift into an affluent but second class status within the burgeoning American empire; for the price of affluent continentalism includes not only second-class status, but also "homogenization" — the eroding of particularistic communities like the French-speaking Canadians, the Indians of Canada, the Eskimos, and many other presently unique groups in Canada.

Meanwhile, the most important perspective for Canadians — both in and outside Quebec — to grasp is the present situation of American society. The prospect appears grim. Let us consider the surge and down-swing of oppositions within American society. In our view, this pattern is a key to contemporary Canadian alternatives.

Nearly a decade ago, the present writer argued that decisive structural change comes from oppositions, and that there had been no major oppositions in American society since approximately the time of World War I.[32] It is too early to assess the opposition role of the American Black revolt: this may yet prove to be America's best hope. In the meantime, we may review the two major confrontations in the United States during the history of that Republic.

The first was that leading to the American Civil War, 1861-65. It consisted of the competitive clash between two increasingly divergent societies — North and South — both based on capitalistic economies which had to expand or perish. By mid-century, the outcome of the contest was no longer doubtful. The northern coalition of commercial and industrial interests, linked with the western farmers, steadily forged ahead in wealth and power. In 1860, with the election of Lincoln, the control of the national government passed to the new order. It only remained to win the Civil War and make the victory official. As usual, the old regime preferred to initiate a desperate counter-revolutionary war rather than to acquiesce

---

[31] *Lament for a Nation* (New Jersey: Princeton University, 1965).
[32] "Decline and Fall", *Monthly Review*, XII (1960), 334-344.

in its own displacement. We quote from historians Charles and Mary Beard.

> Viewed under the light of universal history, the fighting was a fleeting incident; the social revolution was the essential portentous outcome . . . . The capitalists, labourers and farmers of the North and West drove from power in the national government the planting aristocracy of the South. . . . The physical combat merely hastened the inevitable. As was remarked at the time, the South was fighting against the census returns that told of accumulating industrial capital, multiplying captains of industry, expanding railway systems, widening acres tilled by free farmers. Once the planting and the commercial states, as the Fathers with faithful accuracy described them, had been evenly balanced; by 1860 the balance was gone . . . . Viewed in the large, the supreme outcome of the civil strife was the destruction of the planting aristocracy which, with the aid of northern farmers and mechanics had practically ruled the United States for a generation.[33]

No other war in American history, before or since, ever made such an indelible impression on the minds, the memories, and the traditions of the American people and their descendants — both North and South.[34]

The second great opposition in recent American history began to take shape soon after the end of the Civil War. As the immense expansion of post-war American industrialism got under way, nurtured by the new protective tariff, by public subsidies to transcontinental railroads, and by the fabulous resources of the West, rumblings of discontent and revolt appeared among workers, miners, farmers, and various other colonials. Frustrated farmers, excluded from the feast for one reason or another, organized to raise hell instead of corn. Strikers fought pitched battles with police and militiamen across the country. Socialist splinter groups sprang up here and there, and numerous other strange counsels and cults alarmed the ruling burghers. By 1900, a fledgling indigenous Socialist movement led by Gene Debs was under way. In 1912, the various Socialist groups together received 6.3 per cent of the popular vote for the presidency. But since then, the combined Socialist percentage of the American presidential vote has steadily declined. It was seven-hundredths of 1 per cent in 1956.

What happened? Why did the emerging opposition collapse? Why did the opposition to capitalism, generated by capitalism as predicted by Karl Marx, collapse immanently in the United States — where the lack of non-capitalistic alternatives and the absence of anti-capitalistic traditions should theoretically have made for a classic case of socialist displacement of

---

[33] *The Rise of American Civilization,* (New York: Macmillan, 1927), XI, 54, 99.
[34] When the death of latter-day American hero-presidents like Franklin Roosevelt and John Kennedy were memorialized and publicly solemnized, the poem invariably recited was Walt Whitman's great elegy to President Lincoln: "When Lilacs last in the Dooryard Bloomed". The greatest American national crisis evoked the greatest national poem. Subsequent American crises, because they have been lesser, have merely echoed the greatness of that earlier day.

capitalism? The basic reason seems to have been the over-success of American capitalism.

The fantastic resources of the American heartland; the absence of any competing traditions of rival aristocracy; a vast domestic market protected by a high tariff; an endless supply of cheap immigrant labor; friendly politicians in control of the national government (which owned more than half of all land in the nation in 1860) who were eager to help and to share; these are the factors pointed out by the historians Charles and Mary Beard in their *Rise of American Civilization* as the key elements in the "triumph of business enterprise".

We explain American economic and social development, then, in terms of capitalism evolving under unique domestic, geographic, and international conditions — a perspective applicable to any other capitalist society with appropriate modifications in the components. This approach has not prevailed among the majority of American historians and intellectuals. The more common focus has been upon the development of the western frontier. In a famous essay in 1893, "The Significance of the Frontier in American History", F.J. Turner portrayed the westward movement as perennial rebirth, as a movement away from European influence and toward American uniqueness, and as the basis of democracy and prosperity.[35] Despite its genuine insights, this viewpoint obscures at least as much as it reveals. It embodies a large element of nationalistic parochialism. Set in our larger and more realistic frame of reference, however, the Turner thesis helps to bring out the central fact that throughout its course the American republic has resorted to expansion in order to escape its domestic contradictions and tensions. And when the western frontier was essentially closed in about 1890, expansionism had to continue abroad. If the historians missed this key point, the more perceptive business and political leaders of the United States from the earliest days of independence were in no doubt where their interests lay.

And when, much as Marx had predicted, capitalism began to generate the resisting forces of labour organizations and populist agrarian revolts toward the end of the nineteenth century, those thrusts in the case of the United States were turned aside by a combination of sharing the goodies at home and imperialistic expansion abroad. The crisis of the 1890's threatened by the closing of the frontier was resolved in part by extending the necessary economic expansion and investment frontier beyond the national boundaries. Indeed, as William A. Williams, another American historian, has shown, it was the rural colonials — farmers and small town processers in the American hinterland — who pressed most strongly for market expansion abroad. Some of the disappointed colonials moved to the Canadian prairies for a second try.

In other words, interest groups that feel deprived often strive first and foremost to improve their position in the going economic system. With a few adjustments, the system then carries on with some new faces

---

[35] *The Frontier in American History* (New York: Henry Holt, 1921), Chap. i, xii *et passim*.

at the head table. A parallel conclusion was reached by McCrorie in his recent study of the Saskatchewan farmers' movement in the twentieth century.[36] The American farmers got markets; later they received subsidies. American labour turned to "business unionism." The real process was much more complex, naturally.

The foreign expansion of business was decisively and irreversibly reinforced by the effects of two relatively cheap world wars that brought still further American economic growth, and which wrecked the rival British, French, German, and Japanese capitalistic empires. But these same world wars, in destroying America's rivals, also cleared the way for the communist and nationalistic revolutions in Russia and China, thus closing off vast regions of the world to American business expansion, and forecasting an ultimate confrontation between the American empire and the rising new socialist world.

On another level, the domestic Keynesian and social security reforms have likewise bolstered the fairy tale American version of capitalism since the 1930's. In our own generation, the military and space budgets, which Thorstein Veblen would have called waste, have operated as additional investment frontiers. In truth, the limitless sky has become the limit. It all adds up to the most fantastic success story in human history. It staggers the imagination.

My central concern, however, is not the dynamics and contours of American history, but certain consequences that appear to follow from them, in the light of our dialectical premise. Since the first World War, there has been an absence of great oppositions in American society. Competition has been sharp, often nasty, sometimes violent. In our own day, assassination has become a standard political response; consider the cases of Malcolm X, Martin Luther King, the Kennedy brothers, and the hunting down of the Black Panthers. But no new philosophy, with organizational resources and potentially decisive mass support, has arisen to challenge seriously the prevailing pattern of corporate structures and middle class style of life. The hippies have opted out of their own encapsulated thing; some student groups may drop out, turn on, or even sit in;[37] the Blacks — so far — simply riot; the old left is largely defunct; the new left — at least in the foreseeable future — has far less organizational and mass support than has George Wallace's reassertion of traditional White racism. Practically everyone that matters, power-wise, in the United States accepts the traditional American middle class way of life. The protests seem negative; none of them sounds positive — with the possible exception of certain stirrings among the Blacks.

---

[36] All that my friend Roy Atkinson, President of the Saskatchewan Farmers Union, is trying to do by organizing a National Farmers Union is to give farmers an effective trade association such as most other categories of capitalistic entrepreneurs have long enjoyed. A more conservative truly capitalistic goal could hardly be imagined.

[37] The student strikes and the march on Washington in Spring 1970 provoked by the Kent College killings and Nixon's move into Cambodia may have been a step towards organization and mass support on campus however fleeting.

At the moment, the best hope for a great change in American life seems to be in the emerging non-racist socialist humanism of such Black leaders as the late Malcolm X and Elbridge Cleaver. Whether these types can secure the necessary mass support among both Blacks and Whites is still a question mark. Surely no country in the world, for its own interest, has greater need for a social revolution than the United States. And the interest of the rest of the world in a new American revolution is equally compelling. In estimating the American future, therefore, we should reserve judgment on the potential of the Black revolt.

Meanwhile, the present absence of major internal oppositions acts as a block to the necessary structural changes that might adapt the United States to the modern world. The investment frontiers abroad are successively being closed out by the rising revolutionary tides of nationalism and communism. The Soviet Revolution of 1917, the Chinese upheaval of 1949 have slammed the door on American expansion in those vast and heavily populated heartland regions. Latin America could follow suit any day, any year. Yet, in this mounting crisis, there is as yet — apart from the aforementioned murmurings — no dialogue, no positive opposition in American society. On the contrary, there is rigidity and nativistic revivalism. In this perspective, the decline of American society may have set in two or three generations ago. It is interesting to note that Toynbee, in his study of civilizations, puts very early in his grand cycle the shift from a creative to a dominant (i.e. uncreative) minority, even though a long period of increasing national power and glory may follow.

The oppositions to American society and to the American ethos are today external rather than internal. This further impedes meaningful dialogue between Establishment and Opposition, by virtue of the emotional barriers of patriotism, nationalism, and racism. Yet without such a dialogue, without massive and positive oppositions, the United States may well become increasingly obsolete, like the dinosaurs that in a long ago age failed to meet the challenge of their own time. Unfortunately, the United States still bestrides the world like a muscle-bound and inflexibly programmed colossus. It holds the fate of all of us in a finger tip poised above a nuclear push button.

The problem of the United States in 1970 is not primarily Vietnam. "Uncle Sam" could get out of Vietnam tomorrow without fundamentally altering his underlying dilemma. Indeed, the real problem of American society is not even the ghetto-encapsulated Blacks. The crisis, the failure of nerve, the Achilles heel of American civilization surely lies in the colossal, almost indescribable failure — and need — to face up to itself.

> The central issue of the mid-twentieth century is how to sustain democracy and prosperity without imperial expansion and the conflicts it engenders. . . . The way to transcend tragedy is to reconcile the truths which define the tragedy. . . . To transcend tragedy requires the nerve to fail. . . . For the nerve to fail has nothing at all to do with blustering and self-righteous crusades up to or past the edge of violence. . . . For Americans, the nerve to fail is in a real sense the

nerve to say that we no longer need what Turner calls "the gate of escape" provided by the frontier . . . . The traditional effort to sustain democracy by expansion will lead to the destruction of democracy.[38]

So wrote William A. Williams in 1962. Using different terminologies, a number of writers have come to similar verdicts — Veblen, Sorokin, Walter Lippman, Paul Sweezy — to name but a few.

"Over-success as failure" — this is the tragic verdict on the American republic, seen from afar by the present writer in 1970. In all the checkered course of human history, no other national rise has been more brilliant or more meteoric. No nation's fall could be more cataclysmic. It might well engulf not only Canada, but most of the world.

> Once there was a way to get back homeward,
> Once there was a way to get back home . . . [39]

Once upon a time it was not too late to retreat. But not any more.

The dreadful impasse in the United States, the mindless rigidity of American societal development during the last three or four generations — especially since World War I — this is what Canadian society has bought (or sold) into, and is now confronting. That the American Blacks in alliance with other underclass and dissident groups may break through the reigning conservative orthodoxy that pervades the American Establishment (including both major political parties)— is not impossible. But it seems uncertain. Is the consequent drag upon Canadian society inevitably fatal?

Let us first consider the objective pessimism of George Grant, a perceptive Anglo thinker, a dissenting product of the Tory establishment of eastern Canada, and chairman of the McMaster University Department of Religion. He argues that in Vietnam the American empire is destroying an entire nation in order to preserve its domination, and that Canada is an integral and subordinate part of the United States order.[40]

In the light of our dialectical premise, we think there may be something more to be said. Regional and class oppositions have been more prominent in Canadian society during the half-century since the first World War than in the United States. And the half overt, half latent opposition between Canada and the United States still lives.

Today the prime confrontation within Canada, combining partly overlapping regional, ethnic, linguistic, and class oppositions, is that between Anglo Canada and French Quebec. It is wholly possible that Quebec may yet be the salvation of Canadian society, especially if Quebec opts for independence — as seems increasingly likely. And in our dialectical perspective, this domestic confrontation — particularly if Quebec moved decisively toward socialism (as she would almost certainly be compelled to

---

[38] *The Tragedy of American Diplomacy* (New York: Dell, 1962), pp. 303, 307, 309.

[39] The Beatles, *Abbey Road*, 1969.

[40] *Technology and Empire* (Toronto: House of Anansi, 1969), pp. 63, 65.

do, in order to manage successfully her natural and human resources for national French-Canadian survival) — might awake unforeseen reactions and resources in English Canada. To be sure, these reactions might produce either a collapse into the American camp or a spine-stiffening resolution to remain different.

There are only two basic alternatives for Canadian society in the foreseeable future. One is a continued drift toward continentalism which means further absorption into the American capitalist empire. This policy, which since World War II has been pursued largely without public debate by most elements of the Canadian elites — the policy makers in the private, public, and governmental corporations — anti-national and therefore anti-Canadian. The other alternative is a Canadian Castro. This means socialism: expropriation of selected foreign and domestic major corporations, closer control of certain other key industries, and the over-all planning of the use of our major resources for national purposes and public services.

But there may also be intermediate possibilities, such as the watered-down socialism of René Lévesque. According to certain lines of contemporary economic thinking, it is apparently desirable to leave a fairly large private sector in the economy, perhaps along Scandinavian lines, particularly in "small business", but also in a few large scale industries. In principle, however, the choice lies between American imperialism and Canadian socialism.

Compensation for expropriation? In principle, yes. But unforeseeable circumstances would doubtlessly control the amount. At one end of the range of possibilities is a minimal token compensation, based on the argument that past profits should be weighted off against present value. At the other end of the range is full compensation for present value. The pattern could vary for different industries. Here we may revert to a remarkable occurrence in Quebec. Some years back, the Province of Quebec nationalized an American owned corporation — Quebec Hydro — and borrowed the money from the Americans to pay for the take-over. We should all reflect at length upon this significant event. We might just possibly make it financially worthwhile for the Americans (who know a good business deal when they see one) to finance Canadian independence. And we could always hope to scale down the interest rate in due time. In any case, there are other sources in the world for borrowing capital for investment and for compensation. The Americans understand competition — or so they say. Let them compete with France, the Soviet Union, Japan, and so on for the financing of Canadian independence.

Still thinking in terms of metropolis-hinterland oppositions as a core concept in the history and the future of Canadian national development, we may suggest that the coming confrontation between Quebec and English Canada may be the best promise for both parties to that great dialogue. In Quebec's drift and thrust toward independence, it is secondary that a subjected and exploited nationality may some day soon recover its freedom. That would be no more than poetic justice for past wrongs. What really matters is what Quebec may do to stimulate the revival of independent nationalism in the rest of Canada. And even more important, perhaps, is what such socialist and nationalist development in the form of two independent nations north of the American border might do for the United States. That may be too optimistic, of course. Yet the fate of homo sapiens may well rest upon the issue: Can the United States recover — or more accurately, achieve — a national identity and national policy that is compatible with the emerging revolutionary mainstream of the rest of the world? Consider the words of W.A. Williams, American historian in the classic tradition of Charles Beard:

> For the rest of the world, be it presently industrial or merely beginning to industrialize, is very clearly moving toward some version of a society modeled on the ideal of a true human community based far more on social property than upon private property. That is what the editors of *The Wall Street Journal* meant in 1958 when they candidly admitted that the United States was on "the wrong side of a social revolution." The socialist reassertion of the ancient ideal of a Christian commonwealth is a viable utopia. It was so when the Levellers asserted it in the middle of the 17th century, and it remains so in the middle of the 20th century. It holds very simply and clearly that the only meaningful frontier lies within individual men (and women) and in their relationships with each other. It agrees with Frederick Jackson Turner that the American frontier has been a "gate of escape" from those central responsibilities and opportunities. The socialist merely says that it is time to stop running away from life.[41]

All this may seem speculative, of course, but it is not entirely so, given the dialectical promise herein adopted. It is one task of the sociologist to clarify alternatives, regardless of how improbable they may appear in the light of current professional and political orthodoxies. Having said that, it may be well at this point to emphasize the importance of contingencies in social affairs. We may plan our futures, yet much depends on the larger trends of the times. For example, the National Policy that constituted and guided Canadian Confederation over most of the past century was "planned" only in a limited sense. Fowke has put the matter in this way:

> ... The National Policy was not by itself sufficient to make Western development possible on the scale eventually attained. The establishment of the prairie wheat economy, which may be regarded as its first major economic triumph, was accompanied by tremendous economic expansion throughout the entire Canadian economy, and was an integral part of a complex of dynamic forces which pervaded the western world. Professor Mackintosh has spoken of the "con-

---

[41] *Contours of American History* (Cleveland: World Publishing Co., 1961), p. 487. Copyright © 1961 by William Appleman Williams.

juncture of favourable circumstances" which marked the transition from the nineteenth to the twentieth century and which gave to Canada three decades of unprecedented expansion. This conjuncture of world circumstances created the opportunity for Canadian expansion, but a half-century of foundation work along the lines of national policy has prepared Canada for the opportunity.[42]

R. Heilbroner points up the same argument in even stronger terms:

> For the common attribute of contemporary events is not their responsiveness to our designs, but their indifference to them. . . . History less and less presents itself as something we find or make, and more and more as something we find made for us.[43]

Yet part of this deepening impasse may be due to the fact that the United States, like King Canute forbidding the tide, is attempting to stand against and to turn back the rising swell of anti-colonial and communist revolutions that are sweeping much of the world in the twentieth century.

This brings us to our final issue. By contrast with the United States, Canadian society has been characterized as "pluralistic." This means that ethnic and regional differences for example have been more generally accepted, more legitimized than they have been in our southern neighbour. There has not been as much pressure in Canada for "assimilation" as there has been in the United States — though it is easy to exaggerate the importance of the American "melting pot" ideology (in the case of the Negro, and the southwestern Mexican-American, for instance) — just as one may readily over estimate Canadian tolerance for ethnic differences. Canadians seem to prefer Indians and Blacks to keep their distance. Yet the Hutterite communities unquestionably are granted more autonomy in Canada than in the United States. Likewise, the Indians of Canada, however rudely they were shunted onto reservations when the fur trade no longer needed their labour and the eastern Anglo Establishment wanted their land for white settlement, were seldom treated with such overt coercion as were the American Indians. Above all, the English and the French, despite the conquest and subordination of the latter, had to arrive at a *modus vivendi* that involved mutual compromise and autonomy as well as exploitation.

Another way of describing and perhaps of partially explaining Canadian pluralism is to observe the fact that capitalism never developed to such extremes in Canada as it did in the United States. The American colonies broke their ties early with England, and the philosophy of laissez-faire Manchesterism could run wild until the rise of new internal oppositions late in the nineteenth century. Even then, as we have seen, the competitive challenges of the labour and the agrarian movements were blunted by taking the rebels into the feast and paying for this by means of foreign

---

[42] *The National Policy and the Wheat Economy* (Toronto: University of Toronto Press, 1957), p. 70.

[43] *The Future as History* (New York: Harper, 1959) (1968 Torchbook paper edition).

economic expansion. In England, on the other hand, elements of pre-industrial classes and values survived industrialization. The first reforms in the nineteenth century were sparked, not by the "new men of Manchester", but by Tories from the old landed classes motivated by feudal norms like *noblesse oblige*. Something of these restraining values seem to have carried over into English Canada. And French Canada has embodied still other and different traditions.

Now, however, all Canadian particularisms are threatened by what George Grant calls the "homogenizing and universalising power of technology".[44] What kinds of community do the various segments of Canadian society want? This is one of the key questions posed by the Alberta Indian leader, Harold Cardinal:

> The new Indian policy promulgated by Prime Minister Pierre Elliot Trudeau's government . . . in June of 1969 is a thinly disguised programme which offers nothing better than cultural genocide. . . . Indians have aspirations, hopes and dreams, but becoming white men is not one of them.[45]

The Indians, according to Cardinal, want a respected place in Canadian society, but they also insist at least in some degree on remaining Indians.

A similar theme is voiced by René Lévesque, leader of the Quebec independence movement:

> We are Quebecois. What this means first and foremost . . . is that we are attached to this one corner of the earth where we can be completely ourselves: this Quebec, the only place where we have the unmistakable feeling that "here we can be really at home." Being ourselves is essentially a matter of keeping and developing a personality that has survived for three and a half centuries. At the core of this personality is the fact that we speak French. . . . We are heirs to the group obstinacy which has kept alive that portion of French America we call Quebec. . . . This is how we differ from other men and especially from other North Americans . . . [46]

In calling for an independent Quebec, Lévesque is striking out for the survival of a major Canadian particularism. He is arguing that only in their own sovereign state can French-speaking Canadians develop their own special style of life and shape their own institutions. Unlike the Indians of Canada, the independence movement in Quebec has such assets as numbers, concentration of population, organizations of all types, important natural resources, well developed economic enterprises, and so on. The Indians are scattered, divided into over 500 bands on more than 2200

---

[44] *Technology and Empire* (Toronto: House of Anansi, 1969), p. 69.
[45] *The Unjust Society* (Edmonton: Hurtig, 1969), pp. 1, 3.
[46] *An Option for Quebec* (Toronto: McClelland and Stewart, 1968), pp. 14-15.

reservations, further separated into 11 language groups, and for the most part poverty-ridden.

In affirming that the survival of various nationalisms in Canada requires (among other things) a shift to a socialist economy, we must refer to the thesis of André G. Frank concerning "underdevelopment". Although Frank based his analysis on Latin American studies, his conclusions seem equally applicable to Canada:

> Underdevelopment is not due to the survival of archaic institutions and the existence of capital shortage in regions that have remained isolated from the stream of world history. On the contrary, underdevelopment was and still is generated by the very same historical process which also generated economic development: the development of capitalism itself.[47]

The history of the fur trade in Canada is a classic illustration of this thesis. The development of the fur trade tied the Indians to a world market as colonialized workers managed by others. When the fur industry declined, capital migrated to other sectors of the economy, and the Indians were left stranded and by-passed in a world they did not make. Now the Indians are beginning to knock on the door of the modern world. They no longer wish to be a poverty-ridden rural proletariat, they are not content to move into urban slum ghettos. Nor do they wish to be merely "brown white men". They want to be different it seems; they want to be Indian.

The Frank thesis can be applied also to Quebec. Modern economic development came relatively late to Quebec, compared to Ontario, and it came mainly for the benefit of Anglos. Now Quebec is catching up, but Quebeckers, too, wish both to retain their cultural differences and to have more of the economic goodies.

If this approach is valid, it greatly reinforces the argument that the salvaging of Canadian pluralisms requires a socialist economic base. The economic aspect of the issue is essential, but it is clearly not the only essence. There is also among many Indians, the Quebeckers, and perhaps among many other groups such as students and young people as well, a quest for community. Socialism by itself does not guarantee community. There is still the problem of large scale bureaucracy. Much experimentation in making bureaucratic organization more responsive to the control and needs of its members and clients is still needed. But a regime of social property rather than private property seems one obvious prerequisite of the next great phase of North American society. If that society has a future — a big "if" — the American empire must be de-colonialized. What Quebec and the Indians of Canada appear to be seeking to escape from is their dependent and colonial status. English Canada's branch-plant condition relative to the United States economic empire is objectively parallel in certain respects to the hinterland status of the Indians and French vis-à-vis the Anglos

---

[47] The Development of Underdevelopment", *Monthly Review*, No. 18 (September, 1966), p. 23. See also A.G. Frank, *Capitalism and Under-development in Latin America* (New York: Monthly Review Press, 1967).

in Canada. But English Canadians have not yet awakened to their dependency and fate in the homogenizing and expanding American empire.

The coming confrontation between English and French Canada — if it does occur — may help to change all that. Lévesque's insight seems valid, in the light of our dialectical frame of reference.

> As for the other Canadian majority, it will also find our solution [independence for Quebec] to its advantage, for it, will be set free at once from the constraints imposed on it by our presence: it will be at liberty in its own way to rebuild to its heart's desire the political institutions of English Canada and to prove to itself, whether or not it really wants to maintain and develop on this continent, an English-speaking society distinct from the United States.[48]

Looking back and looking ahead, the Canadian Centennial of 1967 may well prove to be a watershed in Canadian history, an interlude between eras. This is the view suggested by our conception of Canadian history and society as a dynamic sequence of oppositions, irregularly and alternately latent and overt between overlapping hierarchies — regional, class, ethnic, urban-rural — of metropolis-hinterland relationships within North American society. Does this schema have any predictive value? If it does, then it could inform policy.

In the present writer's judgment this modified dialectical approach seems to "fit" the Canadian and North American past reasonably well. Whether it will continue to offer a realistic interpretation in the future, only time will tell. Life is full of surprises. Somewhere in his postscript to *War and Peace,* Tolstoy remarks that some interpretations of modern history are like "a deaf man answering questions which no one has asked".

The mythical scientific analyst must assume a completely deterministic premise: If he knew all the factors in a situation and their relative weights and vectors — currently an impossible "if" — he could predict the resultant outcome of that situation. The actor, however, cannot know all the factors in his action situation; therefore he has "choices". Hence we suggest no more than this: A dialectical approach illuminates the past and perhaps also clarifies the future alternatives of Canadian societal development. In other words, it fulfills what C. Wright Mills called the interpretive task of classical social analysis (see p. 17). All we are certain of, at this point, is that for such a purpose the dialectical frame of reference is superior to the orthodox structural-functionalism of academic sociology.

Is it unrealistic to take into account this dialectical perspective as one factor in making policy decisions in various interest-groups in Canadian society? For example, is it reasonable to suppose that Quebec or Canada can "confront" the American colossus and still survive? The answer seems obvious. Why not? We never know until we try. And if nothing is attempted, then the drift into the American empire will simply continue. What the fate and value of American society will be is presently indicated

---

[48] *An Option for Quebec,* p. 28.

in the obscenities now proceeding in Vietnam. American policy in Vietnam — and potentially in Latin America — is like the Assyrian armies that flayed alive thousands of their opponents, only it is mechanized and on a vastly greater and more "efficient" scale. If the heart of American society is Main Street, its cutting edge is in Vietnam, and there is an organic link between the two aspects. This is barbarism, not civilization.

Many turning points of history appear to be a chancy process of "slipping successfully between the icebergs". The collection of puny American colonies was able to achieve its independence from the superior might of the British empire because Britain was pre-occupied by a major war with France. The Bolshevik revolution in Russia succeeded because the hostile western powers, exhausted by a world war, could not muster sufficient force to smother it. Castro led a successful revolution in Cuba, right under the nose of the United States, partly because of American involvements in Asia and Europe and partly because the Americans assumed they could do business as usual with the new leader as they had always done with previous rebels in Cuba and Latin America. When the Americans finally woke up, it was too late.

Contrary to George Grant, therefore, we believe that nationalism in Quebec and in English Canada is not necessarily defeated. But it will require a socialist transformation to salvage and rebuild what remains and even that may not be enough.

Earlier in this paper (footnote 1) it was suggested that "North America" may in certain respects be too small a framework for analyzing Canadian society. The American empire is not merely a hemisphere but a global operation. It seems appropriate for students of Canadian society to take into account so far as possible key developments all over the world.

Looking at that larger picture, the chances for a successful confrontation with the United States may well be better in Mexico or elsewhere in Latin America than in Canada. A "successful confrontation" may be defined as one that leaves the people of the world both alive and fit to live. Mexico has vitality, great numbers, longer and deeper roots in distinctive Indian and Catholic cultures, a revolutionary tradition, and so on. On an even larger canvas, as Sorokin suggested during his last years, the best hope for a viable and humane stabilizing of the world may lie with Oriental societies — Japan, China, and India — especially the latter two. These societies have already made extensive progress in adapting such western patterns as science and technology to their own ancient cultural heritages, and in "kicking out the White man".[49] Indeed, during most of world history the leadership of civilization has rested with the river-valley imperial societies of the near East, India and China. Perhaps the meteoric rise and evident decline of Western Europe during the last few centuries is but a passing episode.

This massive transition, however, could well be cut short by nuclear war, precipitated by the terminal convulsions of the American juggernaut

---

[49] P.A. Sorokin, *Basic Trends of Our Time* (New Haven: College and University Press, 1964), p. 64, and Chap. ii *passim*.

in the face of rising domestic and external oppositions. That would be the end of all of us. Meanwhile, we may offer one final thought. If a new Gene Debs appears to lead a revolutionary transformation in the United States, he may perchance be a Black. In Canada, he will probably be a French Canadian or a western farmer. He — or they — will come from, or be identified with, one or more of the underclass and regional hinterlands of North American society.

2

EDITOR'S INTRODUCTION

In both classical and contemporary sociology, recurring emphasis is given to the analysis of distinctions between the characteristics of rural and of urban communities. The universal population shift away from rural communities and toward urban communities is viewed as one of the major and massive changes occurring in the basic nature of social life.

So much has been written on this topic that most studies in sociology have been either directly or indirectly influenced by it. Researchers generally concur that the urbanization of the world has resulted in sweeping changes in the social and individual life of human beings. More specifically, it has generally been accepted that urbanization of human populations results in the deterioration of traditional social institutions such as the family and religion, and the realignment and bureaucratization of other institutions such as the economic and political systems. Social life has been viewed as fractionalized and atomized while at the same time the individual has been viewed as emancipated from the more confining traditions and customs of the rural milieu.

Political life has been characterized as increasingly liberal and diversified as urbanization progresses and dissolves traditional and "irrational" political loyalties. Thus, radical political movements, be they left or right, tend to be seen as distinctively urban phenomena.

Professor McCrorie, in his discussion of the socialist agrarian movement in Saskatchewan and elsewhere, directly and indirectly challenges some of the foregoing assumptions. Our widely accepted assumptions concerning the major distinctions between rural and urban communities cannot be applied very easily to the changing patterns that are discussed in the following article.

The use of "ideal types" has been particularly extensive in the sociological study of communities. An ideal type is a theoretical concept which maximizes the extreme differences that could possibly obtain in personality and group structure ("absolute" and polar opposites) in order to observe and analyze the actual reality which appears in-between these types and tends to approximate one or the other extreme. In the analysis of communities, the concepts of *rural* and *urban* have emerged as the most popular ideal types. It becomes obvious that these distinctions serve merely as over-simplifications and even distortions with respect to the social changes that McCrorie discusses. Many of the patterns witnessed in agrarian Saskatchewan would normally be associated more with urban than with rural communities. It is especially with respect to political radicalism and social class differentiation that this appears to be the case.

33

In the discussion that follows, it is shown that the social development of Canada was not the result of "natural" economic progress or evolution. The urbanization and industrialization of Canada was due in no small measure to government planning before the turn of the century, and implemented largely through political decisions formulated in Eastern Canada. In the context of these political inducements toward rapid industrialization, the conflict between the relatively urban and industrial East and the basically agrarian West was to be anticipated. The inevitable "back-lash" of the western provinces, especially the development of radical political movements such as the CCF in Saskatchewan and Social Credit in Alberta continue to vitally effect the nature of Canadian society and to underline the conflict within it.

In his comparison of agrarian political movements in both Canada and the Soviet Union, McCrorie demonstrates what will be shown in other articles in this volume; i.e., structural conditions may give rise to somewhat similar consequences even in diverse societies. Thus, the conflict between the hinterland and the metropolis occurred in both capitalist Canada and the socialist Soviet Union, and the rural populations of both countries rebelled against the policies of forced and accelerated industrialization. Differences, however, were also witnessed, for the peasants of the Soviety Union resisted imposed communal economic activities, whereas the farmers of Saskatchewan developed their own communal organizations in order to better defend themselves against the economic exploitation of the eastern metropolis. Differences of this magnitude reaffirm the need for consideration of situational and historical factors in conjunction with structural conditions in social science research.

The paradox of the role of social class with respect to the changes occurring in agrarian Saskatchewan is also discussed. The author shows that it was the members of the "middle class" farmers who most sharply responded to the deliberate policies of industrialization and urbanization, and reacted to feelings of economic and political deprivation by forming economic and political organizations over which they could exercise considerable control. Thus, the owners of very small as well as very large farming enterprises were not so much involved in the radical agrarian movements which developed and continue to demonstrate considerable viatality in Saskatchewan.

In view of all of these factors, it is difficult to evaluate the future of the agrarian movement in Saskatchewan. McCrorie points out, for example, that large scale farming organizations are becoming more and more prominent and that the usual stereotype about the small-time grass roots farmer is rapidly becoming a myth of the past. To what extent will the increasingly large scale organization on the farms relate to the further development of radical political behavior similar to past patterns? It would seem, according to McCrorie's discussion, that at least some modified patterns of radicalism will continue so long as a sense of alienation and deprivation is felt even by the increasingly large scale farming operators, in spite of the usual tendency of economic entrepreneurs to engage in somewhat more conservative behavior. Should this be the case, it appears clear that most of our views of social class and associated political behavior require considerable reconstruction.

The portrait of the evolution of this interesting and multi-faceted agrarianism demonstrates the relevance of historical and situational factors in the analysis of societies and social change. In many ways, it also demonstrates that all groups, regardless of social class or objective economic interests, when faced with long-term situations of alienation, isolation, and feelings of deprivation, may engage in very similar forms of behavior.

As McCrorie's discussion shows, the conflict between metropolis and hinterland has been and remains endemic to the nature of social development and social change in Canada. This important factor, which so clearly distinguishes Canada from the United States, is also suggested in the discussions of Clark, Davis, and Vallee in other articles in this volume.

2

Change and Paradox
in Agrarian Social Movements:
The Case of Saskatchewan

JAMES N. McCRORIE

If one were invited to summarize the Saskatchewan farmers movement in a word, perhaps the term "paradox" would be appropriate. On the one hand, the movement involved a large number of small, independent, capitalistic entrepreneurs. It was rooted within the ranks of the agrarian middle class who believed, for the most part, in the private ownership of land and the means of production; who employed, until recently, seasonal labour; and who produced, from the inception of the agrarian west, a cash crop in the pursuit of profit.

On the other hand, the same farmers came to attack the owners of other industries having some relation to agricultural production. They vigorously quarrelled with banks, and mortgage and insurance companies. They tangled with railway companies, line elevators, and grain merchants. They expressed critical misgivings concerning federal marketing, and trade and transportation policies. They revolted against the political party structure of the nation and questioned, from time to time, the viability and desirability of capitalism. And they threatened, on more than one occasion, to secede from Confederation.

For example, dissatisfaction with the grain marketing system gave rise to the formation of voluntary co-operative elevator companies such as the Grain Growers Grain Company in 1906 (now know as the United Grain Growers) and the Saskatchewan Co-operative Elevator Company in 1911 — both of which sold grain through the Winnipeg Grain Exchange. The integration of marketing with production was further modified with the formation of the Saskatchewan Wheat Pool in 1923-24, a marketing co-operative that by-passed the Grain Exchange and pooled receipts. The fight to persuade the Federal Government to institute and then expand the jurisdiction of the Canadian Wheat Board is both long and complicated, and by no means over.[1]

[1] See H. Patton, *Grain Growers' Co-operation in Western Canada* (Cambridge: Harvard University Press, 1928); V. Fowke, *The National Policy and the Wheat Economy,* (Toronto: University of Toronto Press, 1957); C. Schwartz, *The Search For Stability* (Toronto: McClelland and Stewart, 1959).

Concern with the costs of production, including farm implements, fuel, timber, and credit gave rise to consumer co-operatives, the development of a co-operative wholesale society, an oil refinery, a farm implement co-operative, and credit unions.[2] And if the frequent demand for the nationalization of the railroads, the farm machine industry, the oil industry, and the banks was somewhat inconsistent with co-operative solutions to cost of production problems, it was, on occasion, no less emphatic.

The challenge was no less dramatic within the political arena. The passing threat of the Non-Partisan League in 1917 was a portend of things to come. The formation of the Progressive Party in 1921 gave organizational shape and direction to a growing dissatisfaction with what had become known as the "old line" parties. The birth of the Farmer-Labour Party in 1932 and the Co-operative Commonwealth Federation in 1933 acknowledged the more modest political innovations of the twenties and expanded the attack to include the very nature of a capitalistic society itself.[3]

While this brief inventory of events and developments is incomplete, it suffices to illustrate the paradox of which we speak; a paradox that is highlighted by the 1944 election of the CCF Party to office in a province that was then primarily rural and agrarian.

It was this event as much as any other that has provided a temptation to explain the paradox in terms of class conflict and class politics, to view the farmer as a special category of the urban industrial working class and the farmers movement as an appendage to a large working class political movement.[4]

The traditional discussion of stratification and class politics has been associated with the development and activities of an urban industrial community. In this connection, Marshall discusses a point that deserves mention:

> ... there is a quite different set of conditions which can produce two or more distinct systems of stratification in one society. And that is when society as a whole is not a true unit for stratification in terms of a particular dimension, but must be divided into two or more sections or regional areas, *each with its own stratification structure.* The most familiar example is a society fairly equally divided into agricultural and industrial — or rural and urban — sectors.[5]

Such has been the case of Saskatchewan in the larger Canadian context. The manner in which agriculture was organized and the productive relations which developed gave rise to an agrarian stratification system which was separate and distinct from the urban.[6] Using farm size as a crude

---

[2] See J.F.C. Wright, *Prairie Progress* (Saskatoon: Modern Press, 1956).

[3] See S.M. Lipset, *Agrarian Socialism* (Berkeley: University of California Press, 1959); W.L. Morton, *The Progressive Party in Canada* (Toronto: University of Toronto Press, 1950).

[4] See J.N. McCrorie, "The Saskatchewan Farmers Movement" (Ph.D. dissertation, University of Illinois, 1967).

[5] T.H. Marshall, *Class, Citizenship and Social Development* (Garden City, N.Y.: Doubleday & Co., 1965), p. 140. Italics added for emphasis.

index of class, it can be seen that by 1921, there were at least two distinct economic groups among the agrarian population. (See table below.)

CLASSIFICATION OF FARMS BY SIZE, SASKATCHEWAN[7]

Farm Size	Year	Year	Year	Year	Year
(Acres)	1921	1931	1941	1951	1961
Under 300	34.7	34.7	34.0	21.5	14.8
300-1,279	65.3	59.6	63.2	73.4	76.1
1,280 plus	—	5.7	2.8	5.1	9.1
Total	100.0	100.0	100.0	100.0	100.0

Some 34 percent of the farms were small in size and some 65 percent were of medium size. Between 1931 and 1961, the proportion of small farms declined, the proportion of medium size farms increased, and in the post-war years the proportion of large farms grew dramatically.

The importance of these differences in farm size is easy to minimize. Unlike the agricultural regions of the central provinces, agricultural production in Saskatchewan is dominated by wheat. Drought, grasshoppers, killing frost and hail affect all producers, regardless of farm size. Most are dependent on an international market and an international price over which they have neither direct control nor influence.

Nevertheless, differences in farm size remain and they relate to differences in income, in production and managerial problems, in machinery inventory, in access to credit, and, to some degree, in style of life.

It is of some significance that farm leaders in Saskatchewan were aware of these economic differences within the community and attempted, at the same time, to dismiss them as being irrelevant and insignificant in terms of the issues of the day. Indeed, it became a common rhetorical device to speak of farmers as a "class" and to equate the interests of the agrarian class with those of workers in the urban industrial centres.[8] One

---

[6] Agriculture in the province was organized primarily around the family. Capital intensive productive units have gradually replaced labour intensive units, resulting in smaller families and larger farm units.

[7] Census of Canada, 1961. All figures shown are percentages.

[8] This development, of course, was not peculiar to Saskatchewan. Johnstone notes that toward the middle of the nineteenth century, American farmers felt a close kinship with those who laboured in the cities. Society was viewed as being made up of two classes: those who laboured and those who profited from the labour of others. The term "labour" referred to all creative work with the hands, and included farmers as well as urban workers. The populist revolt of the 1890's was an attempt to weld rural agrarian and urban labour forces together in one political party. It is interesting to note in this connection, the similarities between the Omaha Platform of 1892, and the Regina Manifesto of the CCF in 1933. See P. Johnstone, "Old Ideals and New Ideas in Farm Life", in An Historical Survey of American Agriculture (Washington: U.S. Government Printing Office, 1941); R. Hofstadter, The Age of Reform (New York: Vintage Books, 1960); R. Hofstadter, Great Issues in American History, (New York: Vintage Books, 1960), Vol. II.

of the first and most eloquent advocates of this point of view was E. A. Partridge of Sintaluta, who in his *A War on Poverty* argued that both farmers and workers were victims of an economic system over which they had no control. Moreover, the nature of the system — capitalism — was such that the hardships and problems of workers and farmers would grow worse as time went on. Partridge suggested that farmers and workers should join together and bring about a socialist society in which production for use, not profit, would be the guiding incentive, a society in which those who laboured in the factories and tilled the soil would find their just reward.

Although Partridge's views were not widely accepted in his time, some farm leaders were influenced by them. One of the earliest and most controversial was Louis Philip McNamee of Kelvington, one of the founders and first president of the Farmers Union of Canada (Saskatchewan section).[9] McNamee was impressed with the gains workers had made through the organization of strong labour unions. A former railroad worker turned farmer, he believed that farmers were being exploited by the same group that continually fought the working man, namely, those who owned and controlled large industry and transportation facilities in Canada. During the thirties, McNamee visited Russia. Following his return, he continued to express the view that both farmers and workers were caught up in a class struggle and only the overthrow of the capitalist system would bring any measure of relief.

The birth and coming to power of the CCF in Saskatchewan gave an organizational base to the idea that farmers and workers had common interests and should work together to attain their mutual aims. During the fifties and sixties the Saskatchewan Farmers Union attempted to strengthen and improve the formal relationship that had grown up between their predecessor — the United Farmers of Canada (Saskatchewan section) — and organized labour, particularly the Canadian Labour Congress. The 1946 farm delivery strike and the threat of collective withholding action in the sixties indicated that the tactics appropriate to industrial labour in their struggle over wages and working conditions might be appropriate to farmers.

These developments notwithstanding, two considerations give rise to questions about these ideological claims. We have already mentioned farm size and income differences within the Saskatchewan agrarian community. Studies of the movement suggest that organizational activities within the movement tend to reflect class considerations. For example, farm families active in the CCF, the Saskatchewan Wheat Pool, the consumer co-operatives, and the Saskatchewan Farmers Union tend to come from the ranks

[9] The Farmers Union of Canada (Saskatchewan section) was organized in 1921. Some of its early leaders and members had been active in the Saskatchewan Grain Growers' Association — an educational and agitational organization of farmers that had been formed at Indian Head in 1901. For some, the older organization had become too staid and conservative in its policies. Through the new organization, they hoped to renew a tradition of radicalism associated with the early days of the Association. In 1926, the two organizations merged to form the United Farmers of Canada (Saskatchewan section). The organization changed its name in 1949 to the Saskatchewan Farmers Union.

of the agrarian middle class.[10] Put another way, organizational participation in the movement does not cut evenly across class lines. Low income and high income farmers are not as active in the organizational activities of the movement as middle income families.

We are not suggesting that class differences alone account for variation in organizational participation. There are other considerations to be taken into account.[11] For the present purpose, however, it is sufficient to point out that ideological claims emphasizing the unity of the agrarian community as a "class" are not born out by the pattern of organizational participation in the very movement to which the claims may be attributed.

A second and equally important consideration is a difference in the economic relations and problems related thereto between farmers, on the one hand, and industrial workers on the other. From the inception of the agrarian West, the Saskatchewan farmer has found himself involved in an intricate and ever-changing web of economic relationships with industries producing different but related goods and services. For example, he was dependent on railway companies to ship his product to export position. At one time, he relied on middlemen to store and then sell his grain on the international market. He was obliged to purchase farm implements from companies he did not own, borrow capital from banks he did not control, and sell some of his produce to processors whose interests did not always seem identical to his own.

Conflict was endemic to the situation. The interests of the one were too often incompatible with the needs of the other. For example, the fight on the part of the railway companies to persuade Parliament to revoke the Crowsnest Pass Rates Agreement was always matched by a heated and vigorous reply from farm organizations. The pursuit of higher freight rates on the part of the CPR and CNR was no less than agrarian insistence that lower freight rates on grain remain in effect.

The struggle between the agrarian West and the industrial East over tariffs and trade policy is another case in point. To the western grain farmer, the import of cheaper farm machinery from the United States or other countries was consistent with his own and what he thought to be the national interest. Such a policy was an anathema to eastern Canadian farm machine companies. The one sought freer trade and cheap farm machinery; the other supported tariffs in order to acquire a captive market.

One could consider other historical examples. More to the present point is the fact that labourers were often in conflict with the owners and managers of the same industries. For example, railroad workers were continually struggling for higher pay and better working conditions. The same was true of those who worked in farm machine companies, or pro-

---

[10] See, for example, Lipset, *Agrarian Socialism*, Chap. viii; McCrorie, "The Saskatchewan Farmers Movement", Chap. xii.

[11] *Ibid.* For example, education and ethnic background were found to be related to variation in organizational participation. Not to be overlooked is what we might call a social psychological propensity to find gratification in organizational life; a trait, if we may trust the opinion of hard pressed organizational leaders, that is not widespread among the population.

cessing plants, or terminal elevator companies. In such cases, the object of antagonism was the same for both farmers and workers.

However, the source of antagonism was different. Workers were involved in conflict within a given industry; farmers were involved in conflict between industries. The historical solution for the workers was to gain bargaining power over wages and working conditions within an industry; the historical solution for the Saskatchewan farmer was to gain control over other industries.[12] The worker eventually acquired bargaining rights within an industry; the farmer eventually took over some of the industries with which he was in conflict, integrating them to his farm operation. The worker remained a worker. The farmer became, in some instances, his new employer.

Seen historically, the alliance between farmers and workers was "natural" in the sense that many industries and their practices were viewed with alarm and hostility by farmer and worker alike. It is not surprising that the leaders of farmers sought a common cause with the leaders of labour and that in the process, both thought of their struggle, their interests and their goals as a class struggle, as class interests and class goals.

No less "natural", however, was the antagonism that was to arise when one party of the "alliance" became the employer of the other. It is evident that the farmers' relationship with labour was far more complex than a superficial review of their occasional common struggle and endeavors would suggest. The farmer was not a special category of the industrial labour force. He was and remains a petit capitalist entrepreneur who found himself in conflict with industries producing different but related goods and services. If the object of conflict gave him occasional common cause with labour, the source of antagonism was not identical nor synonymous with the roots of worker dissatisfaction. And the root of agrarian antagonism can be found in the conflict which arises between industries in a capitalist society and in the historical relationship of Saskatchewan agriculture to Canadian industrial development.

Reference has already been made to inter-industrial conflict as it concerns the agrarian population. The profits of any business establishment, be it a family farm or a steel corporation, are affected by the relation of that unit to other economic units producing related and different but indispensable goods and services.[13] For example, the farmer can reduce his

---

[12] We speak here of "historical" solutions to problems of inter- and intra-industrial conflict. Insofar as grain is concerned, the Saskatchewan farmer has experienced some success in vertically integrating the function of marketing with that of production. Such has not been the case in the livestock industry, where packing companies have been more successful in integrating production with processing than the other way around. In the case of industrial workers, the Winnipeg general strike of 1919 was one of the few instances in the history of the Canadian labour movement where worker control and ownership of industry was taken seriously. See D.C. Masters, *The Winnipeg General Strike* (Toronto: University of Toronto Press, 1950).

[13] To be sure, profit is the result of many considerations, including demand, price, the cost of labour, and so on. For purposes of analysis, however, it is convenient to draw attention to the function of inter-industrial competition in this regard.

costs of production by keeping old machinery in repair or by purchasing larger and more efficient implements. But the return on his capital investment will nevertheless be affected by the price he is obliged to pay for either new parts or new machinery. Or, consider the case of the grain merchant during the first three decades of the century. It was in his interest to "buy low and sell high", a practise to which the agrarian population took vigorous exception. In this case, as in others, conflict was inherent in the very nature of the relationship between the two.

This conflict was a problem common to all industrial groups in a changing capitalist society, a problem that has been aptly summarized by Schumpeter.[14] Not simply price competition, but competition over new commodities, new technologies, new sources of supply, and new forms of economic organization; these are the manifestations of competition that strike not simply at profit margins but at the very foundations of existing economic organizations. Thus, the struggle between the grain merchants and grain producers during the past sixty years, as one example, has been of "life and death" proportions. The establishment of the Canadian Wheat Board as the sole marketing agency for most western cereal grains in 1943 not only guaranteed a system of orderly marketing compatible with agrarian needs and interests; it dealt, in addition, a powerful blow to the grain trade in general and the Winnipeg Grain Exchange in particular. The same result has not been characteristic of the relationship between the livestock producer and the processing companies. The failure to establish a hog marketing board in 1964, for example, has enabled the processing companies in western Canada to further integrate production with processing on terms that are compatible with the needs and interests of the meat packing industry.

The consideration of inter-industrial conflict, however, is not in itself sufficient to answer the riddle of agrarian radicalism in Saskatchewan. It is also necessary to consider the history of that conflict in order to appreciate the special circumstances that envelop agricultural production in the West in general, and Saskatchewan in particular.

It is possible to think of Saskatchewan farmers as being *in* industrial society, but not *of* it. They have been *in* industrial society, so to speak, insofar as they consumed its products, contributed to its labour force, provided — through trade — some of the capital necessary for industrialization, were subject to its laws, regulations, and political processes, were involved in inter-industrial conflict, and shared some, if not all, of the general values that pulsated through the larger society. They were not *of* industrial society, so to speak, in that the aim or objective of national policy was the creation of a national urban and industrial society, not a national rural and agrarian or resource-based community.

The decision to develop a viable, national industrial society north of the 49th parallel was both conscious and deliberate. If it was formulated in a period (1870-1879) when some 70 per cent of the population was

[14] J. Schumpeter, *Capitalism, Socialism and Democracy* (New York: Harper and Bros., 1950).

rural based, it was nevertheless an emphatic rejection of that type of community and society. In the words of Sir Leonard Tilley:

> . . . it does appear to me . . . that . . . the time has arrived when we are to decide whether we will be simply hewers of wood and drawers of water; whether we will be simply agriculturalists raising wheat, and lumbermen producing more lumber than we can use . . . whether we will continue our attention to the fisheries and other certain small industries; . . . or whether we will inaugurate a policy that will, by its provisions, say to the industries of the country, we will give you sufficient protection . . .[15]

It is of course convenient to speak of national policy in terms of the tariff legislation of 1879. It is perhaps more accurate, however, to consider in addition, the political and territorial problems facing the nation following Confederation, as well as the economic needs of those engaged in trade and manufacturing in the central provinces.

Confederation represented an attempt to achieve economic and political unity among the former maritime and St. Lawrence colonies.[16] But as Fowke has pointed out, the western expansion of American railroads and settlement in the last half of the nineteenth century threatened to absorb territory west of the Great Lakes and north of the 49th parallel, a development the new Canadian government was determined to prevent. Fowke observes:

> The concept of a British North American domain to encompass northern North America from coast to coast was essentially defensive. It was a defensive nationalism marshalled to secure the frontiers against the surge of expansive American nationalism. More accurately, indeed, it might be designated counter-imperialism, an effort by the St. Lawrence colonies to establish effective empire over the western territories in order to forestall identical action by the neighbours to the south. It was obvious by the middle of the nineteenth century that the empty spaces of the British fur trader in North America would not long continue empty. They would become effectively occupied and developed and the only question was, what would be the economic and political affiliations of the occupiers? . . . The land and immigration policies of the Dominion government were focussed upon the goal of an agricultural west. De facto occupation of the plains would alone give reality to the legal fiction of British ownership.[17]

[15] An address to Parliament by the Minister of Finance, 1879, cited in Fowke, *The National Policy*, p. 65. See also W.A. Mackintosh, *The Economic Background of Dominion Provincial Relations* (Toronto: McClelland and Stewart, 1965); D. Smiley, ed., *The Rowell-Sirois Report* (Toronto: McClelland and Stewart, 1965), Book I.

[16] See D.G. Creighton, *British North America at Confederation,* study prepared for the Royal Commission on Dominion-Provincial Relations, 1939.

[17] G.E. Britnell & V.C. Fowke, *Canadian Agriculture in War and Peace, 1935-50* (Stanford: Stanford University Press, 1962), p. 21.

It is important to recognize, then, that one of the prime objectives of settling the West was to prevent American expansion west of the lakehead and north of the 49th parallel; to affect, rather, Canadian dominion from coast to coast.

But how? The answer lay in the conversion of the prairies from a fur trading domain to an agricultural community based on wheat. It had been argued with creditibility as late as 1857, that the western plains were unfit for agricultural settlement.[18] American expansion west of the Ohio placed this claim in contention. Wheat — a drought resistant grass plant — proved to be a crop of agricultural and commercial promise.

The possibility of creating a wheat economy in what had once been known as Rupert's Land was of more than political significance. The prospect did not escape the attention of eastern commercial interests, ever on the look-out for new export commodities. More important, the tariff policy of 1879, the construction of the Canadian Pacific Railway (1880-1885), and the federal land and settlement policies of the last quarter of the nineteenth century ensured an expanding and captive non-industrial market for central Canadian industry, re-aligning traditional north-south trade patterns on an east-west axis.[19]

In retrospect, it has been tempting to interpret the strong central government concept of the British North America Act, the federal purchase of Rupert's Land in 1870, the Indian Treaties of the 1870's, the national tariff policy of 1879, the construction of the Canadian Pacific Railway in 1880-85, and the suppression of the Riel Rebellion in 1885 — all as parts of a grand and comprehensive national plan.[20]

As we have already hinted, such was never the case. The confederation debates of 1866 represented something of a hasty and ad hoc response to the abrogation of the Reciprocity Treaty with the United States. The strong central government concept of the BNA Act was nevertheless a compromise between a strong legislative and a weak federal union. The national tariff policy of 1879 was a cautious, if conscious departure from the economic policies of Confederation. It was not until the last two decades of the nineteenth century that a clearer policy of national industrialization emerged; a policy in which the development of a wheat economy was functional, yet subordinate to national industrial ends; a policy that was able to take advantage of past decisions and undertakings.[21]

---

[18] See Mackintosh, *The Economic Background,* Chap. ii.

[19] See Fowke, *The National Policy,* Part I; C. Dawson & E. Younge, *Pioneering in the Prairie Provinces* (Toronto: Macmillan Co. of Canada, 1940); H.A. Innis, *The History of the C.P.R.* (Toronto: McClelland & Stewart, 1923).

[20] See G. Stanley, *The Birth of Western Canada* (Toronto: University of Toronto Press, 1963); P.B. Waite, ed., *The Confederation Debates in the Province of Canada* (Toronto: McClelland & Stewart, 1964).

[21] In this regard, the strong central government concept of the BNA Act cannot be overestimated. It is timely to point out that Sir John A. Macdonald viewed the Act as an improvement on the defects of the American Constitution. The provision of a strong central government with residual powers was deliberate; the unintended relevance of this provision for industrialization is apparent. See Waite, *The Confederation Debates,* pp. 40-44.

The establishment of a wheat economy in Saskatchewan required large capital investment, the establishment of marketing mechanisms, credit facilities, and transportation. Apart from investment in land by individual farmers, the necessary capital came from the east or abroad. The marketing, credit, and transportation facilities were built with eastern or foreign capital and designed to serve eastern or foreign needs and interests. The tariff provided a protected market for farm implements and machinery manufactured in the east. Provincial boundaries were drawn up in Ottawa, and the party system of the east was imposed, without modification, on the new western provinces.

In view of these considerations, it is clear that in addition to the hazards of climate, the agricultural community in the Canadian West found itself involved in an economic and political system that was neither of its making nor in accord in every instance with its interests. If, in the attempt to adjust and adapt to this system, the Saskatchewan agrarians considered forming new political parties and nationalizing industries other than their own, it was not so much an attempt to remake industrial society along more humane and enlightened lines (appealing at this might be) as it was an effort to control industrial development in accord with agrarian needs and interests. For it was in agrarian and rural terms, not urban and industrial ones, that the Saskatchewan farmer sought heaven on earth. It is in these terms that the paradox of which we speak must be explained and understood.

It is pertinent to inquire into the extent to which the Saskatchewan "paradox" has been unique. The question is both relevant and demanding, but we can only propose at this time to attempt an introduction to a more thorough and satisfactory answer.

Since 1900, there have been a number of issues which Saskatchewan has shared with farmers in other provinces. The railway and elevator issue at the turn of the century[22] involved the farmers of Manitoba as well as the territory now known as Saskatchewan. The marketing and Grain Exchange question of 1905-10[23] involved farmers in the three prairie provinces, as did the terminal and elevator issue of 1907-12. The trade and tariff issue of 1910[24] brought western, as well as Ontario farmers together in a march on

[22] See Patton, *Grain Growers' Co-operation*, Part I. The issue involved agrarian resentment over preferential treatment given line elevator companies by the railroads in general and the CPR in particular in the allocation of box cars for shipping of grain. The farmers charged that the railroad companies were conspiring with the grain trade to deny the producer direct access to the market.

[23] See Patton, *Grain Growers' Co-operation*, Part II; Fowke, *The National Policy*, Part II. At issue were certain trading practises in which farmers alleged discriminated against the producer, along with the growing demand that farmers, as well as middlemen or grain traders, should have an opportunity to store and market grain through the grain exchange by way of farmer owned grain companies or co-operatives.

[24] See Morton, *The Progressive Party*, Chaps. i and ii. The question of western agrarian opposition to tariffs and the incessant demand for free trade came to a head in 1910 when farmers from the provinces of Alberta, Saskatchewan, Manitoba, and Ontario marched on Ottawa to demand a radical change in federal trade policy.

Ottawa in the same year. Issues arising over credit and banking were common to most Canadian agricultural communities. The question of freight rates, while of more lasting importance to prairie farmers, was nevertheless a frequent concern of eastern Canadian producers. The marketing issues of the twenties involved the three prairie provinces and the struggle to reestablish a government compulsory wheat board during the thirties and forties involved Manitoba, Saskatchewan, and Alberta. Starting in the thirties and continuing through the forties and fifties, the question of prices — in particular, parity prices and the costs of production — was common to most Canadian farmers. The issues which arose in Saskatchewan were often found in other provinces. In some cases, they included the other two prairie provinces; in other cases, they reached beyond the West into the heart of the agricultural East.

The response of farmers to these issues frequently cut across provincial boundaries. The 1909-10 struggle of the Grain Growers' Company with the Winnipeg Grain Exchange involved farmers, organizations, and governments in both Manitoba and Saskatchewan. The 1910 march on Ottawa swept Ontario, as well as the prairie provinces of Manitoba, Saskatchewan, and Alberta. The federal election of 1921 and the electoral successes of the Progressives in Ontario and the prairie provinces, the struggle to organize the wheat pools in the prairie provinces, the 1942 and 1959 marches on Ottawa which swept Alberta, Saskatchewan, and Manitoba were all events which reached beyond the borders of Saskatchewan.

The political affairs of Saskatchewan were very much coloured and affected by developments within the farm movement. The Liberal Party was intimately involved with the movement up until the late twenties, the Progressives grew out of the movement in 1920 and 1921, and the CCF, having developed within the movement, has continued to retain its ties since the 1944 provincial election.

In varying degrees, the pattern is in evidence in other provinces. The United Farmers of Ontario formed a provincial government in the early twenties that clearly reflected the needs and interests of the agrarian community. The former Roblin Government (Conservative) in Manitoba was extremely sensitive to agrarian questions, taking a decided stand in the conflict between the Grain Growers' Company and the Winnipeg Grain Exchange and nationalizing the line elevator companies within the province in 1909. In Alberta, the United Farmers of Alberta elected their own government in 1921, the UFA administration remaining in office until 1935. Moreover, the formation and coming to power of the Social Credit Party (1935) connected the activities and some of the ideological predispositions of the UFA.[25]

In the field of commercial organizations, farmers in various provinces have undertaken to build co-operatives similar in purpose and design to those found in Saskatchewan. We have already noted the organization of

---

[25] See J. Irving, *The Social Credit Movement in Alberta* (Toronto: University of Toronto Press, 1959); C.B. Macpherson, *Democracy in Alberta: Social Credit and the Party System* (Toronto: University of Toronto Press, 1962).

United Grain Growers and the wheat pools in the three prairie provinces. Consumer retail and wholesale co-operatives have developed in all Canadian provinces. The 1945 Royal Commission on co-operatives found that most co-operative business was done in the three prairie provinces although by 1943, co-operative development was expanding and growing in Quebec and Ontario.[26]

Moreover, the Commission noted:

> . . . Canadian co-operatives have always had more to do with the sale of farm produce than with the purchase or sale of any other commodity. Their selling has been more important than their buying: 'marketing more important than merchandising'.[27]

Finally, educational and agitational organizations such as the Saskatchewan Grain Growers' Association, the United Farmers of Canada (Saskatchewan section), and the Farmers Union have been organized and operative in other provinces. In Manitoba, the Grain Growers Association (later to be known as the Manitoba Farmers Union) was formed at Virden in 1903. The United Farmers of Alberta was organized in 1905. In Ontario, the Grange, the agricultural societies, and later the United Farmers (1916) were organized for a similar purpose and in a similar way.

This brief and tentative review of agrarian unrest and agitation in some, but not all of the other provinces, is nothing more than suggestive. As we might expect, the prairie provinces share much in common, and only on occasion do they collectively make common cause with farmers in eastern provinces such as Ontario.

Even within the West there is considerable variation in response to what would appear to be common economic and political problems. One need only consider the development of the CCF in Saskatchewan, Social Credit in Alberta, and the absence — since the 1920's — of any comparable radical political development in Manitoba to appreciate that the historical response of farmers to common economic and political problems in the three prairie provinces is far more complex than first impressions might suggest.

Studies of agrarian movements in the United States and France suggest the same conclusion.[28] In both countries, farmers organized a variety of educational and agitational organizations, marketing, credit, and consumer co-operatives, and they occasionally became involved in direct political action through the formation of new and primarily agrarian political parties.

It is important to point out that regional and commodity differences within rural America and France produced considerable variation in the agrarian assessment of and response to the problems created by industrialization. In the United States, for example, it was in the South and in the

[26] *Report of the Royal Commission on Co-operatives* (Ottawa: The King's Printer, 1945).

[27] *Ibid.,* p. 78.

[28] See for example, C. Taylor, *The Farmers' Movement* (New York: The American Book Co., 1953); G. Wright, *Rural Revolution in France* (Stanford: Stanford University Press, 1964).

West that agrarian hostility to the challenge of urbanization and industrialization reached proportions resembling the Saskatchewan experience.[29] Mention has already been made of the similarities between the Omaha Platform of 1892 and the Regina Manifesto of 1933. The revival of the Non-Partisan League in North Dakota during the thirties and the Nashville Manifesto "I'll Take My Stand" renewed agrarian suspicion of and hostility to the larger industrial society in both the West and South respectively.[30]

In France, where the prospects and value of industrialization were less certain or taken for granted, the agrarian response to the process frequently included attempts to "repeal" the growing urban industrial community and to return to, or develop, a vigorous rural society in its stead. It is not without significance that Marx, observant as he was of the emergence of industrial capitalism, was somewhat perplexed over the attitude of some of the French peasantry to industrialization.[31]

The occasional appeal of the "left" *and* the "right" to some, if not all, French peasants remains a paradox as long as we insist that the peasant is in some manner an appendage to the urban industrial working class. Wright, in a careful study of agrarian France, suggests that such is not, and has never been, the case. The occasional appeal of the left or the right is rooted in the same consideration. Both from time to time, quarrelled with, and took exception to contemporary industrial processes. And it was these processes and their implications for agriculture that was of concern to the peasant.[32]

This consideration is more than evident in post-revolutionary Russia. In 1921, the Russian Government proclaimed the New Economic Policy (NEP).[33] It is not without irony that the Bolsheviks had captured the leadership of a revolution which was in many respects agrarian, and had achieved power in a society that was barely industrial.[34]

The NEP reflected this irony. The civil war that followed the October Revolution of 1917 had decimated the rural countryside and undermined what modest industrial progress Russia had made since the 1890's. To many Bolsheviks, including Lenin and Trotsky, the total collapse of the Russian economy appeared to offer the opportunity of building socialized industry

[29] Hofstadter, *The Age of Reform,* Chap. iii.
[30] Lipset, *Agrarian Socialism,* Chap. vi; C. Vann Woodward, *The Burden of Southern History* (Baton Rouge: Louisiana State University Press, 1960); A.K. Davis, "Decline and Fall", *Monthly Review,* No. 12 (October 1969).
[31] See K. Marx, "The Eighteenth Brumaire of Louis Bonaparte", *Selected Works* (Moscow: Foreign Languages Publishing House, 1962), Vol. I.
[32] See Wright, *Prairie Progress,* Chap. iv-viii.
[33] See E.H. Carr, *The Bolshevik Revolution* (Harmondsworth: Penguin Books, 1966), Vol. II, especially Chap. xix.
[34] Lenin's own appreciation of this point was expressed in his April Theses, delivered upon his return to Russia six months prior to the October Revolution. See V.I. Lenin, "The Tasks of the Proletariat in our Revolution", *Selected Works* (Moscow: Foreign Languages Publishing House, 1960), Vol. II. See also L. Trotsky, *The History of the Russian Revolution* (New York: Simon & Shuster, 1932), Vols. I-III.

from scratch, without the hindrance and obstruction of established institutions from the old regime. The success of this kind of programme depended in no small measure on the ability and willingness of the peasant to produce for the urban market. By 1920, it was abundantly clear that the peasant had no such intention. The requisitioning of food, the control of distribution, and the ban on trade was resulting in subsistence rather than surplus production.

To correct this situation, the Soviet Government designed the New Economic Policy, providing for free trade in agriculture, distribution, and other small scale industries.[35] The new policy at once heightened and postponed the solution to the basic conflict between town and country, between industrialization and agrarian production, between fundamental, long range government goals and objectives, and peasant needs and interests.[36] In the words of one economist:

> During the 1920s . . . there was a persistent problem of getting food for the cities and for export. Insofar as peasants had larger incomes, they were interested in improving their farms and were neither able nor willing to provide funds for industrial development. An increase in industrial investment, in these circumstances, meant mainly an increase in farm prices. City food supplies would tend to become short, and farmers would actually cut back on their deliveries unless manufactured goods were sent to the villages.[37]

This dilemma made its presence felt in the struggle within the Bolshevik Party for power in the years following Lenin's death. Without minimizing the other issues involved, it may be said that the leaders of the Party momentarily divided into two groups: the one advocating an improvement of the NEP and support for the peasantry, especially the more productive kulaks, and the other pressing for more intensive industrialization, primitive socialist accumulation of capital, the exemption of small farmers from taxation, a progressive tax on kulaks, and the gradual and voluntary collectivization of agricultural production.[38] Between 1926 and 1927, an intensive struggle over this and other issues took place. The left or "united opposition" of Trotsky, Zinoview, and Kamenev was defeated by Bukharin, Rykov, Tomsky, and Stalin, who sided with the other three for political if not ideological reasons. At the close of 1927, it appeared that rural agrarian Russia had reasserted herself and had found in Bukharin and his followers, political leaders who were sympathetic to the agrarian community.

The victory was short lived. Within a year Stalin was in the process of reversing himself. Through the instrument of the first Five Year Plan,

---

[35] It should be noted that major industries, finance, and international trade remained under government control.
[36] For a further discussion see I. Deutscher, *The Prophet Armed* (New York: Vintage Books, 1965), Chap. iv.
[37] E. Ames, *Soviet Economic Processes* (Homewood, Ill.: R.D. Irwin Inc., 1965),
[38] Deutscher, *The Prophet Armed,* Chap. v.
Chap. viii, p. 126.

Stalin adopted many of the economic measures proposed in 1926 by Trotsky. In effect, he tipped the balance of the scale in favour of more intensive industrialization and more rigid regulation and control of agricultural production and the allocation of investment. The response of the peasantry was both dramatic and brief. They attacked and in some cases murdered local government and party officials; they withheld their products from the market, slaughtered their livestock, and burned surplus crop.[39] The Government, however, was adamant. With the fall from power of Bukharin and his followers, avenues for protest and pressure within the Party and the Government were closed. The peasant was faced with the choice of collectivization or deportation. By 1934, private agriculture had been largely eliminated; agriculture had finally become functional and subordinate to the process of intensive industrialization.

The relevance of the Russian experience to this discussion can be restated. Mitrany argues and we concur that:

> The startling fact is that Communism has only come to power where by all Marxist tenets it might have been least expected that it could. In every instance, from 1917 in Russia to 1949 in China, Communism has ridden to victory on the back of disaffected peasantries; in no instance has it come near victory in industrialized "proletarian" countries.[40]

And we might add, why? The Saskatchewan experience suggests a tentative answer. Some Saskatchewan farmers were prepared to embrace, and other farmers were prepared to tolerate, if not support, co-operative institutions and a political party with claims to being "socialist" so long as co-operatives and "socialism" promised to solve agrarian problems in a large urban industrial society on agrarian terms. The agrarian support of the October Revolution, the temporary alliance between Lenin (and later, Bukharin) and the Russian peasants appears to be rooted in the same consideration. The break between the peasants and the Russian Government came with the first five-year-plan, not with the New Economic Policy. And it came on the eve of what appeared at the time as a significant victory of the Bolshevik "right" and the peasantry over all that Trotsky and the "left opposition" stood for.

To summarize and conclude, it would seem that the reaction of agrarian communities to the process of industrialization varies from country to country, and from region to region within countries. Where agriculture is clearly subordinated to the process of industrialization, the response of the agrarian community can be dramatic. The cases of Saskatchewan in the larger Canadian context and agrarian Russia come to mind.

In such cases, a paradox would seem to follow. The process of industrialization and urbanization provides the basis of agrarian unrest, concern,

---

[39] Ames, *Soviet Economic Processes,* Chap. viii.

[40] D. Mitrany, *Marx Against the Peasant* (New York: Collier Books, 1961), Chap. xvi, p. 207. (With permission from the University of North Carolina Press.)

and alienation; yet the reaction is in agrarian and rural, not industrial and urban, terms. The farmer is not a worker disguised in boots, overalls, and a cloth cap.

The ideologies that emerge can, in some cases, reflect this situation in rather startling terms. Again a reference to Saskatchewan and Russia is appropriate. Capitalism, in the case of Canada, and communism, in the case of Russia, have proven to be vehicles of industrialization in these respective countries. In the case of Saskatchewan, it is not surprising that many, if not all, farmers should come to associate, if only momentarily, the evils of industrialization with the capitalist system within which it develops, and in attacking the one, condemn the other. In the case of Russia, communism — so-called — was tolerated by the peasantry so long as the Government made some attempt to solve agrarian problems on agrarian terms. The dramatic rejection of the Government and its policies by the peasantry occured at the same time the Russian Government decided to proceed with its plan for intensive industrialization.

Tentative as these conclusions may be, they nevertheless suggest the value in the further undertaking of case studies of agrarian and other rural hinterlands in Canada. The relevance of such studies to a better understanding of industrialization and the nature of Canadian society is apparent.

Urbanization
and
Industrialization:

Causes and Consequences

3

EDITOR'S INTRODUCTION

An important consideration in the analysis of Canadian society is the accelerating urbanization of its population. Over the last century, the proportion of the Canadian population living in cities has increased from less than 10 per cent to about 70 per cent.[1]

The general magnitude of Canada's urbanization, including some regional and provincial differences, is indicated by the following table:

URBAN (METROPOLITAN) POPULATION INCREASE FOR CANADA AND PROVINCES, 1951-61*

	Number	Per cent increase
Canada	2,526,911	44.8
Nfld.	22,218	32.4
P.E.I.	—	—
N.S.	50,015	37.3
N.B.	17,226	22.0
Que.	718,984	41.1
Ont.	1,032,609	45.8
Man.	119,176	33.4**
Sask.	—	—**
Alta.	297,533	93.2
B.C.	269,150	39.9

*Source: Abstracted from Yoshiko Kasahara, "A Profile of Canada's Metropolitan Centres", *Queen's Quarterly*, LXX, Autumn 1963, reprinted in Bernard R. Blishen, et al., eds., *Canadian Society* (Toronto: Macmillan of Canada, 1968), p. 68.

**What appears to be relative lack of urbanization in Manitoba and Saskatchewan is misleading. Leroy Stone, *Urban Development in Canada* (Ottawa: Queen's Printer, Dominion Bureau of Statistics, 1967), p. 38, shows that for the period 1941-1961, the prairie provinces generally manifested the greatest increase in rate of urbanization in Canada.

Some interesting variations and patterns are indicated by this composite picture. Although Ontario, British Columbia, and Quebec have a relatively high proportion of their populations residing in cities, the rate of urbanization in the prairie provinces, generally, and Alberta,

[1] See Leroy Stone, *Urban Development in Canada*, 1961 Census Monograph, Dominion Bureau of Statistics (Ottawa: The Queen's Printer, 1967), pp. 16-17. This estimate is perhaps a liberal one, for it considers population centres of 2,000 and over. On a more cautious or conservative definition of "urban", (20,000 and over), Canada had 52 per cent of its population in such centres in 1961.

in particular, is higher than that of the older industrial provinces. The maritime provinces have generally lagged behind, along with the Northwest Territories.

Many social changes that have occurred or are developing in Canada are related to urbanization. Not only has the Canadian metropolis affected institutional and individual life, but it has also altered the nature of social, economic, and political life in the Canadian hinterland.

The hinterland has not simply been changed because of the diffusion of urban influences. Such diffusion, including the increased "urban" character of small towns and rural areas, brought about by centralization, mass marketing, and the mass media, is widely acknowledged among students of community life, especially in the United States.[2] In Canada, industrial-urban centres have brought about changes in the hinterland in additional ways for reasons that are peculiar to the nature of Canada's urbanization and industrialization. On the one hand, the direct meeting of "urban" and "rural" through the development of Canada's northern industrial cities, discussed by Clark in the following article, gave rise to economic and ethnic conflicts which both highlighted and increased the limitations of a capitalist system; similar problems of the same magnitude did not develop in the United States where large-scale industrial development was generally exclusive to the larger metropolitan centres. On the other hand, as suggested by McCrorie elsewhere in this volume, populist agrarian movements, although they have occurred in the history of the United States, are still being generated in Canada and are of significant political magnitude. These movements are largely centred around reaction and opposition to the economic establishment of Canada's metropolitan East.

There are, however, similarities between the United States and Canada in terms of certain social consequences of urbanization and industrialization if only urban dwellers are taken into consideration. Changes in social institutions, as well as new and developing forms of social deviance, have been witnessed in the cities of both countries.

These changes were the concern of "Chicago-School" sociologists of the 1920's and 1930's, including Robert Park, Louis Wirth, Harvey Zorbaugh, Ernest Burgess, and many other contemporaries and students, all of whom were concerned with developing general theories about the urban community.[3] They tended to accentuate the vastness of changes in social life brought about through urbanization. While in some respects, they romanticized and idealized cities for their potential to enhance the human condition, they generally emphasized the disorganizing processes of urban life, especially the disintegration of traditional social institutions such as the family and religion, the indi

[2] See, for example, Arthur J. Vidick and Joseph Bensman, *Small Town in Mass Society* (Princeton: Princeton University Press, 1958).
[3] For a review and evaluation of some of these theories of community, see Maurice Stein, *The Eclipse of Community* (Princeton: Princeton University Press, 1960).

viduation and isolation of human existence, the emergence of racial and ethnic conflicts, and the increases in criminality and deviance.

Studies conducted by the "Chicago-School" sociologists, as well as more recent studies, have generally tended to confirm some of the expectations of a relationship between urbanization and social disorgranization.[4] It was shown that the urban family was smaller, more mobile, and had less "control" over the behaviour of individual members than the rural family. Urbanites appeared to be more oriented to spheres of influence found outside of the family and kinship confines. Religious organizations and religious beliefs and practices were also found to be of less relevance to the urban-dweller than to his rural counterpart. Even if the formal religious institution and organization had some relevance, they had, in the urban environment, become highly bureaucratized and secularized.

These institutional changes were commonly associated with the apparent concentration of criminality and deviance in large urban areas in the United States.[5] In that country, generally higher rates of criminality and deviance appeared to characterize urban life in contrast to smaller communities and rural areas.

While it appears that the association between urbanization, institutional deterioration, and criminality has been generally considered as truistic, there is good reason to suspect it and, perhaps, even to refute it. Hartung,[6] for example, has argued that the differences in crime rates between urban and rural communities, may be simply attributable to differences in the visibility of crime and reaction to it; while offenses in the city are frequently observed and reported, and thereby enter into the criminal statistics, the same offenses in the rural community may be handled "informally" (by family and friends) and thus never appear in the criminal records. Hartung also suggests that the actual extent of criminality is generally no different between urban and rural communities.

Clinard[7] has suggested, but not yet fully developed, a somewhat different approach to the explanation of the association between urbanization and criminality. He suggests that it is not urbanization itself which might be related to high rates of criminality, but instead, the *rate* of urbanization; the higher the rate, the more extensive the institutional deterioration and, consequently, the higher the rate of

---

[4] A comprehensive range of these, and other areas of urban research may be found in Paul K. Hatt and Albert J. Reiss, Jr., eds., *Cities and Society* (New York: The Free Press, 1957), and Scott Greer, et al., eds., *The New Urbanization* (New York: St. Martin's Press, 1968). See also Sylvia Fava, ed., *Urbanism in Word Perspective* (New York: Thomas T. Crowell Company, 1968).

[5] For a brief discussion and critique of some of these interpretations, see Marshall B. Clinard, *Sociology of Deviant Behavior* (3rd ed.) (New York: Holt, Rinehart and Winston, Inc., 1968), pp. 80-114.

[6] Frank E. Hartung, *Crime, Law and Society* (Detroit: Wayne State University Press, 1966), esp. pp. 93-124.

[7] Clinard, *Sociology of Deviant Behavior*, p. 105.

criminality. Thus, Massachusetts, which has shown relatively little recent urban growth, has a lower crime rate than California, which has had one of the highest urban growth rates in the United States.

Both of these alternative approaches to the explanation of urbanization and criminality have some relevance to a brief discussion of patterns in the Canadian scene.

As suggested by Clark some time ago,[8] the early development of Canadian cities was characterized by extensive institutional deterioration and high rates of criminality and deviance. Much of this pathological behaviour was "hidden", simply because it was handled "informally"; the formal control agencies, including the police, became operative and effective in detecting criminality during later stages in the development of Canadian cities.[9]

In view of the absence of reliable criminal statistics and formal social control agencies during the early stages in the development of Canadian cities, it is difficult to determine whether relatively recent urbanization in Canada has, in fact, "caused" increases in criminality.

The statistical evidence suggests a generally strong relationship between urbanization and criminality in Canada. Giffin[10] has shown that the crime rates for Canadian cities have been generally higher than the rates for rural areas, including both adult criminality and juvenile delinquency. These differences, while not as clear as those generally found in the United States, suggest a similar pattern. Also, *rates* of urbanization of the different Canadian provinces were found by Giffin to be generally associated with criminality and delinquency, although the differences were not strongly significant, statistically. However, no association between delinquency and the relative size of urban communities in the various provinces was found. In view of this limited evidence, it can be suggested that the size of the city is not related to different rates of criminality; it appears to be more a matter of growth than absolute size.

Alberta, for example, which is not highly urbanized compared to Ontario and Quebec, but has a much higher rate of urbanization, also has a relatively high rate of delinquency and criminality.[11]

The relationship between criminality and institutional deterioration has not yet been systematically examined in Canada, but there is evidence that shows that social institutions such as religion and the family have been greatly affected by urbanization, similar to the pattern in the United States.

The secularization and bureaucratization of the Church, especially with regard to the religious attitudes and practices of the urban middle

[8]S. D. Clark, *The Social Development of Canada* (Toronto: University of Toronto Press, 1942), pp. 248-263 and 380-472.

[9]For a discussion of the evolution of the police as an agency of formal social control in Canada, see W .H. Kelly, "The Police", in W. T. McGrath, ed., *Crime and Its Treatment in Canada* (Toronto: Macmillan of Canada, 1965), pp. 109-135.

[10]P. J. Giffin, "Rates of Crime and Delinquency", in McGrath, *ibid.*, pp. 59-90.

[11]*Ibid.*, pp. 70, 72, 87.

classes in Canada, has been documented by a number of authors.[12] With massive urbanization in Quebec, beginning in the 1920's, and accelerating, especially since World War II, the influence of the Catholic Church has declined considerably; the virtually monopolistic control of Quebec's educational and welfare systems by the Church has been broken,[13] and an increasing number of young French Canadians are either neutral or anti-clerical.[14]

The secularization of religion in Canada, generally, is also reflected by the increased participation of the clergy of all faiths in politically related activities, especially through urban renewal and community action programmes which are designed to provide more economic opportunities and power for the urban lower classes in this world instead of the world to come.

The structure and functions of the Canadian family have also been altered drastically by the pervasive processes of urbanization — similar, again, to the pattern in the United States. The Canadian family, especially among both French-Canadian and English-speaking urban middle classes,[15] has become smaller, more mobile, and less relevant in terms of effective social control over individual members. The traditional *extended* family (consisting of three or more generations in the same household) is no longer a characteristic pattern.[16] It is especially among the French Canadians that family structure and functions have been most clearly altered because of urbanization. It has been found that the French Canadian family in urban areas has become *nuclear* (consisting of only two generations in the same household); this change is reflected by the fact that the French Canadians' knowledge about kin beyond their immediate family members has diminished considerably during a short span of time.[17]

In some ways, the impact of urbanization on the institutions of the family and religion has resulted in a *demographic* convergence between French Canadians and English-speaking Canadians. During the last several decades, the long-term trend in Canada has been the gradual decrease in fertility rates, although the French Canadians had

---

[12]See, especially, J. R. Seeley, et. al., *Crestwood Heights* (New York: John Wiley & Sons, Inc., 1963), pp. 212-216, 352-355, and Stewart Crysdale, "Urbanism and Its Relationship to Religious and Theological Perspectives", in *Canada: A Sociological Profile*, ed. W. E. Mann (Toronto: The Copp-Clark Publishing Company, 1968), pp. 368-380.

[13]Fernand Dumont and Guy Rocher, "An Introduction to a Sociology of French Canada", in *French Canadian Society*, eds. Marcel Rioux and Yves Martin (Toronto: McClelland and Stewart, 1964) I, pp. 194-197.

[14]*Ibid.* The increasing anti-clericalism of the young French Canadians was in ample evidence during my research visit to Montreal early in 1970.

[15]See Frederick Elkin, *The Family in Canada* (Ottawa: The Queen's Printer, 1964), esp. pp. 31-71.

[16]*Ibid.*

[17]See a discussion of the relationship between urbanization in Quebec and variations in kinship recognition by Marcel Rioux, "Kinship Recognition and Urbanization in French Canada", in Rioux and Martin, *French Canadian Society*, pp. 372-385.

been maintaining relatively high fertility rates.[18] During the past decade, however, the fertility rate of the French Canadians has decreased to one below the national average. This demographic convergence has occurred largely because an increasing proportion of French Canadians were becoming urbanized, while an increasing proportion of English-speaking Canadians were becoming suburbanized.[19]

Although it is legitimate to suggest that the massive modifications of traditional social institutions such as the family and religion brought about by urbanization merely indicate a functional and healthy accommodation to new and different social requirements, there is little doubt that considerable stress is experienced by individuals who are undergoing the transition from rural to urban life, especially among members of the first and second generation migrants. In the Canadian West, especially, where massive urbanization has occurred during a relatively short period of time, institutional deterioration, economic maladjustment, social isolation and alienation, appear to be common among urban residents who were "socialized" in relatively small rural communities.[20]

The pattern of the impact of urbanization on social institutions appears similar in Canada and the United States; the extent of this impact, however, seems greater in the United States than it does in Canada. The Canadian family, generally, is larger than the family in the United States.[21] The Canadian fertility rate is also higher.[22] Moreover, urban crime rates in Canada are considerably below those in the United States.[23] These differences may be attributable to the perpetuation of ethnic pluralism in Canada, whereby the relative social-cohesion within different ethnic groups tends to be perpetuated for a longer period of time, thus counteracting institutional deterioration which is more characteristic of "assimilationist" societies such as the United States. Moreover, the considerable post-war immigration to Canada, including a relatively high number of immigrants from urban communities in other societies, has, in some ways, minimized the problems of urban adaptability. On the one hand, the urban background of many of these immigrants has "prepared" them for urban life in Canada. On the other hand, some evidence indicates that immigrants to Canada,

[18] Jacques Henrepin and Nathan Keyfitz, "Les Tendances demographiques au Canada et aux Etats-Unis", Canadian Review of Sociology and Anthropology, II, No. 2 (May, 1965), p. 80.
[19] See Nathan Keyfitz, "Human Resources in Canada: Population Problems and Prospects", in Contemporary Canada, ed. Richard L. Leach (Toronto: University of Toronto Press, 1968), p. 23.
[20] Richard J. Ossenberg, Community Opportunity Assessment: Calgary Study (Edmonton: Human Resources Research and Development, Government of Alberta, 1967).
[21] Arthur P. Jacoby, "Some Family Problems in Canada and the United States: A Comparative Review", in Social Problems in Canada, ed. Richard Laskin (Toronto: McGraw Hill of Canada, 1965), pp. 280-284.
[22] Henrepin and Keyfitz, "Les Tendances".
[23] Based on a comparison of data presented by Giffin, "Rates of Crime and Delinquency", passim., and Clinard, Sociology of Deviant Behavior, p. 100.

in comparison with immigrants to the United States, tend to perpetuate their institutional distinctiveness longer,[24] largely in response to the Canadian encouragement of ethnic pluralism or the "mosaic".[25]

But urbanization in Canada, similar to the United States, has both accentuated and "caused" severe problems of economic inequality, expressed in severe social class differences, which provide the potential for revolutionary social movements. The magnitude of urban poverty in Canada is not unlike that in the United States, and is attributable to the economic system common to both countries. The poor in Canada are beginning to express increasingly militant sentiments with regard to their conditions of absolute or relative deprivation.[26] Urban community action programmes designed to resolve some of the problems of economic and social inequalities have had little impact thus far, largely because of the lack of political and popular support. This condition cannot be perpetuated without the inevitable development of considerable social conflicts and revolutionary social movements. Canada's *vertical mosaic*,[27] as a major facet of Canadian pluralism, cannot continue without significant reactions and repercussions.

Some similarities and differences between Canada and the United States with respect to urbanization have been discussed. Urbanization in both countries has brought about certain structural similarities. Yet, the distinctive aspects of urbanization and industrialization in Canada remain to be analyzed, including the influence of historical antecedants, peculiar aspects of Canada's ecology, and, especially, the role played by elites in the shaping of Canadian cities. Professor Clark's discussion provides a beginning for an understanding of these factors in the evolution of Canadian society.

[24]One of the most striking examples of this was provided by Rudolph Helling, "A Comparison of the Acculturation of Immigrants in Toronto, Ontario, and Detroit, Michigan", unpublished (Doctoral dissertation, Wayne State University, Detroit, 1962).

[25]Richard J. Ossenberg, "The Social Integration and Adjustment of Post-War Immigrants in Montreal and Toronto", *Canadian Review of Sociology and Anthropology*, I, No. 4 (November, 1964), pp. 202-214.

[26]This is a dominant theme in the numerous reports about the public hearings held by the Canadian Senate Committee on Poverty throughout 1970.

[27]John Porter, *The Vertical Mosaic* (Toronto: University of Toronto Press, 1965).

3

The Position of
the French-Speaking Population
in the Northern Industrial Community[1]

S. D. CLARK

GENERAL CONSIDERATIONS

Much of Canadian history is a history of the relations of English and French in the structure of Canadian life. In this article, attention is focussed upon the position of the French-speaking population in one particular segment of the Canadian society — the industrial society of northern Ontario and Quebec as this society has developed over the past thirty years.

The industrial society of northern Ontario and Quebec exemplifies in striking form the nature of the situation which develops when economic control becomes lodged in the hands of powerful corporate establishments. The hold of the ruling group cannot be easily broken, and especially by persons of a different ethnic origin. The financial capital as well as the management and skilled personnel for these corporate establishments came from English-speaking Canada or the United States. As a consequence, it was English-speaking persons who controlled the economic and political life of these communities from the beginning. The French-speaking population which made up a large part of the labour force (and a large part of the total population) found itself almost wholly dependent, economically and politically, upon the English-speaking population. In the structure of power, the two ethnic groups began by occupying extreme polar positions — the one group clearly dominant, the other subordinate.

Yet, in the development of the new industrial communities of northern Ontario and Quebec, no ethnic group was in a more potentially strategic position than the French Canadians to take advantage of the opportunities offered. The northern areas of Canada had long been known to French Canadian fur traders, voyageurs, and explorers. With the extension of railway lines into northern Ontario and Quebec, great numbers of French Canadians moved into these parts of the North to settle. Already by the turn of

[1] Based on data collected by the author during his field work in the communities discussed.

the century, within the province of Quebec, settlement had spread north eastward up the Saguenay Valley to the lower end of Lake St. John, and north westward up the Ottawa Valley into the areas east of Lake Timiskaming. Across the border in Ontario, a large French origin population also established itself early.

Given the character of development of the lumbering and mining industry and even of the pulp and paper industry throughout the North, the active participation of the French in these industries might have been expected. Many of the industries of the North were established by enterprising individuals who started out with little influence or capital. Few of these individuals, however, were French Canadians. In all the industrial communities of the North, the French made up an important part of the population very easily; but it was as unskilled workers, not as industrial entrepreneurs, that they settled in these communities. The penetration of the North by the French-Canadian population was made by settlement on the land.

Political and church leaders in Quebec had been highly successful in persuading people to settle on the land, and, for a time, in keeping them there. In Ontario, the provincial government, anxious to promote the industrial development of the North, had held back large blocks of land as pulpwood preserves, and, where settlement was permitted, had limited it to townships along the railway. But in Quebec wherever roads could be built and land cleared, farm settlement had been encouraged. Government and Church combined to provide extensive aid to the new settler and to keep the development of new farm areas under close control. Settlement took place through the establishment of "colonies", with much of the structure of the farm community established before people moved in; here there was no haphazard scattering of farm population over a great area. The use of the land survey system, long familiar in southern Quebec, offered assurance that individual farm families would not live in isolation, separated from farm neighbours and the church. The systematic creation of new farm colonies extending out from old secured, in the end, the effective establishment of great blocks of farm settlements, stretching for miles across the North.

The methods of colonization employed had two important results. Vast areas of the North were opened up for farm settlement which would have been left lying waste had dependence been placed upon individual enterprise; and early abandonment of northern farms, in face of the hardships experienced, was discouraged. But the price paid was a heavy one. Substantial government assistance made farm settlement in the North appear deceptively easy. Virtually no capital on the part of the individual settler was required, and continued government subsidies encouraged the settler for years after settlement to remain on the farm, however meagre the returns. Church efforts to provide for the social and spiritual needs of the pioneer farm population of the North conspired to the same end. People were persuaded by the substantial benefices from the State and the Church to undertake and to continue the effort of farming in the North when, if left to their own resources, they would either not have made the effort at all or, having made it, would have quickly given up. What was established, throughout vast areas of the North, was a farm industry which could not support the population which was made dependent upon it. The immediate effect was to create for the growing industrial communities a large pool of part-time workers. Ultimately, the effect was to provide these communities with their main source of labour.

It was a ruthlessly exploitative type of economy which developed in the North. In the early development of the mining and pulp and paper industries, there could be little concern for the well-being of the people involved or for the communities of which they were a part. For the promoters of new industrial enterprises, there was the promise of great riches but always the threat of financial disaster as well. Where success or failure depended so much upon the realization of immediate profit, the drive to keep down labour costs was intense.

RURAL AND URBAN CONTRASTS

For a large part of the labour force, however, in the early industrial development of the North, an important protection was offered. In time of economic boom, the North faced the problem of an acute shortage of labour. Most of its workers had to be recruited from outside. The Canadian city offered no certain supply and it was from other parts of Canada and from the world beyond that its early workers largely came. The diversity in the background of these workers, their isolation in the North, and their lack of any form of trade union organization placed them in a weak position in dealing with unscrupulous employers. There were few industrial communities which did not experience in the early years of their development labour troubles leading often to open conflict and violence. Labour was exploited in the North as was the North's physical resources. But so long as labour maintained the attribute of mobility, its exploitation could be carried only so far. It was upon highly mobile types of workers that the northern industrial community largely depended for its early supply of labour. Workers sufficiently mobile that they could be recruited were mobile enough that they could not be kept for long if conditions of work proved intolerable.

For a time, it was in the character of a camp that the northern industrial community developed. The promoters who reaped the profits of industrial development left little or nothing behind. The fine homes they built themselves were built in Toronto, Montreal, or other such old established centres, and it was here that their benefactions were made. They invested little in the community of the North. Indeed, even the physical plant which their industrial enterprise required could readily be dismantled and moved on to other places. The abandoned mine shaft or mill soon became a familiar sight in the North. So did the abandoned shacks or dormitories which had once housed workers, the wooden community hall and the various other physical structures that had given a crude shape to what had once been a community. The North grew and prospered — up to a point — by avoiding any investment that could not be realized upon quickly and wholly. In this regard, there was no great difference between the industrial promoters in the North and the vast majority of workers. If the employers of workers came and went, so did the workers.

As industrial enterprises grew in size, however, and large numbers of workers were required, an increasingly high price was paid for the failure to build up a stable work force. An acceptance of responsibility by these larger employers for the welfare of the community in which they operated was a reflection of their realization that if workers were to be persuaded to remain in the North, they had to be given a stake in it. Very early in the development of many of the industrial communities of the North, the problem of attracting trained personnel had led to the providing of company houses and recreational facilities for senior company officials. There quickly became established around the mine or mill or in the nearby town a compound of well-built and painted homes, situated on treed lots, with streets circling and leading to an attractive company recreational centre (by northern standards) and an inn for visiting company executives. From the provision of such amenities, it was a short step to the company's acceptance of at least some responsibility for the providing of homes and various community services for the body of its workers. Thus emerged, in various degrees of completeness, the company town.

In superficial appearance, there was a vast difference between the company town and the town which grew up with no company participating in its development. It took the visitor to the company town, however, no great time to discover that the shacks, unpaved streets, ill-kept stores and such, so characteristic of the booming northern industrial community of early years, had not been eliminated by the company town. The "camp" had simply been pushed outside the town's borders.

A substantial economic outlay would have been made by northern industrialists had they undertaken to provide decent housing and social amenities to the whole body of their workers. In the end, they might have been forced to, had they continued to depend upon the recruitment of workers from the outside world. Kitimat, in the interior of British Columbia, could only be established by making available in the community all those amenities and facilities, including a high standard of housing, provided by the old established urban community; and, even then, a serious problem of labour turn-over was not avoided. In northern Quebec and Ontario, industrialists, in their failure to accept the costs of providing decent housing and community amenities for a large part of their work force, continued for some time to pay the price of depending upon highly mobile types of workers who could as easily move out of the North as they could move in.

But for the industrial community of northern Quebec and Ontario, the northern farm settlement soon came to offer a supply of workers that could be relied upon to remain in the North, almost regardless of the conditions of work, and it was a supply not quickly exhausted. Throughout the years 1900-1955, farm settlement in the North proceeded alongside industrial development. As older established farm settlements began to give off population to nearby industrial centres, new farm settlements came into being.

There was provided, as a consequence, a continuous and increasing supply of workers for the growing industrial communities of the North. And these were workers almost completely lacking the attribute of mobility. The northern farm settlement destroyed in the individual the capacity to move. It was not the highly mobile people who settled in the North in the first place. They were people who were moved to the North through the combined efforts of the State and the Church; and once there, they had no means of getting out. For a time, substantial subsidies kept them on the land, but when circumstances forced them to seek a livelihood elsewhere, they had neither the means nor the will to venture far afield. Part-time work off the farm offered a means of making the transition from farm operation to industrial employment. When the move was made from part-time to full-time work off the farm, there could result no great change in the individual's manner of life. For many northern families, the shack of the bush farm was given up for the shack of the town, but, other than that, conditions remained much the same. A population made economically defenceless by years of struggle in farming in the North was now made economically defenceless by being pushed into marginal forms of employment in the northern industrial community.

In this regard, there was no important difference between the population recruited from farm areas of the North that was French in origin and the population that was not. The immobility of the population was primarily owing to its farm experience as such. What gave distinctiveness to the population that was French in origin was simply its size. English-speaking people did settle in the farm areas of the North but, apart from those who located in that fertile farm area stretching north of New Liskeard to Englehart, few remained beyond two or three years. The marginal farm lands of the North were occupied predominantly by French Canadians.

Where as in mining towns, such as Cobalt or Timmins in the early years of their development, virtually the whole population was compelled to live in make-shift quarters and little effort was made to make of the community anything more than a place of temporary residence, there was nothing in the social position occupied by the French-speaking population which distinguished it from the rest of the population. In those industrial communities, however, where capitalist enterprise played a more responsible role and an effort was made to provide those workers in demand with attractive living conditions, a very marked difference developed between the way of life of certain sections of the population and other sections. The company town offered itself as an attractive place to live, but it was made attractive only by the development outside its borders of places of residence for those who could not afford to live within it. What emerged in such an industrial community was an exceedingly sharp division of social classes. Housed within the company town limits, very largely, were the personnel the company valued. This was personnel which could not be recruited locally and included plant managers, engineers, accountants, technicians and such. Housed outside the town limits was that great mass of marginal industrial workers, persons without the skills or aptitudes which made them of any great value to the industrial enterprise. Increasingly, this mass of industrial workers came to be made up of people moving into the industrial community from northern farm settlements and thus it came to be made up of people of French origin.

What was achieved in the company town industrial community was a relatively stable work force. People from the outside were given a large stake in the community. They were provided with a house, a good school, a hospital, pleasant shopping facilities, and various other community amenities. More importantly still perhaps they were brought close to the seat of power in the community. The head office of the company may have been a long way off, but within the community itself company and town tended to become one. The people who ran the town, and the people who lived in it, were scarcely distinguishable. The fraternity of the company became the fraternity of the town. It was, as a consequence, with pleasant and important people that one associated. In a curious paradoxical way, the company town knew no social class boundaries. People could boast, with reason, that "in the North" it did not matter what was a person's family background or how much money he had. Everyone mixed freely and easily with everyone else; that is, with everyone else within the company town's limits.

The consequence was a high degree of "settling down" on the part of people who were recruited from the outside world. There was also a settling down of the large unskilled labouring force recruited by the northern company town industrial community. For these people, not a great deal was offered in the way of community facilities or a structure of community life. But the industrial community of the North was one easy to move into and find a social place. Beyond the built up area of the community lay great stretches of virtually waste land. Squatting in many cases was possible, but even where land had to be bought it commanded no great price. With building lots readily available and rough lumber near at hand, houses could be built cheaply and quickly. In every northern industrial community there grew up a type of residential area which seemingly knew no outward bounds. Streets, if such they could be called, wandered off into the woods, eventually perhaps to come to an end on the approach to a small river or lake. For people who early moved into the northern industrial community, the small frame houses and shacks which sprang up were intended to serve as nothing more than temporary living quarters, but, where the community took on a company town structure, the residential areas outside the company town limits, as well as within, began to assume an air of permanency. The social cohesiveness of the community within gave a social cohesiveness to the community without.

It was the rural background of the population which set off the residential areas developing outside the company town so sharply from the town itself. The company town was given a highly urban character. It was not permitted to grow, as most towns have grown, from a rural village to an urban form. It was made an urban community, whole and complete, from its beginning. Absent were those forms of kinship and neighbourhood association, and the physical apparatus giving expression to such forms, found in the normal small town. Everything about the company town was urban, including its population. Economically, socially, and politically, the company town developed from the industrial enterprise which had been responsible for bringing it into being. The company personnel set the tone of the community, and this was a personnel highly urban in social background. The plant managers, engineers, accountants, technicians, and even skilled workers were the product of an urban environment. In the nature of their social aspirations, tastes, attitudes and values they stood in sharp contrast to people of rural background.

Thus the two cultural worlds of the northern industrial community were the two cultural worlds of urban and rural. The urban, by the nature of the large-scale economic enterprise which developed in the North, was highly urban, while the rural, by the nature of northern farm settlement, was highly rural. Characteristic of the urban cultural world was the engineer, with his casual dress, easy social manners, conversational skills, and ambition to get ahead and do well by his family. Characteristic of the rural cultural world was the farmer or farmer's son turned truck driver, the construction worker or casual labourer, with a style of dress much less smart, manners more awkward, vocabulary more limited than his urban compatriot, and with an ambition that appeared to take little account of the future. Differences such as these, it is true, showed up whenever rural and urban were brought together; but these differences had a new prominence that they did not have in the old established urban community. Not only was there a greater polarization of the two ways of life, but the juncture of the two ways of life was more suddenly brought about.

The conflict of urban and rural would have arisen whatever the ethnic identity of the population had been. Indeed, in the early development of the northern industrial community, ethnic differences in the population had little social significance. A heavy premium had been placed upon individual enterprise; among the more enterprising in the community were often European immigrants, socially uprooted in their homeland and determined, in the new land, to get ahead. The North was a great social leveller, where all that counted was a man's willingness to work hard, make money, and take his place in the social life of the community. A large part of the whole population of the North, in the early years of its industrial development, was a socially uprooted population. The people who settled there, whether Canadian or foreign born, had left the world they had known behind and were, in effect, making a new start in life. Where success was measured by standards that had nothing to do with where a man had come from or what he had once been, ethnic differences had little place.

It was thus not ethnic differences as such which figured prominently in the structure of social life of the northern industrial community. The differences assumed an ethnic guise only because the population of rural background was one predominently of French origin. The Irish family from Pontiac County, or another such rural area, was as little adapted to the conditions of life of an urban-industrial society as was the French Canadian family. Unlike the European immigrant family of rural background, the Canadian rural family, in moving to a nearby urban-industrial centre, experienced no sudden change in its way of life, no break with its past. It carried into the new industrial-urban environment the values generated and sustained by a rural environment. It was these values, not values of ethnicity, which set off the family of rural background from its highly urban neighbours. Given the fact, however, that the Canadian population of rural background in the northern industrial community was predominantly of French origin, it was inevitable that the resulting conflict of values would become translated into ethnic terms.

In relation to the Anglo-Saxon population, the position of the European immigrant appeared as disadvantageous as the French; indeed, more so. Though the family of French origin may have occupied a frame house, crudely constructed, it was often located on a large lot, and there was much fresh air and play space for children. Few of the pleasures which had been enjoyed in the rural community had to be given up with residence in this type of urban area. There was no crowding here — great open spaces lay beyond the built up outer reaches of the community — and there was no concern about the demands of unreasonable landlords or city authorities. In contrast, it was a crowded condition which characterized the down-town residential area where the European immigrants dwelled.

But it was this very crowded condition which largely determined the character of mobility of the European immigrant resident. The European immigrant was soon forced out of the down-town residential area in search of living space. That is not to say that place of residence alone contributed to the mobility of the European immigrant. There was nothing he brought with him — not even his language — which was of much use in making his way in the new world. What he sought on his settlement in the urban-industrial community was not a place in which to settle, but a place from which to move. His character of residential mobility reflected his character of economic and social mobility.

Unlike the European immigrant, the family from a nearby farm area sought in the northern industrial community a place to settle down. The residential area on such a community's outskirts was an easy place to move to but a difficult place to move from. A condition of residential immobility became closely related to a general condition of economic and social immobility. The rural-reared person turned urban resident sought to cling to the conditions of life he had known in the rural community. He wanted a home he could call his own and this he could most readily find in areas outside the constructed parts of the community; he wanted the type of job where he could be his own boss and this was best secured by exploiting the simple skills he had brought with him from the farm rather than by acquiring new skills. The hammer and saw, the ability to drive — and repair — a truck or car, and a great resourcefulness provided the person from the farm with the means by which he would acquire a house and a vocation in the new industrial community of the North.

For the less mobile rural-reared person, however, the avenues of advancement were severely restricted. In no paradoxical fashion, the northern industrial community was at one and the same time a wide open and a tightly closed community. It was a wide open community in making it possible for people to live wherever and however they wanted to live beyond the boundaries of the restricted company town area and to engage in a wide variety of economic pursuits outside the range of operation of the major industrial enterprise. But it was also a tightly closed community where the opportunities for economic — as well as political and social — advancement were almost wholly determined, at least for a very long time, by the major industrial enterprise. It was very largely only people associated with the major industrial enterprise of the community who could get ahead, become economically better off, and politically and socially more important. The industrial development of the North had involved the recruitment of a personnel with particular managerial and technical skills, and it was to this personnel that the larger rewards went. The system of preferment extended from the industrial enterprise to embrace the whole community. The people who were important in the company — or to the company — were the people who became important in the community.

As the northern industrial community developed, a broadening of its economic base did occur. New ways were to be found for achieving economic success. Even the most rigidly structured company-town industrial community could not for long wholly control the economic, and political, and social life of the community. If opportunities for advancement were denied within the structure of the company town, they could develop in the community outside. Ultimately, the lines separating the closed industrial community of the North from the open became, up to an important point, obscured. There were soon large areas of economic endeavour over which the company could exercise no control. People became rich — and up to a point, politically and socially important — by engaging in such enterprises as selling real estate and insurance, operating a garage or taxi service, expanding a corner grocery into a large retail establishment, or building and operating a motel on the outskirts of the community. There occurred in time in all northern industrial communities a widespread shift in social class alignments.

But there were important limits to the system of social mobility which developed. Where economic advancement was denied within the bureaucratic establishment of the major industrial enterprise, it would only be achieved by operations carried on in peripheral areas of the community. Characteristically, it was in enterprises like construction, automobile sales and repairs, trucking, the taxi business, real estate and insurance, the building and operation of motels, or (where political influence could be brought to bear) in the management of governmental enterprises like liquor stores or employment agencies, that the person possessed of the simple skills and resources of the rural-reared could find opportunities for economic advancement. Such enterprises required no great amount of capital to get started, made no heavy demands in the way of educational or social skills, and offered to the individual a great deal of independence. Very often there was a moving about from one such enterprise to another.

For the most part, enterprises of this sort had two important limitations. They could not be expanded beyond a certain point; and they involved catering to the wishes and tastes of the dominant population element in the community (that is, the English). There were not many enterprises owned by the French which represented a very large capital investment or which involved the employment of a great number of workers. And there were not many enterprises, unless they remained, as in the case of the corner grocery store, very small, which could afford not to adapt itself to the demands and the pressures of the dominant English-speaking community. The consequence was the failure on the part of French-speaking people engaged in such enterprises to take any important lead in securing an improvement in the economic and social position of the French-speaking population in general.

It was, indeed, a happy-go-lucky type of middle class business person who was produced by the northern industrial community. He was a person ready to accommodate himself to the immediate economic and social position he found himself in. If such an accommodation meant catering to the English-speaking element, speaking their language and adopting the role of a good-natured social subordinate, no great objection was taken. A large measure of profanity and braggadocio served to cover up an awkwardness of speach and manners upon the part of even some of the most successful of French-speaking business men in the North. Viewed in relation to the social class structuring of the community as a whole, the weak economic and social position of the French-speaking business middle class was apparent.

What economic success was achieved by a small number of French-speaking persons in the northern industrial community only threw into bolder relief the inferior economic and social position of the French-speaking population as a whole. Only a very small middle class could develop in the North. Opportunities for the vast majority of the population were limited to occupations of a working class nature. For persons settled in the North, the extent to which there existed opportunities for satisfying wage employment was of crucial importance, while for those young persons who were not yet a part of the work force, the opportunities to move out of the North were of primary importance. On both counts, the French-speaking population did badly. The French-speaking population, very largely, was to be found in the lower strata of the occupational hierarchy, and compared with other population elements in the community, only a very small proportion of its new generation of workers was being prepared to take their place in the larger working world outside the North where most of the opportunities for economic advancement lay.

THE INFLUENCE OF ELITES ON SOCIAL STRATIFICATION

The social system which had been long operating in the northern farm settlement was extended to the northern industrial community. Within this social system, the Church had occupied a central position. The dominant concern of the Church had been to maintain the Catholic attachment of the population, more than its ethnic attachment. The stability of the rural society had depended upon the population developing no high social aspirations. People had been neither encouraged nor anxious to concern themselves with the management of the affairs of the community at large. Control of such crucial undertakings as that of education had been left largely to the Church, and through this control the Church had been able to determine the shape of the rural society.

When movement from the farm inevitably came, its effects were minimized, paradoxically, by the very lack of preparation of the population for non-farming ways of life and of work. The settlement of the French-speaking population on the outskirts of the northern industrial community made possible its escape from the responsibility of participating in the management of the community's affairs. Two systems of power were able to emerge in the northern industrial community without seriously clashing: that of the major industrial enterprise and that of the French-speaking Catholic Church.

The first interest of the major industrial interest, of course, was that of cheap labour. Trade-unionism developed slowly in the North, and met vigorous resistance from the campanies operating in northern communities. The reliance for long upon a work force made up largely of European immigrants strengthened the hand of industrial employers in their efforts to keep unions out of the North. The immigrant dominated trade union had been highly vulnerable to the charge of acting as an agent of the Communist Party.

In the end, however, the demands of trade-unionism could not have been withstood by even the most resolute of employers if dependence had continued to be placed upon the European immigrant for a supply of labour. It was the displacement of the European immigrant by the French-speaking rural migrant in the industrial work force that made possible, until very recent years, the maintenance of non-union labour conditions in the North. The French-speaking Catholic Church openly opposed trade-unionism.

The interest of the major industrial enterprise in maintaining a supply of manual labour continued for long to coincide with the interest of the Church in maintaining the Catholic attachment of the population it served.

The major industrial enterprise was the representative of a body of shareholders, and, as such, its major concern was the maximization of profits by, among other means, keeping down labour costs. But it was also the representative of a body of people on the ground, people concerned about the kind of community they had to live in, and, what was a dominant concern, about the future of their children. Within the industrial enterprise, there was no sharp, clear line separating one class of people from another with respect to such a concern. Indeed, if it developed greater strength among certain elements of the work force than others, it was among those occupying positions in the middle range of the occupational hierarchy. Those at the very top could isolate themselves from and remain largely indifferent to what was offered by the community.

This is not to say that there developed easily and quickly a sense of community on the part of the North's industrial work force. For a long time, the major industrial enterprise showed little readiness to entrust to the population the management of the affairs of the community in which it was situated. The town's officials were appointed by the company, or the election to office of the right people secured by the exercise of its influence; and the major institutions of the community — educational, recreational, cultural, and religious — were established through the company's support and under its direction. Even the houses people lived in and the stores in which they made their purchases could be company owned. But as the northern industrial community developed, there occurred an important shift of control of the community's affairs from the company to the community itself. Those people who were important in the company — its plant managers, engineers, accountants, and such — became important also in the town. It became their interests as residents of the community which determined how the affairs of the community were managed.

The consequence was a strengthening drive to secure improvement in those facilities of the community which touched closely upon the welfare of the people, and particularly of the new generation. It was, of course, the middle class which took the lead. Persons of the middle class not only possessed the most power, but they were the ones most alive to what was important for their welfare. Community facilities, such as those of education, became of vital concern to a people who, themselves enjoying the economic and social prerogatives of middle class occupations, were acutely aware that in the northern industrial community opportunities for advancement into middle class occupations for young people were exceedingly limited.

It was not always easy to persuade the industrial worker of the importance of such a community facility as education, but among the English-speaking element of the working class population at least no powerful institutional vested interest stood in the way. Schools, recreational centres, libraries, churches and such were made ready to serve the needs of the whole population. If their establishment in the beginning was largely owing to the support of the major industrial enterprise in the community, the community as such, in the end, was compelled to accept the responsibility for their maintenance and extension.

But such involvement of the major industrial enterprise (or of the people associated in an important way with this enterprise) in the institutional life of the community extended only to the limits of the community as an English-speaking and largely Protestant social complex. The northern company town was almost wholly and completely a Protestant town. The company management as well as the company's work force at all the higher occupational levels was Protestant. Thus the community institutional structure established with company support was one designed primarily to serve the needs of the English-speaking Protestant (and somewhat more awkwardly the English-speaking Catholic) population within the community's borders. The drive to extend to the whole population the benefits of those community facilities giving expression to the values of the middle class stopped short at that line separating the French-speaking Catholic population.

This population, whether situated outside the limits of the company town community or within, from the beginning was made a part of an institutional structure sharply distinguished from that of the company town community. Two distinct social worlds came into being, and there was no serious clash between them for a long time. The system of power of the major industrial enterprise, and given expression through the growing influence of a middle class largely associated with that enterprise, was seldom brought into a position of opposition to the system of power of the French-speaking Catholic Church. The schools, neighbourhood associations, and fraternal and religious societies built up to serve the needs of the French-speaking population secured the considerable separation of the social world of the French-speaking from the social world of the English-speaking.

There did develop, of course, certain serious points of strain. Even under the most ideal circumstances, the two social worlds could not be kept wholly separate. The working world that developed in the northern industrial community operated to a very considerable extent to secure the separation of French-speaking and English-speaking people. In the pulp and paper industry, the French became predominantly woodlands workers; in the mining industry, workers above the mine. Yet, while the working world of the French-speaking population developed largely apart from that of the English speaking population, the two worlds could not remain wholly apart. French-Canadians did become mill workers or miners. They entered other lines of employment which had no ethnic identification. The working world of which they became a part was an English-speaking world. In it, the English language occupied a dominant position; the values, social aspirations, manners of behaviour and thought associated with the English-speaking social world predominated. In order to progress, the French Canadian found himself becoming more of an English Canadian. Support of trade union activities, at a point in time when such activities were still dominated by English-speaking persons, could represent a serious break with his culture for the French-Canadian worker.

A second point of strain developed from the socially ambiguous position of the French-speaking middle class which was produced by the northern industrial community. This middle class owed its position to the successful building up of peripheral types of enterprises which were neglected or disdained by the English. Opportunities for economic advancement which characteristically were seized by the European immigrant proved not wholly unattractive to the French. Like many European immigrants, many French Canadians got ahead by developing a capacity to adapt to the tastes and demands of a public, not always reputable, prepared to pay for what it wanted. The consequence was to shift those persons, now middle class in social position, into the social world of the English-speaking. For such persons, intermarriage with the English could represent the break with their culture and race.

A third point of strain in the relation of the social world of the French-speaking to the social world of the English-speaking developed around the activities and the demands of young people. It was, of course, in communities situated within the English-speaking province of Ontario, that this strain assumed its most severe form, but there was no escaping it even in the predominantly French-speaking communities of Northern Quebec. On the street, if not in the school and the home, French Canadian youth came in contact with English Canadian youth. Indeed in the social gatherings on the streets and in restaurants, the lines separating the French from the English became almost completely blurred. Friendships developed across ethnic lines, ideas flowed back and forth, and with them manners of speech and behaviour, values, tastes, beliefs. Young English-speaking persons became more French, but not nearly so much as young French-speaking persons became more English, so long as the world outside, where the greater glamour and power was to be found, was predominantly English speaking. For the young French-speaking person there was a great deal that the English-speaking world had to offer, or so it appeared.

In the end, the Church was bound to fail in its effort to keep the French-speaking population of the northern industrial community Catholic by keeping it working class, just as it was bound to fail in keeping the French-speaking population of the rural community Catholic by keeping it immobile. Neither the working class urban society, nor the rural society, possessed the means to sustain itself beyond a certain point. The rural society sought survival by extending outside its boundaries, but ultimately it could only persist by the transforming of a large part of its population into an industrial urban population. In like manner, the French-speaking population in the industrial urban community could only so long depend upon manual occupations as a means of securing a livelihood. Every new wave of migrants from farm areas resulted in a further building up of a supply of workers to fill what manual labour positions were available in the industrial community. On the one side, increasing numbers of French-speaking workers were forced into the ranks of the unemployed to become a serious force of strain in the structure of the French-speaking working class urban society. On the other side, avenues of advancement out of manual occupations were seized by the more enterprising (or more exposed) elements of the French-speaking population. In the efforts of French-speaking workers to improve their working class position by participation in trade union activity, in the move of French Canadian persons into middle class positions, and in the assimilation by young French Canadians of English values and ways of thinking, the social system of the northern industrial community built up around the French-speaking Church met serious challenge.

Yet, like the rural society, the French-speaking society of the industrial urban community was almost totally lacking in the means of broadening its basis of support. Its population had neither the resources nor the will to develop those instruments necessary to secure its economic and social advancement. The institutions of the community built up about the Church offered the population little opportunity to secure experience or training in the management of its own affairs or in the development of means of community improvement and self-betterment. As a result, the points of strain which did develop could lead to no serious effort to remake the society. French-speaking persons who moved close to the English-speaking world of work, business and pleasure — industrial workers, middle class business men, young people — were persons very largely without power. What economic or social success they achieved gave emphasis to their marginal character, in both the French-speaking and English-speaking societies. Such was particularly the case of French-speaking youth.

In the associations of the street, the young French-speaking person could "get ahead." His very facility in the two languages gave him an advantage in aspiring for recognition and social prominence. He could develop the reputation of being a good fellow, with a wide circle of friends and acquaintances. But success stopped short at the point where the limits of the associations of the street were reached. Beyond those limits, the young French-speaking person became almost wholly dependent upon what the French-speaking urban industrial society of the North had to offer him. A very large number of his English-speaking associates moved on to a world outside. The young French-speaking person, unless he was one of a fortunate few (such as the boy who made good in hockey and ended up with the *Canadiens*), knew no world beyond the industrial North, possessed no means by which he could move from the associations of the street to the associations of the adult world, and maintain the status he had won for himself in the associations of the street.

The French-speaking industrial worker or middle class person who moved ahead by conforming to the demands of the English-speaking world of industry or business came to occupy a position almost as greatly limited in power and influence as that occupied by the French-speaking young person. Until a new type of leadership emerged, and the associations (trade unions, chambers of commerce, and such) to which the French-speaking industrial worker or small business man was made to belong became transformed, the success achieved by individual French-speaking persons in the world of industry or business could lead to no important broadening of the sources of power in the French-speaking society of the northern industrial community. The associations of work and business remained for long a part of the English-speaking world. They had no place in the structure of social life — or of power — of the French-speaking community. Thus French-speaking persons who were attracted into their ranks were made marginal to their own society. For long, they remained marginal as well to the other society — the society of the English-speaking industrial and business world.

For the great mass of French-speaking people of the northern industrial community no means of advancement out of a world of manual labour and relative poverty existed. The very distance of the North from the older developed areas of the South operated as a formidable barrier to movement from the North to the South. The social structure of the English-speaking northern industrial community was built up in a way to overcome this barrier. It was the determination of those English-speaking persons brought in by northern industrial enterprises to provide for their children the education that would make them as mobile as they themselves had been when they settled in the North. Through the leadership of these middle class elements, the benefits of such an education were made available, to an important degree, to the whole population of English-speaking young persons. In contrast, the social structure of the French-speaking northern industrial community was built up in a way to take advantage of the physical isolation of the North, to make more formidable the barrier of movement from the North to the South. French-speaking young persons were discouraged to look beyond the North for opportunities for employment. Education, as it developed in the French-speaking northern industrial community, had as its object the limiting of the young person's capacity for mobility. Young persons, apart from a favoured few, were provided an education appropriate for a people engaged in manual occupations.

The development of a capacity for mobility in the French-speaking population could come only with the movement into the northern industrial community of French-speaking persons possessed of such a capacity. People had to want to get ahead, and even more had to want their children to get ahead, before they could become interested in the creation and support of instruments of social mobility. There was required a willingness to give up benefits of the present for future benefits, a willingness to be taxed for something that offered no immediate returns. A working class population could not easily be persuaded of the advantages of supporting a costly system of education. In this regard, there was no great difference between the English-speaking society of the northern industrial community and the French-speaking society. In neither society did the mass of the population display any very great interest in education. But in the English-speaking society there developed very early around the major industrial enterprise a powerful middle class whose position depended upon perpetuating those advantages it had enjoyed through education. A middle class of this type developed very slowly in the French-speaking society.

With the growth of urban population, a number of French-speaking professional people did settle early in the North. But scattered throughout the North, their number in any one community was exceedingly small. The middle class of the northern industrial community developed strength from two important sources. The first, of course, was the major industrial enterprise, with its dependence upon having on the spot a body of managerial and professionally trained people. The second, and scarcely less important, was the complex of secular institutions which, though standing apart from the major industrial enterprise, was essential for the life of the community in which this enterprise operated. The school system, with its ever growing body of professionally trained teachers, stood close to the centre of this complex of secular institutions.

The French-speaking middle class was without either of these two important sources of support. The major industrial enterprise was dominated by English-speaking interests. For long, the complex of institutions operating in the community of French-speaking people was dominated by the Church. The result was that until very recent years the French-speaking professional middle class remained socially isolated in the northern industrial community. They could make a place for themselves only by becoming a part of the larger and predominantly non-French-speaking middle class of the community. This, in fact, is what most of them did. Successful French-speaking doctors or lawyers took up residence in the English-speaking residential areas of the northern industrial community. Many of them participated actively in the secular life of the community in which they lived. Some even "passed over" to the point of sending their children to an English-speaking school. Where accommodation to the English-speaking world was not carried this far, dependence could be placed upon the French-speaking world outside. The child of the French-speaking professional family of the North characteristically was provided an education by schools and colleges in older French-speaking centres of southern Quebec. The adjustment of the French-speaking professional middle class to the French-speaking society of the northern industrial community was made largely by socially isolating itself from it.

Such an adjustment or accommodation was possible so long as this middle class remained small in numbers. But, even before there was any important change in the power structure of the northern industrial community, there occurred a substantial growth in the size of the French-speaking middle class. French-owned industrial and commercial enterprises established themselves in the North, and new types of professional services came increasingly into demand. The Quiet Revolution in the North found its beginnings in the strengthening influence of this new French-speaking middle class.

In establishing a position of influence and power, there was no certain direction that the French-speaking middle class might have moved. An effort could have been made to transform the French-speaking society into an English-speaking society, and, up to a point, such an effort was made. To progress and even more to provide the conditions which would assure the getting ahead of the next generation, the French-speaking middle class could find tempting the acceptance of the demands of the English-speaking world.

But if this class had the most to gain from accommodation to the English-speaking world, it had also, in the end, the most to lose. Its constituency primarily was a French-speaking one. The doctor, in becoming less French and more English, could only hope that his patients would likewise, or else he could be threatened by their loss to a doctor remaining yet French. Increasingly, the vested interest of the French-speaking middle class in ethnic separateness took hold. Growing support of such separateness from outside, particularly in those communities lying within the province of Quebec, steadily swung the balance in a direction away from accommodation.

What occurred was an intensification of the division between French and English within the northern industrial community, on the Ontario side of the border as well as the Quebec. For a long time, it had been possible to talk about the state of harmony which existed in the relations between English and French. French-speaking church leaders could so talk, as well as English-speaking business and political leaders. The ethnic issue did not intrude itself into community affairs or into the affairs of business or politics. There were, it is true, antagonisms which found forceful expression at the face-to-face level of social relations. Few French-speaking children failed to escape the experience of having such epithets as "Frenchy" or "Frog" hurled at them on the street. There was among the English-speaking population a deeply rooted prejudice against the French. French-speaking people were considered priest-ridden, unreliable, lacking in ambition. But feelings of animosity on a personal level did not seriously disturb the relations between the two population groups on a community level. French and English did "get along" very well in most of the industrial communities of the North as these communities developed over the years.

Such communities, of course, were dominated by the English-speaking population. It was English-speaking people who occupied most of the important positions in the community and lived in the best residential areas. They were financially the best off. The division that existed was not an ethnic but a class division. The great mass of French-speaking people were poor, and powerless, not because they were French, but because of the circumstances that led to their settlement in the North. The prejudices directed against them were essentially class based prejudices. The rich can never approve of how the poor live. On the other hand, however, what were faults of the French-speaking at the level of personal relations, became virtues at the level of collective group relations. The French-speaking did not press, as did the European immigrants and workers of English, Scottish and Irish origin, their disadvantageous social class position. The bitter industrial disputes which developed in the North touched scarcely at all on the issue of French-English relations. The antagonisms which were engendered of an ethnic sort were directed against the worker of European origin.

The growth in the northern industrial community of a French-speaking middle class had no important effect upon the underlying social class structure of the community. The French-speaking middle class persons who took up residence in the North were persons with interests, tastes, aspirations and values not different from those of the English-speaking middle class. They were persons highly urban in background, and, even more perhaps than the English-speaking, highly class conscious. But there was one important difference between the French-speaking and the English-speaking middle class. The English-speaking middle class could serve its best interests by protecting its class position. The French-speaking middle class felt compelled to protect its ethnic position as a means of serving its class position.

Thus it was French-speaking persons, most like the privileged class of English-speaking persons, who played up most vigorously the differences between French-speaking and English-speaking. There was nothing strange about this. An underprivileged population can be appealed to in social class terms, as well as in regional terms. Indeed, in the North, both of these types of appeal came very much into play. The development of trade unionism represented an effort to give to the underprivileged population of the northern industrial community a greater sense of social class, while northern politicians were not slow to take advantage of the regional appeal – the North was made to appear, with some justification, an area neglected or discriminated against by governments far removed. But both appeals inevitably involved the making of the northern industrial society into a society more English-speaking. They offered little that would have secured a strengthening of the position of the French-speaking middle class.

In contrast to a social class appeal, the ethnic appeal offered no challenge to the existence of an autonomous French-speaking community, or in a direct way, to the position of the Church within this community. Thus it could have as its end the creation of an urban society that was French-speaking without making it less French or in any true sense less Catholic. This is not to suggest that the French-speaking middle class, as it gained in influence in the northern industrial community, had clearly in view the end it sought to serve in making an ethnic appeal. Nor is it to suggest that the Church, in making itself a party to such an appeal, had a full appreciation of the consequences. What the French-speaking middle class of the northern industrial community sought was a betterment of its own position. But the betterment of its own social position depended upon a betterment of the position of the French-speaking population as a whole, if rejection was an accommodation to the English-speaking world.

The position of a middle class depends upon two important conditions: first, the opening up in the society of an increasing number of career lines appropriate for middle class persons; and, second, the development of institutional means by which a middle class can perpetuate itself from one generation to the next. In the northern industrial community, the attainment of the first of these conditions involved an attack upon the system of power built up around the major industrial enterprises; the attainment of the second upon the system of power built up around the Church. It was the attack upon the system of power built up around the major industrial enterprises that was made to rely so heavily upon the ethnic appeal.

RECENT DEVELOPMENTS

It is not possible here to detail the changes which have occurred in the economic, political, and social structure of the northern industrial community within the past few years. What is clearly apparent is the shift which has taken place in the centres of power in the community. Brought under attack has been that whole complex of institutions built up around the major industrial enterprise. Recently the English have been overwhelmed by the weight of numbers of the French who have now been provided with a new and vigorous leadership of middle class people. In many of the industrial centres of the North today, it is the English-speaking population which finds itself isolated, deprived of influence and power. A new type of leadership has taken hold and is extending its influence beyond the community of French-speaking people into the industrial society of the North as a whole. Institutions which began as English-speaking and then were made English and French have now become almost wholly French. In many communities of the North, it is the English residents, not the French, who are compelled to learn a second language, or move out.

It could not be expected that this shift in the balance of power between the English and French would occur without conflict, struggle, and the generation of feelings of bitterness between the two groups. The northern industrial community did become caught up in the issue of French-English relations. The major industrial enterprise, particularly when situated within the Province of Quebec, offered itself as too good a target for political attack. But within these communities the ethnic issue had something of a manufactured quality about it. The reason was to be found in the fact that at no time did the French-speaking population occupy the position of a minority ethnic group. What had developed here were two distinct and separate social worlds: the social world of the English dominated company town community, and the social world of the French-speaking community outside. For a long time, it was the English dominated company town community which possessed the greater economic and political strength, but gradually the situation became reversed, notwithstanding the fact that the major industrial enterprise continued to be controlled by the English. In the end, the company town ceased to be a company town, and at that point the two social worlds of English and French came close to becoming one. The English dominated company town community was in effect swallowed up by the French-speaking community outside. The result was to make of the English-speaking population a minority ethnic group, something the French had never been.

In the northern industrial community, the French-speaking middle class has come close to the attainment of the first of those conditions upon which its position depended: the opening up in the society of an increasing number of career lines appropriate for middle class persons. It has come close to the attainment as well of the second condition: the development of institutional means by which a middle class can perpetuate itself from one generation to the next. It was upon the accomplishments in the field of education that the success of the Quiet Revolution in the northern industrial community came ultimately to depend. There could be little gained in forcing a change in the "management" of community affairs if, within the French-speaking population, there was not a sufficient number of persons ready to take over. What was required was a very considerable raising of the general educational level of the French-speaking population.

In the effort to attain such an objective, it was not possible to avoid an attack upon that system of power within the French-speaking community built up around the Church. To a very considerable extent, however, concern with the issue of English-French relations served to divert attention away from the issue of Church control of education. Support of education offered itself as the most effective means of securing for the French-speaking population a position of equality with the English. Thus the appeal to this population in ethnic terms operated as a powerful force in the making over not only the system of power of the larger community, long dominated by the English, but the system of power of the French-speaking community itself. Education became a vital weapon in the struggle of the French-speaking population to overcome the dominance of the English-speaking.

It is too early yet to assess the full consequences of the Quiet Revolution in the northern industrial community. What certainly is apparent is a general improvement in the position of the French-speaking population. This is a population which is becoming better housed, better provided with the comforts and amenities of life, better educated, and better employed. The time may be not too distant when this population will be generally better off than the English-speaking population. But any comparison of the state of the two population groups made in such terms can be highly misleading. The truth for both the English- and French-speaking populations was that beyond a certain point, there was nowhere to go in the North. Viewed from the perspective of the older generation the North may have appeared a land with bountiful opportunities. As older developed areas declined, new areas opened up. The economic growth that resulted encouraged the establishment of new types of business enterprise and offered a large and expanding market for goods and services of various kinds. Workers, business men, and professional people crowding into the North could indeed, prosper and become rich.

But for the new ascending generation, the North had not a great deal to offer. The northern industrial community may have changed markedly in character, but it was still a single enterprise type of community. What businesses and services developed remained very much dependent upon the one major enterprise about which the community was built. The result was to impose a sharp limit upon the development within the North of opportunities for individual advancement. There was no room in the northern society for a middle class beyond a certain narrowly restricted size. Where the demand for middle class positions developed across a broad front, the demand could be realized only by movement out of the North.

It was by this means that the English-speaking middle class in the North was able to maintain and improve its economic and social position from one generation to the next. For the English-speaking population, the North was never viewed, except at most for the older generation as a permanent home. The new generation rising up was directed to look to the outside world for opportunities for advancement. In the development of such an attitude of mind, education was an important influence, but there were other influences even more important than education. Indeed education, in its character, reflected much more than determined the English-speaking attitude of mind. The English-speaking young person was given no strong feeling of commitment to his ethnic group, culture, or community of which he was a part. His was an individualist ethos. For him the appropriate career line was the one that promised the greatest individual advancement, whatever the consequences for attachments to ethnic group, culture, or community. For such a young person, thus, the northern community could be abandoned without painful struggle when he was offered outside more promising opportunities.

Not all English-speaking young persons, of course, were motivated to the same extent by such an individualist ethos. There were some for whom attachments to their social group were a decisive consideration. But over all, there was in this regard a great difference between the English-speaking and the French-speaking population. For the French-speaking population the North did tend to be viewed in a very real sense as its home. For long, it is true, this character of immobility of the French-speaking population could be attributed to its lack of preparation to make its way in the outside world. Without the skills required in a highly industrialized and urbanized society, French-speaking persons were made dependent upon the kind of jobs the North had to offer.

But it was more than its lack of skills which tied the French-speaking population to the North. The commitment of this population to the North developed out of its commitment to its ethnic origin and to its religion. The French-speaking person was made to feel concerned about remaining French and Catholic. The ethnic consideration transcended the consideration of self advancement. About the individual was built a whole network of obligations which, in tying him to his ethnic group and religion, tied him to his community.

In its reliance thus upon the ethnic appeal, the Quiet Revolution was almost bound to fall short of the ends it sought to achieve. The hope was to secure for the French-speaking population a position of equality with the English. In the effort, however, to accomplish such an object this population was committed more fully than ever to its ethnic origin. The effect of the ethnic appeal was to secure an advancement of the French-speaking population, but in a way that was in certain respects highly illusory. In the northern industrial community this population did move up, but not in any real sense at the expense of the English. For the French, the lines of advancement remained limited very largely to what the North had to offer. For the English, it was to the outside world that the really important lines of advancement led.

What was crucial to the position of the French-speaking population were the opportunities for advancement opening up to the middle class. In the emphasis given to education, there was a clear sense of the importance of preparing an increasing proportion of the French-speaking population for middle class occupations. The French were made ready to seize from the English a large range of middle class positions. In this regard, the results achieved by the Quiet Revolution could appear impressive, certainly in the northern industrial community.

In the effort to take over "the management" of the affairs of the northern industrial community, however, there was revealed something of the illusory character of the accomplishments of the Quiet Revolution. Though technological changes and the introduction of new business methods had led to a considerable upgrading of the labour force in such industries as mining and pulp and paper, the number of senior management positions within the corporate establishment, appropriate for middle class persons, remained still exceedingly small. At no time had the English-speaking middle class in the northern industrial community made itself dependent upon such positions in seeking to make available to the ascending generation opportunities for advancement which the English-speaking middle class, itself, had enjoyed. English-speaking youth, if they wished to get ahead, moved out of the North. The result was that there were no limits to the growth of the English-speaking middle class from one generation to the next. The benefits of a "middle class" education could be extended to an ever increasing portion of the total population, without exhausting the number of positions appropriate for middle class persons. In the case of the French-speaking middle class, it would be an exaggeration to suggest that, in its drive to secure an improvement of education, it had in view only the end of making available to the ascending French-speaking youth those middle class positions which the corporate establishment of the northern industrial community had to offer, but to the extent that such was the case, very sharp limits were set to the real accomplishments of the Quiet Revolution.

It was, of course, upon a very narrow economic base that the northern industrial community was built. The business establishment here could not extend far beyond the major industrial enterprise. In most industrialized centres of the North, there was in each community only one "company" that really counted. It was this concentration of economic activity about the one major industry which imposed such sharp limits upon the growth of a middle class. A large portion of the population here had no means of improving its social position in any important way, except by getting out.

Yet in the character of the society of the northern industrial community, there was much that was like the character of the society of the Canadian community at large. It was upon a very narrow economic base that the Canadian community was built. Throughout Canada's development, there has been a concentration of economic activity about a few large business establishments. In its control of these establishments, the English-speaking middle class has consolidated its position. But, no more than in the northern industrial community has this class made itself dependent upon the corporate establishment in seeking to extend the benefits it enjoyed to new generations of middle class people. To a very large extent, the English Canadian middle class has grown and prospered by taking advantage of the opportunities for advancement offered by economic and other types of enterprise across the border in the United States; also within the Canadian society there has been a continuous opening up of new lines of economic endeavour throughout the country's development. The role played by individual enterprise in the development of the north country offers a conspicuous example.

In the effort to secure improvement for the position of the French-speaking population in Canada, it is not difficult to understand why the first line of attack has been upon the bureaucratic establishment of government and business. It was in the control of this establishment that the dominance of the English-speaking population made itself most felt. But, in the concern to "take over" from the English, the French-speaking middle class may make impossible the realization of the very ends the Quiet Revolution was directed to serve. French Canada has never been without a bureaucratic establishment. It was a bureaucratic establishment centred very much around the Church but extending in an important way after Confederation into the area of provincial government. For a long time, it was on this bureaucratic establishment that the French-speaking middle class depended. In its effort to consolidate thus its middle class position (reflected in the elitist conception of the role of education), the French-speaking society failed to develop strength in the whole broad area of economic development. The drive to secure an improvement in the position of the French-speaking population clearly has been directed to the end of broadening substantially the base of support of the middle class. Yet it may be questioned whether in fact there has come any real change in the sense of dependence of this class upon types of support which, while offering protection to its position, promise few substantial gains to the French-speaking population as a whole.

4

EDITOR'S INTRODUCTION

The study of occupations in connection with that of ethnic groups is particulary important and crucial in a plural society such as Canada. In any society it is of considerable sociological interest to know the representation of the different ethnic groups within the occupational world relative to their proportion within the population. The occupational fate of ethnic groups holds one of the keys to the understanding of the dynamics of development and the change occurring within an overall society. In Canada, an analysis of the distribution of ethnic groups in the occupational structure helps to evaluate the validity of the goal of ethnic diversity and economic equality.

Social science studies of occupations have multiplied in recent years, concomitant with the multiplication and proliferation of the various occupational specialties, a pattern which is clearly shown by Hall. There have been studies which focus on factors relevant to the preparation of various specialisits for different occupational positions — and the consequence of these positions for the incumbents. Such studies have led to a much clearer understanding of the extent to which an occupational role can "condition" a person. Indeed, the study of occupations had demonstrated that the period of social learning (referred to as socialization in sociology) extends considerably beyond the first several years of development. Attitudes and political behavior of individuals change largely because of occupational change and, indeed, profound personality changes may occur among individuals as a consequence of a change in occupational affiliation.

Much of the attention of social scientists, especially sociologists, has been directed toward an understanding of the extent to which occupational changes in industrial societies represent significant shifts in "occupational mobility". Occupations, being considered as significant (if not exclusive) indicators of social status, reveal an important aspect of the social class structures of societies. Are certain occupations more vital to the continued existence in growth of a society than others? Does upward mobility (the movement from a "low status" to a comparatively "high status" occupation), whether within one's life time or between generations, reflect evolutionary social change in terms of the long held and still commonly endorsed myth of the "survival of the fittest"? Or, does occupational mobility (either upward or downward) reflect the peculiarities of certain societies based upon traditions, power structures, or ideological commitments?

To what extent can any society do anything about the efficiency of its occupational allocation among the diverse social, ethnic, and religious groupings within it?

Professor Hall argues that an understanding of the past, present, and emergent patterns of the distribution of different ethnic groups within the occupational hierarchy provides the essential basis for bringing about planned change in future occupational evolution. This argument is indeed a sound one, but still leaves mute the answer to the question of "what do you do about it?" once you discover that certain inefficiencies and injustices have been and continue to be perpetuated. Again, the answer to this question depends to a large extent on the nature of the society in which it emerges. However, before turning to this strategic issue, certain aspects of occupational changes in Canada, as discussed by Professor Hall, should be noted.

As pointed out by Professor Hall, Canada, similar to all industrial or "post industrial" societies, has witnessed fantastic proliferation of occupational specializations, both in terms of the number of specialized occupations and the sub-specializations within these specializations. Indeed, the proliferation has been so pervasive that specialists within a particular occupational category may be as far removed from each other in terms of understanding and communication as are specialists who could be considered as being within different occupational categories. This occupational proliferation, as pointed out by Hall, is one of the consequences of the dramatic shift in population from rural communities to urban communities, or, similarly, the shift from agrarian based occupations to urban-industrial based occupations. The great magnitude of this change (within less than under a century in North America) is an important development in the understanding of contemporary problems and conflicts in all industrial societies, including Canada. Generalized occupations, as witnessed in the average homesteading farmer, where the common known expression "Jack of all trades" probably originated, have given way to specializations which are so highly and specifically defined as to defy the imagination.

In view of the enormity of these development, it seems hardly possible to develop a theory of social stratification (which is so largely dependent upon analysis of occupational prestige) based on a static or conceptually constrained evaluation of occupational ranking. According to one commonly held sociological theory of social stratification (or social class structure), the individuals or groups who hold occupational positions of prestige and power derive their status through factors such as the "functional importance" of their positions and the amount of training and talent necessary to achieve them.[1] While this theory has been considerably discredited,[2] no coherent and acceptable sociological theory of social stratification has emerged. The general view of

---

[1] The initial elements of this theory were posited by Kingsley Davis and Wilbert E. Moore, "Some Principles of Stratification", *American Sociological Review*, April 1945, pp. 242-249.

[2] See Melvin M. Tumin, "Some Principles of Stratification: A Critical Analysis", *American Sociological Review*, April, 1953, pp. 387-394, and Jack L. Roach, et. al., eds. *Social Stratication in the United States* (Englewood Cliffs, N.J.: Prentice-Hall, Inc., 1969), *passim.*

social class stratification based largely on the perpetuation of vested interest groups, as dramatically developed by the American sociologist C .Wright Mills,[3] and modified and applied to the Canadian scene by John Porter,[4] serve as a welcome relief to the widely held notion that occupational prestige and accompanying power are largely dependent upon individual initiative and the survival of the fittest.

Professor Hall shows clearly that there has been and continues to be a tendency for disproportionate representation of various ethnic groups in the Canadian occupational hierarchy. While he emphasizes the disproportionately low occupational representation of French Canadians, both historically and today, it is clear, according to other studies, that most non-Anglo Saxon groups are disproportionately represented at the lower rungs of the occupational-prestige hierarchy.[4]

One peculiarity about Canada noted by Professor Hall — the relatively great extent to which new occupational positions in Canada are filled through massive post-war immigration — is an important point of analysis. There can be little doubt that a nation which is developing so rapidly its economy as Canada is requires a deliberate, rational, and dynamic policy of attracting immigrants. However, it may be suggested that the Canadian emphasis on immigration to enable fulfillment of the rapidly increasing occupational opportunities is partly an attribute of the somewhat "elitist" policy of education which has marked the development of Canada in the past. If there had been a greater emphasis on the provision of occupational and educational opportunities for non-Anglo Saxon groups in the past, perhaps the current policy on attracting immigrants would have been somewhat inhibited.

It may also be noted that the gap between the demand and supply of various occupational categories may be partly attributable to the tendency for all occupational groupings, particularly the professions, to deliberately limit membership.

Professor Hall clearly shows that there are severe problems of inequalities with respect to the ethnic composition of Canada, new occupational positions, and the extent to which unity may be jeopardized by these inequalities.

[3] C. Wright Mills, *The Power Elite* (New York: Oxford, 1957).
[4] John Porter, *The Vertical Mosaic* (Toronto: University of Toronto Press, 1965).
[5] The research publication of the Royal Commission on Bilingualism and Biculturalism, which may precede or coincide with the present volume, will clearly demonstrate this pattern of ethnic disproportionality.

4

The Canadian Division of Labour Revisited

OSWALD HALL

In this article, it is argued that the study of occupations on the Canadian scene today turns out to be in a fundamental sense also a study of ethnic relations and of large scale organizations. All three studies have become welded into a common mass. It is to this mass that the term "the division of labour" applies.

Canada is a multi-ethnic society. Ethnic groups tend to measure their success in terms of the occupations into which they fit. Success in climbing the occupational ladder is one of the most visible measures of life success for the members of any group of people. But on the other hand, the striving for occupational success is a two-edged weapon because occupations inevitably become identified with the ethnic groups that dominate within them. This is so much the case that to mention the police, the construction worker, or the judge is to call to mind the ethnic group that most probably practises these occupations. Occupations become recognizably stained by the groups who predominantly practise them. In short, both ethnic groups and occupations are notably intertwined; they are also both subject to some very profound continuing changes.

Occupations in our time are largely rooted in large scale organizations. It is now but a small and still declining fragment of the work force that is self-employed. The trend appears to run toward progressively larger forms of work organization. As a consequence, it is a genuine question as to whether the work of a person today is an occupation in the usually accepted meaning of the term or whether it is more realistically to be seen as an office or a position in some large form of organization. In other words, it is difficult to estimate what one does in his occupation, or what he derives from it, without knowing something in detail about the organization for which he works. To be labelled a "manager" or a "salesman" or a "supervisor" tells little unless one knows whether one is dealing with a corner restaurant or a pharmaceutical laboratory. The people who gather census data are becoming progressively aware of the need to supplement occupational titles with information about the specific locale and organizational setting of the occupation.

The student of society who studies occupations finds that all of these matters are knotted in an awkward way. One can't discuss occupations very far without raising the query as to the ethnic membership of those in them. Similarly the analysis of the way in which large organizations are manned leads one back to discover which groups generate in their members the ambitions and the expertise to handle the jobs in those organizations. Moreover, if one is impressed by the role of technological change in modifying work organizations, one is again pushed back to discover which groups in society are producing the kinds of people who stimulate and develop technological changes.

These matters have of course a marked relevance if one wishes to understand the so-called "developing" societies. In them, the effort to accelerate development is in large part a search for the blend of specialized occupations and distinctive work organizations that can spiral the underdeveloped country upward to a "developed" state. There can be little doubt that these matters are elusive. To understand the Canadian scene, it is useful to bear in mind Canada's affinity with other underdeveloped countries.

One of the first points to emphasize in any discussion of the division of labor is the extraordinary rate at which new occupations have come into existence, and the way others have splintered or disappeared. If one goes back to 1790 it would be the case on this continent that approximately 90 per cent of workers made their livings off the land. Each nine farm workers, in a manner of speaking, could provide the surplus to "support" one urban dweller. By the time of the 1940 Census, the situation was inverted; one worker on the land was producing enough foodstuffs to feed nine workers in urban employment. Such a shift represents a revolution of sorts — a revolution in production, in the technology of farming, and in demographie as well.

We do not have a current census of the actual number of occupations practised at any point in time. The heroic effort in the thirties to produce a specialized dictionary of occupational titles drew together a list of between 17,000 and 23,000 occupations, depending on how precise were the definitions given to occupational labels. How fast these have multiplied in recent decades is a matter for conjecture, but the pace has been swift. In some areas of work, it is estimated that the members of occupations increase by 20 per cent per decade.

On the Canadian scene, we have some data on this, stemming from the Department of Manpower in Ottawa. In their efforts to count only the technical and professional people, they have come up with some 800 titles in these occupations. It would appear that sociologists, though among the recent occupational newcomers, now number over forty specialized sub-groups. Psychology is represented by over 50 sub-specialists, while engineering, once restricted to four sub-groups, now requires 115 titles to describe its sub-divisions. The fields of science have increased even more substantially. The biological sciences are represented by at least 150 specialized titles, while the physical sciences yield over 250 sub-groups. A great many of these specialized occupations are of very recent vintage. It is eminently clear that the study of occupations is one of the areas of social life in which change is immensely rapid. The challenge to the social scientist is to make order out of the luxuriant growth that occurs here.

The proliferation of occupations is intimately related to changes in the standard of living, particularly the utilization of new goods and services.

This kind of change is almost taken for granted on this continent, although its import is so great that perceptive writers refer to it as the "Revolution of Rising Expectations". It is a matter that injects urgency into the problems of developing areas. And even in developed countries it adds a distinctive flavour to the generation gap. What one generation looked upon as frills and luxuries to another generation is part of the normal expectations of a standard of living. Currently we seem to be witnessing a shift in the standard of living whereby the provision of services is as important as, or more important, than, the production of goods. Such changes have an unmistakeable relevance to the structure of occupations for any society. It adds to their number, and affects the relevance of each class of occupations.

The provision of services seems to offer almost infinite possibilities for the refined sub-specialization of occupations. Most of us recognize this phenomenon when we seek medical aid. It is probable that illness will send one not to a doctor, but to a specialist. The numbers of medical specializations are impressive. A modern medical school recognizes over thirty specializations, many of them in the process of sub-dividing. Nor is medical specialization the most impressive feature of healing. In a hospital, one can find approximately four kinds of "paramedical" workers for each kind of doctor in existence. All in all, a modern hospital system will manifest between 150 and 200 distinctive occupations. Once medical care involved the doctor and the nurse; present-day medical services involve the participation of a veritable army of recently derived specialized occupations.

Many of the occupations that provide services have a common ancestor with those which provide goods. They are the result of an enhanced technology. The impact of this factor is continually recognized in the debates about automation. These discussions revolve around the recognition that changes in technology in our society are dramatic and consequential. So much is this the case that one can talk about a "technological" revolution in somewhat the same way that one talks of an "industrial" revolution.

Although revolutions are fascinating to discuss, they are awkward to define. Indeed the industrial revolution was scarcely discovered until decades after it had gotten well underway. It began in social stress and social dislocation, in unrest and turmoil, in the discovery of distinctive social problems. But it was long before writers and thinkers could draw all these matters to a head and say "What has occurred is a revolution".

What people refer to as a technological revolution is readily distinguishable from the classic industrial revolution. In essence, the latter was a matter of putting new forms of power to work with dramatic effects on the range of goods available and on the usefulness of human labour. What we see currently is the application of scientific knowledge on a vast scale which is capable of generating ways of performing more complex tasks with more complex materials. Unlike the industrial revolution which was limited by the available raw material and sources of power, the new revolution is limited only by the current state of available scientific knowledge. The latter seems to be an infinitely expanding resource rather than a limited and contracting one.

In the early stages of the industrial revolution, it was easy to envisage the specific occupations, such as the role of the fireman feeding coal to a boiler to produce the steam to operate the machines of the mill. It is less easy to comprehend the ingredients in the atomic furnace than can perform the same tasks. What is essentially different is the blend of scientific knowledge made available by a small host of specialized scientists coupled with the expertise of highly trained technologists who can put the scientific knowledge to disciplined use. One reason why it is difficult to export the industrial revolution to underdeveloped lands is precisely the fact that developed societies have moved into this more complex stage where mature science and highly developed technology are essential parts of the total mix.

Some writers now doubt that the term "industrial society" is any longer appropriate to designate the more highly developed countries of the world today. When they use the term "modern", they have in mind a set of changes that have been added on to the simple notion of industrialization. A modern society is one in which occupations associated with industry decline relatively to those that provide services; moreover the industrial occupations have become transformed by the impact of science and technology.

It seems clear that the writers who now discuss a "post-industrial" society are making two sharp distinctions. In part, they are referring to a society that has mastered the arts of producing goods and can now devote resources to the provision of a high level of services. And in the provision of both there has emerged a high level of scientific enterprise along with the relevant technologies to put the scientific knowledge to work. To state their idea in this form is a way of calling attention to a bundle of changes that have gone on in the field of occupations and to emphasize the emergence and spread of occupations of a technological and professional character.

The above matters all shed useful light on the world of occupations. Some of the changes generate whole sets of novel occupations. This in part is what is meant by automation, although in much of the discussion the emphasis is on the holders of expendable occupations rather than the incumbents of new occupations. It can be readily argued that the more difficult problems lie in the latter area; i.e. how to train and/or find the kinds of workers who can perform the bundles of tasks involved in the new technological occupations. The current debates over the ills of automation have tended to obscure this more consequential problem.

On the other hand there is no doubt that specific occupations may suffer total eclipse. A recent case was the firemen on locomotives. With the introduction first of the mechanical stoker and later of diesel power the functions of the fireman evaporated. As was noted at the time, the firemen could not and did not accept this fate without a high degree of unrest and conflict. At that time hardly any one noted that a similar fate had overtaken an earlier member of the train crew, the oiler. When technical change caught up with him both he and his oil can became obsolete.[1]

In both the above examples, the process we are noting is similar to the survival of a species. Change occurs within an occupation or in its

---

[1] Editor's Note: It has been observed by some students of occupational change that unanticipated jobs at times replace those made obsolete; e.g., the displaced "fireman" became an important "co-engineer" and observer.

environment that may favour its development or may lead to its disappearance. In the social world, however, these changes are always more complicated. The struggle of occupations to survive becomes elaborated into a struggle for prestige. The people who practise occupations come to apply invidious evaluations to the worth of their occupations and other occupations. Given enough time for consensus to arise, the occupations of a society would presumably form a prestige hierarchy in which each occupation is accorded a ranking which differentiates it from those above and below it. A number of scholars have set themselves the task of establishing these patterns for Canada and the U.S. As might be expected the task is very tricky when occupations are in a condition of flux and development. It is still more complex when established occupations are in the process of being invaded by new kinds of people whose color, age, religion, language, sex, or social class add a new dimension to an occupation.

OCCUPATIONS AND ETHNIC GROUPS

The study of occupations is in one sense a part of the study of demography. It is a study of peoples, their numbers, the conditions under which they can increase or decrease, and the charges that go on inside a population that modify its composition over time. The typical case on this continent is the study of increasing populations. There are parts of the world where populations are stable and others where populations are undergoing decline. But the basic concerns of demographers on this continent have been the problems of increasing population.

The natural increase of a population may be highly inadequate to meet the demands for workers to fill the occupational needs of a society. In Canada, this has been dramatically evident. Our cradles have never produced enough of the appropriate kinds of people to fill the available occupational niches. As a consequence, we have maintained a continuous policy of immigration. This has been a selective policy, one which has admitted specific occupational groups while excluding others. Particularly, we have used migration recently as a means of recruiting for highly specialized occupations. If one searches in a rural area for a doctor, the probability is that he has migrated to Canada in the not distant past. We bring our rural doctors from Britain and from many corners of the globe.

In many occupational fields, we depend extremely heavily on migrants to do the work. In the technical and professional fields, to which reference was made earlier, there have been periods in which approximately 80 per cent of the new recruits to many of these have been found in this fashion. Our own young have either not sought or not found the training needed for such occupations, and the migrants from other countries have poured into the country readily. It need hardly be said that our policy of providing jobs for workers trained elsewhere at high cost can quickly become a cause for ill-will among countries which recognize the importance of their scarce, highly trained workers. More recently, we have begun the task of recruiting and training these ourselves and are discovering how costly and demanding is the enterprise. But in the areas where the demand for workers is most pronounced, as in the expanding health occupations, even these efforts fail to keep up with the demands for the services involved.

The recruitment of workers by migration into specific occupational fields is, of course, no guarantee that such occupations will thereby find their ranks filled. The jobs may be filled for the moment, but the new workers may soon aspire to and seek employment in thoroughly different occupations. And most certainly there is no assurance that their children will seek employment in the occupations for which their parents were brought to this country.

On this continent, a major part of the drama of social life has revolved around "getting ahead" in the occupational world and making certain that one's children do likewise or better. An important segment of urban sociology has been concerned specifically with such matters. The cities of this continent have been marked by successive waves of migrants which on their arrival found a distinctive niche in the occupational and residential structure of the community. But no sooner were they established than they or their children sought other occupational and residential areas, at times propelled upward by still newer waves of migrants of different tongues and perhaps different social class. Such waves of immigrants fitting into distinctive occupational niches have created a highly visible pattern to urban society. The recent volume *Beyond the Melting Pot*[2] documents these patterns for a number of American cities.

What is distinctive about Canada, in contrast with the United States, is that the paths for migrants have been much more complex. The American model has been one of "assimilation" with the newcomer eventually transformed into a "100 per cent American" — or so the theory has postulated. The Canadian model has no term comparable to "Americanization". Ours is a dual society, and the immigrant has been constructed to move toward one or the other of the two founding groups. He could choose to be "French" Canadian or "English" Canadian, but hardly both. Moreover each of these choices has been of a highly fateful sort; once the migrant had proceeded with a choice, there has been little possibility of his reconsidering and turning to the alternative.

The choices that migrants make in this regard are consequential not only to themselves but to the host groups. Each choice represents an addition to one group at the expense of the other. Each choice is in effect a symbolic gesture; it is a vote of confidence in the future of one of the host groups rather than the other. In the course of events, the two host groups have not attracted migrants in equal fashion. By and large, migrants have moved to areas where English speech prevailed and have identified themselves accordingly. But even where they have gravitated to areas of French speech, as in Montreal itself, migrants have opted for the English language and have sent their children to English schools. The reasons for this are uncertain. It may be that the English language, on the global scale, has become so dominant in the working world that it is almost an automatic

---

[2] Nathan Glazer and Daniel Patrick Moynihan, *Beyond The Melting Pot* (Cambridge: Massachusetts Institute of Technology, 1963).

choice for present-day migrants. Or it may be that the holders of important positions in Canadian industrial life are predominantly English speaking, and that their high visibility influences the choice of language of newcomers to Canada. Whatever the basis, the choice made by the migrant has conspicuous consequences not only for himself and for his children, but for each of the host groups in the society.

The occupational field is one in which much of the basic structure of Canadian society is sharply visible. In it, the relative places of the two historic founding groups are sharply illuminated. Through the occupational field the long term impact of immigration, not only on the immigrants themselves but on the two founding groups, comes into sharpened focus.

Until now, the relationship of the two founding groups in the work world has been far from one of equality. The weight of numbers would make equality a difficult achievement. Leaving aside this consideration there are other advantages that weight matters heavily in the English direction. One of these that deserves more attention than it has received to date is the form of organization within which work is carried on.

Earlier a reference was made to the fact that much of present-day employment refers to large scale organizations. The self-employed individuals now form a very meagre minority of the work force. Most workers are organization men. But organizations vary among themselves. At one extreme, they are hardly distinguishable from the family. Indeed the family farm and family business are distinctive typical ways of organizing work. But they seem less efficient, in terms of capacity to compete and survive, than are the modern corporations. The latter seem to be almost unlimited in their capacity for growth, particularly as seen in the modern multi-national corporations. The emergence of business corporations and their distribution between our founding groups have a profound impact on our occupational division of labour.

Among the many consequences the one to note here is the way in which the corporation develops specialized occupations within it. Some of these have been obvious, ever since Adam Smith discussed the technology of pin-making. They reflect the functions involved in the productive process. Others stem from the internal needs of the corporation itself; the need to co-ordinate workers doing different things, the need to supervise the quality of work, the need to plan rationally over prolonged time spans all result in the emergence of specialized supervisors, co-ordinators, and managers who add to the specialized occupations found in the corporation. A further group comprises the people who function to invent the future for the corporation, the engineers and scientists in research and development whose work at any point in time may be deciding a future ten or fifteen years distant.

The corporation is a most potent instrument for influencing the structure of a society. It yields a vast range of specialized occupations, and incidentally modifies the lives of those who enter them. It generates a very broad income scale, from those on lowly shop floors to those in the lordly board rooms. It creates a parallel prestige scale for those earning various levels of income. It creates within itself a very powerful group of people who, through science and technology, do much to create the future for the corporation and its enveloping society.

From the standpoint of a society like our own, a dualistic society, the corporation poses two problems of major importance. The first is: To what extent do the corporations become identified with one language group rather than the other? The second has to do with the positions within them occupied by those who speak one language rather than another. Of all the hazards faced by the language groups in our society, it is likely that those posed by the emergence of large work corporations are the most consequential. The corporation constitutes the grid on which the nuances of ethnic relations are played out.

The corporation, as compared with other forms of work organization, is an exceedingly durable affair. In human terms it is well-nigh perpetual. Because of its control over its future and more particularly its devices for recruiting and retiring personnel, it has a fantastic advantage over family businesses that are restricted to the resources that families find among their own members. Mr. Galbraith's recent book on the "New Industrial State" is a mine of information about the nature of corporations in North America and their effects on that society.

For the Canadian sociologist, a major challenge of the modern corporation is to comprehend the kind of occupational mix it generates. A further challenge has to do with the ethnic (language and culture) mix it generates within itself. Since these are interrelated, what is of basic interest is the sort of occupational-ethnic mix that we are developing in the wake of the growth of large corporations.

In spite of the elegant work done three decades ago by E.C. Hughes in this field relatively little is still known about these matters. A recent study of the construction industry in Montreal[3] indicates that it has become highly stylized ethnically as far as its four major components are concerned. The control and operation of large industrial engineering equipment is almost entirely in the hands of the Anglo-Saxon group in the community. The financing of construction is in the hands of this group and the Jewish group. Small scale contracting has become very much a special field for French Canadians, who employ Italians in substantial numbers. The organization of real-estate has fallen very largely into Jewish hands — they predominate heavily among the real-estate businesses of the city.

We are discussing here only the overall ownership or control of these sectors of the industry. It is a matter of real interest to see what sort of inner structure one would find in each sector — whether the sectors have equally homogeneous or heterogeneous work forces attached to them.

It should be noted in passing that the flow of any group into an occupational field depends not only on the opening of opportunities, but the way in which members of an ethnic group idealize specified occupations. It is abundantly clear that members of society may idealize farming as a desirable pastoral style of life long after it has become a mechanized in

---

[3] See P. Briant, *"The Construction Industry in Montreal"*, an unpublished report for the Royal Commission on Bilingualism and Biculturalism.

dustry; or that its member may downgrade the tasks of the accountant and inventor long after they have become essential functions of a social order. Occupational selection is never a simple affair. It depends on the availability of specific kinds of occupations at the time workers are making their initial choice of a life work; it depends on the kinds of training and education that the candidates possess by the time they start off into the occupational world. It depends also on any restraints or discrimination imposed by those in a position to admit candidates into the preferred occupational niches in society. It likewise depends on any cultural restraints which people inherit along with the rest of their culture, which inhibit their seeking to enter specific kinds of occupations.

One of the profound anomalies of the Canadian scene is the discrepancy in the ways in which French-speaking Canadians and English-speaking Canadians are represented in the occupational world. Whether one observes the two groups on the national scale, in a distinctive province like Quebec, or in the metropolitan centre of Montreal a set of discrepancies come to light. They show up in the differences of income for each group of an order of 15 to 20 per cent. (People of British origin tend to stand at the top of the income scale while those of French origin are distributed at the lower end — markedly lower than most of the groups who have migrated to Canada.) They are reflected in the levels of formal education reported for workers of each language group. They appear dramatically in the data on ownership and control of industry in Canada. And they appear, too, in the exploration of life in the corporation where French-speaking Canadians become more rare as one moves upward in the hierarchy of the corporation; the use of the French language in business affairs tapers off in such structures in a similar fashion.

These anomalous discrepancies stand out vividly in the Province of Quebec, the heartland of French-speaking Quebec. Since approximately 80 per cent of French-speaking Canadians live in Quebec comprising about 80 per cent of the total of that province, the situation exemplifies a very large part of the total Canadian picture of the relative positions of the two language groups. The studies of the division of labour undertaken in Quebec in the mid-thirties by E.C. Hughes, S.M. Jameson, and W. Roy demonstrated the kinds of anomalies noted above. More recent efforts by N. Keyfitz and D. Rennie have documented the earlier patterns. More recently a series of studies by A. Raynauld and by other social scientists in Quebec universities have indicated how persistent the division of labor in Quebec along the language axis has been. For purposes of illustration, two sorts of data are valuable: the facts concerning ownership and control of industry, and those concerning the distribution of each language group in the larger industrial and commercial corporations.

In relation to ownership and control of industry the data for this decade, as they are being assembled for the Royal Commission on Bilingualism and Biculturalism, show that French-speaking Canadians in Quebec are represented strongly in only a very few segments of the economy. In agriculture, they account for over 90 per cent of the ownership of farms; in retail trade, they account for about 60 per cent of the field; in the field of construction, referred to earlier, they represent about one-half of the total. In all the other fields, they constitute a minority of the sector and in some cases a small minority. For example in wholesale trade, they account for only 40 per cent of the total, and the same situation applies to transportation and communication. In manufacturing, their representation is about one-fourth of the total, while for financial institutions, it is closer to one-fifth. For the mining industry, the representation is very small, a mere 2 per cent in the hands of French Canadians.

Of course each of the sectors mentioned above is made up of many sub-groups and among them one would find some wide fluctuations in representation. In food processing, woodworking, and furniture, the French-speaking Canadians own or control about double the average for all manufacturing. On the other hand, for iron and steel and electrical equipment and transportation equipment, the representation is about one-half of the average figure of 25 per cent. (In the petrochemical industry they have no representation; incidentally, neither have English-speaking Canadians, because the field belongs in toto to non-Canadians.)

Since ownership and control belong decisively to a minority group in the province of Quebec it is relevant to inquire into how the two language groups are represented in the work force of the corporations. Those owned and controlled by French-speaking Canadians have predominantly French-speaking work forces. But how does the matter stand for those corporations owned and/or controlled by English speaking persons? Do their personnel selection policies result in a random selection of each group to the posts at each level in the corporation, or do the anomalies noted above extend within the corporation.

In general, the anomalies are readily detected in the corporations. By and large the proportion of French-speaking personnel at the salaried levels in the manufacturing corporations is one-half of that at the wage roll level. And the higher one looks into the corporation, the smaller is that representation. At the higher levels, it thins out again to half of what it is at the lower levels of the salaried group. Parenthetically, there is a corresponding decline in the use of the French language as one proceeds up the occupational ladder of the corporations.

It is useful to pursue this matter further by envisaging the corporation as an orderly system of occupations, some involved in production, some in sales work, some in personnel, some in finance, some in research and development to name the main functional groups in the modern industrial corporation. Again one can find the anomalies repeated on this scale. Production and sales are areas where French-speaking Canadians have a higher representation than they have in research and development work. Notably, the latter is a field where some facility with science and a high level of technological expertise is characteristic.

This article began with the assertion that the study of occupations in Canada is in a fundamental sense a study of ethnic relations. Not only are the two intertwined but they are mutually affected by the same influences, notably the impact of large scale work organization, scientific knowledge and technological change, and the immigration policies in effect in the country. The effort to generate hypotheses regarding occupations and occupational specialization will necessarily involve variables of the above mentioned character.

The article can close on a more practical note, on a question of some urgency in Canada at present. When a minority group becomes aware of its disadvantages in the occupational field, what measures can it take to modify its situation? What are the various elements in its environment which must be manipulated in order to bring about any substantial change in its current status? If it espouses the goal of equality of occupational opportunity, what range of phenomena must be equalized to reach that goal? An improved theory of occupations would shed light on what is now a baffling question.

Pluralism
and
Conflict

in Ethnic Relations

5

Social Pluralism in Quebec:
Continuity, Change and Conflict

RICHARD J. OSSENBERG

PLURALISM AND METHODOLOGY

The complexity of social pluralism in Canada is best illustrated in the case of Quebec which could be considered as a situation of *double pluralism*. In many ways, Quebec is a plural society within a plural society, consisting not only of the widely recognized differences which separate English-speaking Canadians and French Canadians, but also, and of equal importance, the pervasive and enduring differences which separate French Canadians from each other.

The existence of severe schisms within the French Canadian population, based essentially on social class differences, largely accounts for the apparent ambiguities, inconsistencies, and contradictions which have marked the evolution of Quebec. Social scientists as well as the Canadian public generally have been perplexed by developments in Quebec largely because of their lack of recognition of the internal dynamics in the evolution of the French Canadian population.

The general image of the French Canadians is that they are of one culture, sharing geographical, linguistic, historical and general "style of life, similarities which clearly distinguish them from English-speaking Canadians. This image, interestingly, is held by many English-speaking Canadians *and* French Canadians. Among the latter group, it is especially those associated more or less directly with Quebec's Quiet Revolution and the separatist movement who find the façade of a "common front" to be compatible with ideological goals.

It cannot be denied that the image of French Canadians as one culture has a certain degree of validity. The "boundaries" of the French Canadian population, consisting essentially of geographical concentration in Quebec Province, and linguistic homogeneity, place them in considerable contrast to the English-speaking Canadian population generally. But the emphasis on this obvious contrast has obscured the existence of a myriad of factors which have always fragmented the French Canadian population in Quebec and continue to plague their search for cultural identity.

Why have the schisms within the French Canadian population been considered as relatively negligible in comparison to those which separate French Canadians and English-speaking Canadians generally? Canadians of all ethnic origins, similar to people throughout the world, tend to think of cultural and ethnic differences in terms of "we" and "they" contrasts, thereby exaggerating the cultural homogeneity of both "groups". Social scientists have largely incorporated this imagery with regard to studies of ethnic relations, although anthropoligists have been somewhat more alert to the existence of internal differences within all ethnic groups than have sociologists, by virtue of their more direct and sustained contact with minority groups. There has been a general tendency, especially marked among sociologists, to over-emphasize the cultural homogeneity of minority ethnic groups, although there have been exceptions, including the studies of Wirth[1] and Cayton and St. Clair Drake[2].

There are, of course, many situations which tend to bring about relatively high degrees of cultural homogeneity and mutual identity among members of minority groups, including competition and conflict with other ethnic groups, sometimes resulting in "nativistic" or "revivalistic" movements which maximize internal social cohesion and solidarity and thereby reduce or eliminate internal divisiveness. However, these social situations have not yet ameliorated the schisms within the French Canadian population which are deeply rooted, and virtually "institutionalized" because of the peculiar nature of Quebec's double pluralism.

It would be misleading to suggest that the internal divisions among the French Canadians have been completely ignored. Among French-speaking sociologists, including Guindon[3] and Pinard[4], the existence of divisive social class differences has been candidly acknowledged and analyzed. Some English-speaking analysts[5] have also recognized the existence and relevance of social class and other differences which have differentiated French Canadians. The existence of social class differences among the French Canadians has figured largely in many of the discussions that I have had with both French-speaking and English-speaking scholars, but the general tendency, as indicated by published studies, appears to emphasize the "one culture" image of the French Canadians.

But it is not only the existence of social pluralism within Quebec that has accounted for difficulties in the analysis of that Province; it is also

[1] Louis Wirth, *The Ghetto* (Chicago: University of Chicago Press, 1929).
[2] Horace Cayton and St. Clair Drake, *Black Metropolis* (Chicago: University of Chicago Press, 1947).
[3] Hubert Guindon, "Two Cultures: An Essay on Nationalism, Class, and Ethnic Tension", in *Contemporary Canada,* ed. Richard H. Leach (Toronto: University of Toronto Press, 1968), pp. 33-59.
[4] Maurice Pinard, "One Party Dominance and Third Parties", *Canadian Journal of Economics and Political Science,* XXXIII (August, 1967), pp. 358-73.
[5] See, for example, Mason Wade's discussion of class conflict during the Asbestos strike of 1949 in Quebec, in his *The French Canadians: 1760-1967* (Toronto: Macmillan of Canada, 1968), II, esp. 1107-1109.

the perpetuation of long established historical patterns which continue to be relevant to an understanding of contemporary developments. The imperative need for analysis of social-historical materials in the scientific study of societies, especially those characterized by ethnic pluralism, has been recognized[6] but generally ignored by social scientists, especially functionalists who believe that group dynamics can be understood on the basis of structural conditions alone. Many of the fallacies of this assumption have been pointed out by van den Berghe.[7]

Two theoretical problems involved in the study of Quebec, which are applicable also to the general study of Canadian society, have thus far been discussed; the general absence among Canadian social scientists of a systematic conceptual model of Canada as a plural society, and their general neglect of historical considerations upon both of which I have elaborated elsewhere.[8] A third problem remains: the lack of a comparative framework in the analysis of Canadian pluralism. Similar to their colleagues in the United States, Canadian social scientists have only rarely attempted to analyze their society in terms of contrasts with, or similarities to, other societies. Even those few attempts which have been made to do so, including those by Lipset and Naegele, have been very general and impressionistic, as pointed out by Davis in this volume.

French Canadian scholars in their analysis of Quebec have been somewhat more likely than their English-speaking colleagues to consider the comparative frame of reference. Guindon's comparison of French Canadian separatism with nationalist and separatist movements in other societies,[9] provides a number of new and interesting hypotheses concerning the social evolution of Quebec. Pinard[10] has examined reasons why radical left wing political ideologies have not yet developed among lower class French Canadians, in contrast to the political behaviour of the lower social classes in other societies. But sociological studies by French Canadian scholars have not generally dealt with comparative materials, a consequence, perhaps, of their preoccupation with factors exclusive to internal evolution.

My purpose in this chapter is to analyze the social evolution of Quebec and some of its contemporary dynamics. Most of the discussion hinges heavily on a theoretical framework of social pluralism in Quebec, social-historical considerations, and, finally, a comparative analysis.

[6] See entire issue of *Annals of the New York Academy of Science*, XXXCIII, No. 5 (January, 1960). Most of the articles contained therein point out the importance of historical factors in an understanding of ethnic pluralism in the Carribean.

[7] Pierre L. van den Berghe, "Toward a Sociology of Africa", *Social Forces*, XLIII, No. 1 (October, 1964), 11-18.

[8] Richard J. Ossenberg, "The Conquest Revisited: Another Look at Canadian Dualism", *Canadian Journal of Sociology and Anthropology*, IV, No. 4 (November, 1967), 201-218.

[9] Guindon, "Two Cultures . . .", esp. pp. 57-59.

[10] Maurice Pinard, "Working Class Politics: An Interpretation of the Quebec Case", *Canadian Review of Sociology and Anthropology*, VII, No. 2 (May, 1970), 87-109.

QUEBEC: A CASE OF DOUBLE PLURALISM

The most basic and enduring difference among French Canadians has been that of social class. Although English-speaking Canadians have been "elitist" in their relationships with French Canadians, emphasizing Anglo Saxon cultural, economic, and political superiority, there has also been a strong elitist tradition within the French Canadian population. Social class differences between French Canadians are no less severe than those social class differences between French Canadians and English-speaking Canadians generally. The existence of general social class inferiority among the French Canadians compared to the Anglo Saxon population of Canada, and even relatively recent non-Anglo Saxon immigrant groups, has long been recognized by people "in the know", and increasingly being acknowledged by Canadians everywhere. The relative disadvantages of the French Canadians with regard to their comparative social class standing in both Quebec and Canada generally, has been documented by Hughes,[11] Porter,[12] and The Royal Commission on Bilingualism and Biculturalism.[13] Studies in Quebec, conducted by French Canadian scholars, including deJocas and Rocher,[14] and Dofny[15] have also demonstrated the existence of generally low social class standing among French Canadians. The evidence is irrefutable: French Canadians stand, and have stood, at the lower rungs of the Canadian social class system. This is the fact of Canadian social structure which has been central to the debates, issues, and controversies concerning Canadian confederation both inside and outside of Quebec. It has added credence and viability to the separatist movement.

The social class inequalities within the French Canadian population, especially in Quebec, while of the same magnitude of those separating French Canadians and English-speaking Canadians generally, have been ignored, played down, or obscured by the "larger" issues of Canadian confederation. The objective evidence for these internal French Canadian social class differences has been presented[16] and there can be no debate over their existence. Yet, these internal social differences have not been systematically studied in an attempt to analyze the essence of Canadian pluralism.

[11] Everett C. Hughes, *French Canada in Transition* (Chicago: University of Chicago Press, 1943), esp. Chapter. vii.
[12] John Porter, "The Economic Elite and the Social Structure in Canada", *Canadian Journal of Economics and Political Science,* XXIII, August, 1957 377-394.
[13] Report of the Royal Commission on Bilingualism and Biculturalism, Book III.
[14] Yves De Jocas and Guy Rocher, "Inter-Generation Mobility in the Province of Quebec", *Canadian Journal of Economics and Political Science,* XXIII February, 1957, 58-66.
[15] Jacques Dofny and Muriel Garon-Audy, "Mobilités professionnelles au Quebec", *Sociologie et Sociétés,* I, No. 2 (November, 1969), 277-301.
[16] *Ibid.* See also Jacques Dofny and Marcel Rioux, "Social Class in French Canada", in *French Canadian Society,* eds. Marcel Rioux and Yves Martin (Toronto: McClelland and Stewart, 1964), I, 307-318.

The French Canadians, as a minority group in Canada, have experienced the development of an internal social class stratification system in much the same way as many minority groups in plural societies undergo the process of an internal stratification system which, more or less, is distinct from the stratification system of the dominant ethnic group(s).[17] This stratification system within the minority French Canadians has basically inhibited the emergence of a strong ethnic identity and solidarity, and thereby weakened the appeal of the separatist ideology — an ideology which, at least until very recently, has been peculiar to the relatively new French Canadian middle class.[18] Internal stratification systems among minority groups are detrimental to them because status differences tend to encourage internal rivalries and conflicts, which would under conditions of ethnic solidarity and union be focussed on the dominant groups.

Although there are similarities between the French Canadians and minority groups found in other societies, there are also significant differences. It appears probable, for example, that the internal social class cleavages among French Canadians have been and remain more severe than those found among minority groups elsewhere. For various reasons, to be discussed presently, the high degree of internal cultural and economic differentiation among French Canadians, beginning with the latter phase of the colonial era of New France, distinguishes them from other minority groups in different colonial situations which tended to encourage greater solidarity among themselves.[19]

Before turning to a consideration of the historical roots of contemporary pluralism in Quebec, and how it might be compared to the pluralism found in other societies, I shall briefly outline what I think are the major dimensions and profiles of social class differences between French Canadians today.

In the last decade, the most "visible" social class within French Canada, from the point of view of both academic and popular interest, has been "the new middle class". The French Canadian "new middle class" is both real and, at the same time, a product of the mass media. It is real in the sense that, especially since World War II, an increasing proportion of French Canadians have entered into the world of white collar occupations, ranging from clerical to academic.[20] The "new middle class" has been a product of the mass media in the sense that its sympathies toward separatist movements have been identified with the French Canadian population generally, while the anti-separatist sentiments of the majority of French Canadians in lower social class positions have been obscured.

---

[17] See George M. Foster, *Traditional Cultures and the Impact of Technological Change* (New York: Harper, 1962), p. 41, and entire issue of *Annals of the New York Academy of Sciences,* XXXCIII, No. 5 (January, 1960).

[18] See Guindon, "Two Cultures", pp. 57-59.

[19] For evidence relating to the greater solidarity among minority groups in other plural societies, see Franklin Frazier, *Race and Culture Contacts in the Modern World* (New York: Alfred Knopf, 1957), pp. 294-295.

[20] Dofny and Garon-Audy, "Mobilités professionnelles . . .".

The "new middle class" of French Canadians has been properly identified as the main thrust behind the contemporary separatist movement.[21] The "hard-core" of this group is found among the intelligentsia, especially students and faculty at the University of Montreal. But the separatist sentiments are diffusing to French Canadians generally found in the upper level white-collar occupations, especially in the Montreal area — where the clash of economic interests, ethnic differences, and a sense of "relative-deprivation" are far more pronounced than they are in more static areas such as Quebec City.

This new French Canadian middle class, with some exceptions to be discussed later in this chapter, is relatively isolated from the other two major social class status groups — the old French Canadian elite, and the majority lower class French Canadians.

The relatively small old-elite French Canadians consist of persons generally of long-standing professional status (physicians, lawyers, merchants, chartered accountants, corporate directors, some university professors) some of whom could trace their heritage to their progenitors of the old days of the seigniorial estates. This group also includes members of the higher Catholic clergy who, like their colleagues, shared a somewhat conservative orientation toward the problems of the lower-class French Canadians. As a group, the old-elite French Canadians generally held power within the French Canadian population and received considerable deference from the Anglo Saxon elite. Since the Quiet Revolution of Quebec, which is most frequently traced to the election of Jean Lesage as Provincial Premier in 1962, the old-elite are becoming increasingly marginal, in view of the great advances made, both economically and politically, by members of the "new middle class". As pointed out by Clark elsewhere in this volume, the French Canadian old-elite are being forced into a position of ambivalence and compromise because of their need for maintaining favourable relations with the Anglo Saxon elite as well as French Canadian clientel.

Of special interest to my analysis is the relatively large French Canadian lower class (about 50 per cent).[22] This group has experienced a large degree of "apartheid" from both upper status French Canadian classes, the old-elite, and the new middle class. Meaningful social relations and political rapport between the French Canadian lower classes and members of the upper status groups have been as minimal as that between French and English Canadians generally. It has been the lower class French Canadians who have inhibited, thus far, the growth and influence of the new middle class based separatist ideology. The political behaviour of the lower class French Canadians, generally contradictory to the aspirations of the new middle class, including the 1970 provincial election, has

---

[21] Guindon, "Two Cultures", pp. 57-59.

[22] This is a very crude estimate based on my impression of figures presented by de Jocas and Rocher, "Inter-Generation Mobility", and the considerable upward mobility of the French Canadians since the time of this study (see footnote 16).

been amply documented.[23] Very recent developments suggest the potential for these historically-based social class differences to become modified, thereby assuring an unprecedented degree of social solidarity among French Canadians generally. These developments, among others, will be discussed following an exploration of the historical antecedents which gave rise to the double pluralism of Quebec.

CHANGE AND CLASS DYNAMICS IN THE EVOLUTION OF THE FRENCH CANADIANS

The French settlers in North America during the French colonial regime, lasting from about 1608 until the British conquest of 1759, were a highly differentiated group of people. The evolution of New France was dynamic, and had far reaching consequences for all classes of its population. Social stability in the colony may have been an aspiration, especially among members of the higher Catholic clergy, but never a reality.[24] The basic economic and social conditions of the colony could not possibly have given rise to the stable and socially integrated society which has been at the center of the images of New France portrayed by both English-speaking and French Canadian scholars alike.[25]

There was never one dominant economic system throughout the entire history of New France which could conceivably have led to general social integration. The system of seigniorial estates, which had been intended to be the primary economic resource in the French colony, has been interpreted by contemporaries[26] as well as subsequent analysts[27] as a failure and, at best, a severely limited success. The seigniorial system, roughly modelled from the already antiquated quasi-feudal system of land tenure in France, had little potential of success in the new colony. Both economic and social factors mitigated against it. On the economic level, the seigniorial estate system, which was intended primarily to offer the basic economic sustenance of the French colonists and, coincidentally, to provide the basis for social integration among them[28] offered virtually no economic rewards in comparison to the rapidly developing North American fur trade. The French Canadian *habitants* (often considered to be the

---

[23] For evidence pertaining to this general pattern, but not including the 1970 election, see Pinard, "Working Class Politics", *passim*. Concerning the 1970 elections, analysis of the votes in various social class differentiated ridings indicated the continuation of the traditional differences in party preference, although not as sharply as before.

[24] See S. D. Clark, *The Social Development of Canada* (Toronto: University of Toronto Press, 1942), pp. 76-94, *passim*.

[25] Ossenberg, "The Conquest Revisited".

[26] Concerning the analysis of contemporary documents attesting to the failure of the seigniorial estates, see Victor Coffin, *The Province of Quebec and the Early American Revolution* (Madison: The University of Wisconsin, 1896).

[27] William B. Munro, *The Seigniorial System in Canada* (New York: Longmans, Green, 1907). See Also Guy Frégault, *Canadian Society in the French Regime*, Historical Bulletin No. 3 (Ottawa: Canadian Historical Association, 1954).

[28] See Munro, *ibid.*

approximate equivalents of feudal vassals, and the bulwark of French Canadian traditionalism) had no particular allegiance to the feudal land-lords, the seigniors. Consequently, mobility of the *habitants* from one seigniorial estate to another, in response to the expectation of greater economic and social rewards, was a common pattern.[29] Moreover, there were numerous instances of habitants breaking their contractual obliga-tions to remain on seigniorial estates in order to become more directly associated with the lucrative fur trade by "specializing" as *voyageurs* or *coureurs de bois*.[30] In contemporary sociological parlance, the *voyageurs* and *coureurs de bois* were the ideal male "role-models" for French colonial youth throughout the entire history of New France, whether simply de-scribed as such by analysts such as Guindon[31], or condemned as such by archbishops.[32]

Not only was the fur trade the dominant economic system in New France; it also was so extensive and lucrative, that a number of social historians have suggested that French colonial merchants, engaging in the fur trade, had far more influence in the French court, by the time of the British conquest of 1759, than the elite of the *ancien regime,* including the higher clergy of the missionary Church.[33]

It is also of interest to note that the fur trade was conducted largely on the basis of illegal enterprise, consisting mainly of sales to the English colonists in the south, in sharp contradiction to the officially proclaimed bans on such enterprise. The following excerpt, taken from an account of the day (1679) graphically illustrates the magnitude of this "deviant be-haviour".

> I return, Monseigneur, to the problem of the disobedience of the *coureurs de bois* and I must not hide from you the fact that it has finally reached such an excess that everybody boldly disobeys the ordinances of the King, that they no longer hide themselves, and that with surprising insolence they assemble to go to trade in the country of the savages . . . It is thus, faithful Monseigneur, and everyone agrees, that there is almost general disobedience in the country. The number in the woods has increased to almost five or six hundred not including those who go out every day. They are the ones most capable of doing good and defending the colony. They have Duluth at their head and are all ready to strike a bad blow and undertake not only to carry their skins to the English, as they are already doing, but even to shift there the trade of the savages.[34]

Such an account, which must be considered as somewhat conservative in view of the vested interest of the elite to play-down such instances of

[29] Frégault, "Canadian Society"; see also, Edgar McInnis, *Canada: A Political and Social History* (New York: Rinehart, 1959), pp. 1-140, *passim.*
[30] *Ibid.*
[31] Hubert Guindon, "The Social Evolution of Quebec Reconsidered", *Canadian Journal of Economics and Political Science,* XXVI, November, 1960, 533-551.
[32] McInnis, *Canada,* pp. 35-55.
[33] See Munro, *The Seigniorial System,* esp. 42-45.
[34] Du Chesneau to the Minister in 1679, Public Archives of Canada, Series C"A. 47-56, as quoted in Clark, *The Social Development of Canada,* p. 64.

deviance among the French colonists, is at direct variance with the generally assumed deferential and conforming behaviour of the lower status French Canadian settlers.

The dynamics and relative chaos of the French colonial economic system was reflected in other social institutions. The general image of the stable and tradition-oriented French colonial family, at all status levels, is in variance with the objective historical facts. The family and kinship system in New France could hardly be considered a system at all. Not only was there extensive (and officially banned) cohabitation between French Canadian males and Indian females, but even the "approved" marital arrangements left some doubt as to their contribution to a stable and socially integrated French colonial culture. The economic inducements offered for marriage and the bearing of children encouraged marriages of convenience, and had little to do with the desire for perpetuation of lineage. The following portrayal of one popular method of mate recruitment is indicative of the considerable departure from kinship-formation traditions which occurred in the largely "open-ended" milieu of the French colonial era:

> Several ships were sent hither from France (about 1665), with a Cargoe of Women of an ordinary Reputation under the direction of some stale old Nuns, who rang'd them in three classes. The Vestal Virgins were heap'd up (if I may so speak) one above another, in three different apartments, where the bridegrooms singled out their brides, just as a butcher do's an Ewe from amongst a flock of Sheep . . . I am told that the fattest went off best, upon the apprehension that those being less active, would keep truer to their Ingagements, and hold out better against the nipping cold of the Winter . . . After the choice was determined the Marriage was conclud'd upon the spot, in the presence of a Priest, and a public Notary; and the next day the Governor General bestow'd upon the married couple, a Bull, a Cow, a Hog, a Sow, a Cock, a Hen, two Barrles [sic] of salt meat, and eleven Crowns; together with a certain Coat of Arms call'd by the *Greeks* Kepara.[35]

Accounts of the arrangements for marriages of the French colonial military elite suggest similar non-traditional arrangements.[36]

Even if these accounts were considered to be dramatic exceptions to the general rule, it should be noted that Garigue, who has expressed his view that the French Canadian family throughout the evolution of Quebec was the main integrating and stabilizing institution has also stated that the French colonial family, in contrast to the traditional French family, was rather "nuclear" in structure and was characterized by generally liberal and democratic relations between husband and wife, parents, and children.[37]

---

[35] Baron de Lahontan, *New Voyages to North America*, ed. R. G. Thwaites (Chicago: n.p., 1905), pp. 36-38, quoted by Clark, *ibid.*, p. 52.

[36] See Clark, *ibid.*, p. 53.

[37] Philippe Garigue, "The French Canadian Family", in *Canadian Dualism*, ed. Mason Wade (Toronto: University of Toronto Press, 1960), pp. 181-200.

The social and economic conditions of New France did not encourage the formation of a highly stable kinship system; the rapid expansion of the fur trade, involving an increasing number of *habitants,* the increasing geographical decentralization because of the fur trade, and the extensive sexual relations and arrangements between colonists and Indian mates or mistresses[38] were among the most important factors.

The authority and influence of Catholicism during the colonial era were also considerably eroded because of the rapid social and economic changes. Additional factors, not yet fully studied, entered into the picture. It is rarely recognized, for example, that "until 1627 Canada welcomed Catholics and Protestants alike and the latter exercised an important economic influence".[39] These Protestants, who were most likely Huguenots, may have had considerable influence in encouraging the developing "Protestant ethic" capitalist motivation which appeared to provide much of the attraction of the fur trade. This hypothesis remains to be tested.

Quite apart from the role that the Huguenots may have played in the decline of Catholic authoritarianism and traditionalism, there appears to be considerable evidence attesting to the pattern of secularization of the colonial society. Expressions of concern by the clergy over the generalized disobedience and rebellious behaviour of the *coureurs de bois, voyageurs,* and *habitants* proliferated during the latter half of the life of New France.[40] Moreover, there is considerable evidence indicating the existence of conflict, both within the clerical hierarchy, especially between younger and older clergy, and between the clergy generally, and colonial administrators and the military cadres.[41]

These extensive changes in the colonial social institutions brought about a situation whereby the *ancien regime,* consisting of clergy, military, and colonial administrators, was virtually powerless in exercising social control over the general colonial population by the time of the British conquest of 1759.[42]

Not only were the social institutions of New France undergoing massive disruption; significant demographic changes, all of which tended toward the secularization of the colonial population, were also relevant. Population expansion because of the fur trade correlated with increasing population concentration in the major cities of Montreal, Three Rivers and Quebec, where merchants and tradesmen conducted their enterprise – either in connection with the fur trade or with the developing shipbuilding and forest industries.[43]

---

[38] See Clark, *The Social Development of Canada,* pp. 22-44, *passim.*
[39] Frégault, *Canadian Society in the French Regime,* p. 3.
[40] Ossenberg, "The Conquest Revisited".
[41] *Ibid.*
[42] *Ibid.*
[43] See Frégault, *Canadian Society in the French Regime,* p. 12; and Philip Garigue, "Change and Continuity in Rural French Canada", in *French Canadian Society,* eds. Rioux and Martin, p. 125.

THE BRITISH CONQUEST: COLONIAL PLURALISM, ELITIST COLLUSION, AND CLASS CONFLICT

The British conquest of New France in 1759, the subsequent emphasis on colonial ethnic pluralism, and collusion between elite of the French *ancien regime* and British colonists resulted, in effect, in the termination and, in some ways, the reversal of social changes that had been taking place in New France. But the general sense of deprivation and frustration among the majority of the French population, because of these factors, led to extensive insurrections and near open rebellion, initially directed against the French *ancien regime* and, later, against the British colonial system.

Before going into the evidence for these interpretations, I will outline, briefly, some typical colonial policies which have characterized the nature of ethnic relations in other plural societies, in order to place the British conquest, and its aftermath, in a comparative context.

There are many different ways in which colonial powers have related to conquered and subordinated groups. Generally, two contrasting categories of colonial policy have been identified; the policy of *direct rule,* whereby the goal is for the social, economic and political absorption of the conquered peoples, and the policy of *indirect rule,* where the emphasis is on ethnic pluralism, involving institutional separation between the colonial power and the subordinated groups, in an attempt to either reinforce or endorse the traditional elite group among the conquered peoples.[44] It is this latter form of colonial contact which is of relevance to my analysis of French-English relations following the British conquest. It was the form of colonial contact which characterized almost all of the British colonies,[45] and the situation in Canada was no exception.

It is therefore of some interest to discuss some of the essential characteristics of this typical British colonial policy in order to discuss its ramifications with regard to relations with the French.

There remains some disagreement over the motivations of colonial powers, such as Britain, in encouraging indirect rule or pluralism. On the one hand, it is argued that indirect rule, with its recognition of the traditional authority figures in the subordinated group, enhances administrative efficiency and, coincidentally, minimizes ethnic conflict because of its recognition of the cultural traditions of the conquered peoples.[46] On the other hand, the motivations for the colonial policy of indirect rule have been viewed as an effort to assure the social, economic, and political superiority of the colonial power. This is the interpretation which, I

---

[44] For a discussion of these different kinds of policies, see Franklin Frazier, *Race and Culture Contacts,* pp. 52, 185.

[45] *Ibid.,* p. 52.

[46] For a discussion of this point of view and others, see Raymond Kennedy, "The Colonial Crisis and the Future", in *The Science of Man in the World Crisis,* ed. R. Linton (New York: Columbia University Press 1945), 306 ff.

believe, has the greater logical and empirical support, especially in its application to the Canadian scene. With regard to this interpretation, Brown bluntly states the essence of its relevance:

> The European prefers the native to remain native, realizing that a collapsing native culture means Europeanized natives who will inevitably demand status in the European system . . . The white man wants the services of the native, but resents him as a co-participant in the social order.[47]

It was the Quebec Act of 1774 which symbolized the application of this typical British colonial policy in Canada. In essence, the Quebec Act specified conditions of ethnic pluralism in the future evolution of Canada; specifically, it put back into power members of the French colonial elite, including the Catholic clergy and the seigniors and, in addition, provided them, at least theoretically, with more power than they had ever enjoyed throughout the history of New France.[48] Thus, the *ancien regime,* which had little control over or respect from the French colonists, was restored.

I have attempted to document elsewhere the immediate as well as long-range consequences of this policy of pluralism symbolized by the Quebec Act.[49] My argument has been, and remains, that the policy of pluralism resulted in extensive reactions among the majority of the French Canadian population, ranging from universal instances of *habitants* revolt on the seigniorial estates, extensive cooperation given by the *habitants* to the American colonial expeditions in Canada, and, finally, the Papineau rebellions of 1837-38. It is my thesis that all of these reactions had in common the popular basis of resentment and frustration among the majority of the French Canadian population. More specifically, these resentments were directed largely against the French authority figures, notably the seigniors and the clergy. The evidence of collusion between Catholic clergy and the British colonial administrators is extensive.[50] Evidence for the disaffection of habitants from the control of the Church, at least up to the Papineau rebellions, is equally impressive.[51]

The almost immediate manifestation of conflict among the French Canadians following the conquest can then be seen as attributable to two essential factors: On the one hand, it represented the continuation of class conflict which, as I have suggested, marked the history of New France; on the other hand, this historical conflict was intensified and sharp

---

[47] W. O. Brown, "Culture Contact and Race Conflict", in *Race and Culture Contacts,* ed. E. B. Reuter (New York: McGraw-Hill 1934), 43.

[48] For a more extended discussion of the provisions of the *Quebec Act,* see Ossenberg, "The Conquest Revisited".

[49] *Ibid.*

[50] See Coffin, *The Province of Quebec.*

[51] *Ibid.* and Gustave Lanctot, *Canada and the American Revolution, 1774-1783* trans. Margaret M. Cameron (Toronto: University of Toronto Press 1967). It is interesting that these authors, who are diametrically opposed in their interpretation of the meaning of the mass disaffection of French Canadians, both agree about its extent.

ened by virtue of the consequences of the Quebec Act. On a comparative basis, therefore, the policy of pluralism in Canada was far less successful than the same policy when it was applied to other colonial situations, at least over the short run. The essential difference between the Canadian situation and that of other colonial situations where the British encouraged pluralism, was that the colony of New France had a comparatively high degree of economic and social change and, consequently, no continuous or pervasive leadership structure.

These were some of the historical factors which, I believe, still influence the nature of "double pluralism" in Quebec. Internal French Canadian social class differences have survived and continue to plague French Canadian solidarity.

Developments since the several decades following the conquest until the 1940's are beyond the scope of this paper. However, there is increasing, albeit still limited, evidence attesting to the survival of internal French Canadian conflicts, manifested in different ways. The usual image of the tranquility of French Canadian parish life, with the emphasis on "cow-church-and-state" orientations of the inhabitants, is being challenged by more recent reconstructions which indicate that authority figures, such as the parish priest, were far less relevant to the values and aspirations of French Canadians than has generally been assumed.[52]

Before discussing some more contemporary manifestations of the double pluralism of Quebec, I wish to briefly address myself to the possible reasons for the existence of different interpretations of the evolution of Quebec, in addition to those mentioned by Guindon.[53]

DIFFERENCES IN INTERPRETATIONS

Interpretations of the same society differ between observers, depending on theoretical orientation, ideologies, and station in life. Problems in the analysis of Canadian society are largely attributable to these factors. An interesting critique of the conceptual biases of French Canadian historians has been provided by Cook.[54] Equally significant biases on the part of English-speaking interpreters of the evolution of Quebec have been discussed by Brunet.[55] However, in spite of the differing interpretations between French and English-speaking analyses, there appears to be a general convergence with respect to the historical social integration within the French Canadian population. This convergence I refer to, for want of a

---

[52] See, for example, Philippe Garigue, "Change and Continuity in Rural French Canada", in *French Canadian Society,* eds. Rioux and Martin, pp. 123-136. While Garigue's notions have been criticized by colleagues, his reconstruction of parish life appears to have as much merit as the conventional interpretations held by his detractors.

[53] Guindon, "The Social Evolution of Quebec Reconsidered".

[54] Ramsey Cook, *Canada and the French Canadian Question* (Toronto: University of Toronto Press, 1966), esp. pp. 119-142.

[55] Michel Brunet, "The British Conquest: Canadian Social Scientists and the Fate of the Canadians", *Canadian Historical Review,* June, 1959, pp. 93-107.

better term, the *golden age* image of the evolution of Quebec. Why is it that French Canadian and English-speaking scholars generally seem to agree that the French Canadians, prior to and following the conquest, constituted a generally homogeneous ethnic group, where conflict was exceptional instead of characteristic?

As far as French Canadian scholars are concerned, I believe that there are two reasons for such an analysis. First, the elitist tradition among French Canadians (many French Canadian historians were members of the higher clergy, or otherwise upper-status groups) naturally perpetuated the notion that the masses were generally content under a rigid and authoritarian social system. Secondly, the notion of French Canadian ethnic identity, so central to contemporary separatism, would be brought into question by highlighting the actual long-standing internal conflicts.

The image of the golden age portrayed by English-speaking analysts is, I believe, attributable to somewhat different reasons. As far as historians are concerned, they, like the French Canadian historians, have come from upper status backgrounds, and therefore support the golden age image. Moreover, English-speaking sociologists in Canada have, with few exceptions, adopted a generally functionalist theoretical interpretation of human behaviour, whereby social consensus and integration are perceived to be the "normal" states of society. Conflict situations are thus likely to be perceived as sporadic instead of endemic to a society. In addition, they tend to deny the relevance of historical factors in affecting contemporary patterns.

THE PERPETUATION OF DOUBLE PLURALISM IN QUEBEC

Since the 1920's, Quebec and French Canadians in particular have experienced massive social and economic changes. Urbanization has been one of the obvious changes. The emergence of the Quiet Revolution has been another manifestation of contemporary social dynamics. Yet, in spite of these developments, with their far-reaching consequences, some of the historical patterns, especially as they apply to internal social schisms among the French Canadians, continue to have considerable influence.

The early post-war period in Quebec was marked by a rapid transition from some of the long sustained traditions, but intermingled with this transition were some of the forms of social coercion and constraint which had marked the nature of pluralism since the conquest.

For the first time in Quebec, the frustrations of the lower class French Canadians found some outlet through the syndicated Catholic labour unions which provided at least a partial organizational basis for economic and political action, a basis which had been absent before. It is not surprising therefore, that the latent long-term protest of the French Canadian lower class, found, at least temporarily, some political expression which was mobilized by the *Bloc Populaire* in 1944.[56]

---

[56] See Pinard, "Working Class Politics", p. 22.

The historical influence of Anglo-French elitism and collusion, at the expense of the lower class French Canadians could be seen even during this rapid post-war transitional period. The very fact of the involvement of the Catholic Church in the labour unions symbolized the carry-over of historical patterns which continued to have influence until at least the beginning of the Quiet Revolution in the 1950's and early 1960's.

Although there was a carry-over of at least the attempt of the Catholic clergy to exercise control over the French Canadian population, there were also very significant threats to the basis for its power. Urbanization, with its inevitable weakening of traditional social institutions, was the most pervasive factor in this threat. Another factor was the increasing manifestation of internal conflict within the Church, especially between the older and younger clergy. While this internal conflict had marked the entire evolution of the French Canadian Catholic hierarchy, it was during the rapid transitional post-war period that it found its fullest and most explicit expression.

Social reform programs related specifically to the problems of the French Canadian lower classes were increasingly and actively supported by renegade priests. Referring to the initially reformist *Bloc Populaire* Party, Wade states: "But if the *Bloc Populaire* found little favour with Cardinal Villeneuve and Archbishops Charbonneau and Vachon of Montreal and Ottawa, it was clearly welcomed by the lower clergy.[57]

Archbishop Charbonneau's later support for the causes of the French Canadian lower classes occurred only a short time after his expression of anti-reformist sentiments. And Charbonneau's change of orientation was in connection with the most significant manifestation of social unrest among French Canadian workers during the first decade of the post-war period; the Asbestos strike of 1949. The Asbestos strike, lasting for several months, was not only an expression of economic grievance; it was also an expression of lower-class resentment against *both* Anglo-Saxon Canadian *and* American domination of the Quebec economy; in a sense, it was thus an even more "sophisticated" expression of French Canadian nationalism than that found in the separatist ideology of the "new middle-class" which was to emerge later. Speaking of the Asbestos strike, and social and economic conditions, generally, Charbonneau, during a sermon he gave in 1949, stated: "The working class is a victim of a conspiracy which wishes to crush it, and when there is a conspiracy to crush the working class, it is the duty of the Church to intervene."[58]

But even during this period of rapid change, ideological realignments, and social conflicts, Charbonneau's sentiments were too *avant-garde* to be considered compatible with the elitist vested interests of his colleagues in the higher Catholic clergy. An increasingly militant French Canadian lower class, especially in Montreal, posed definite threats to the maintenance of cohesion, stability, and loyalty, all of which are conditions that the institutional Church depends upon for existence everywhere. It was not surprising, therefore, that the Church, with the active support of the provincial

[57] Mason Wade, *The French Canadians: 1760-1967*, (Toronto: Macmillan of Canada, 1968), II, 956.
[58] Quoted in *ibid.*, pp. 1108-1109.

government, "evicted" Charbonneau by transferring him to the British Columbia hinterland, where his conversion to lower class insurgency could pose a threat only to the king of beasts.

The continuing collusion between Anglo Saxon elites and French Canadian elites was perhaps best illustrated by the Duplessis regime. Although it is now widely held that the Duplessis regime in Quebec was riddled with corruption and was economically and culturally retrogressive, it is not so widely known that collusion between the Anglo Saxon industrial elite and the Union Nationale, under Duplessis, was responsible for this condition. Speaking about the Duplessis regime (especially its activities in 1945), Wade has observed:

> Meanwhile the Union Nationale's electoral war chest fattened, as non-French Canadian companies sought and won, at a price, the right to exploit Quebec's immensely rich natural resources, the great pool of unorganized or weakly organized labour accustomed to a lower standard of living than English-speaking North Americans, and the manifold advantages of an accommodating government in an era elsewhere characterized by extensive governmental regulation of business.[59]

The reciprocal support between the Duplessis regime and the Catholic Church[60] was but another indication of the perpetuation of the elitis tradition.

EMERGING TRENDS: THE FUTURE OF DOUBLE PLURALISM IN QUEBEC

During the time of the rapid social changes occurring in the immediat post-war period of Quebec, the basis for Quebec's most visible expression c discontent — separatism — was evolving. The "new middle class" was bein formed through a combination of factors; first, increasing urbanization an industrialization in Quebec "opened" or "widened" the middle class whit collar, clerical, and administrative categories among French Canadian thereby somewhat "softening" the theretofore rigid French Canadian clas distinctions. Although the upward social mobility of the French Canadiar during that time was not as extensive as that for English-speaking Quebec kers, there can be no doubt that it did occur.[61] Secondly, the education institutions of Quebec became increasingly secularized and geared to a urban-industrial economy, giving rise to an increasing group of intellectu elite. Through extensive upward mobility and the consequent feeling

---

[59] *Ibid.,* p. 1107.
[60] For some views indicating the existence of this relationship, as well as sor reservations concerning its extent, see the diversity of interpretations provid by several observers, reprinted in Cameron Nish, ed., *Quebec in the Duples. Era* (Toronto: The Copp Clark Publishing Company, 1970), pp. 105-12?
[61] See Dofny and Garon-Audy, "Mobilités Professionnelles".

"relative-deprivation" among the French Canadian new middle class — vis-à-vis their English-speaking counterparts — the Quiet Revolution gathered momentum.

The election of Jean Lesage as Provincial Premier in 1962, with his reformist economic policies and "Quebec pour les Quebecois" slogans, reflected the changing social structure of Quebec, especially that of the French Canadian population. The policies of Lesage were directly geared to the newly discovered aspirations, as well as deprivations of the French Canadian middle class.

But even the Quiet Revolution did not escape the influence of the historical French Canadian internal pluralism, especially with respect to social class differences. The economic reforms of the Liberal Lasage government were extensive, including the government takeover of Quebec Hydro, but these reforms were apparently not seen by members of the French Canadian lower classes, either rural and urban, as having any particular relevance to or benefits for them. The Union Nationale, under Premier Daniel Johnson, was re-elected in 1966, largely through the massive support of the French Canadian lower class.

The Quebec provincial elections of 1970, with the Liberals again returning to power under Robert Bourassa, reflected still further changes in the dynamics of French Canadian pluralism. However, the situation then and now is far more complex than ever before. The considerable support for the separatist *Parti Quebecois,* which won only seven seats but received 24 per cent of the popular vote (closer to one-third of the popular vote if the French Canadian voters are considered as a separate grouping), suggested a degree of French Canadian nationalism not realized before. This contemporary nationalism also reflects a softening of the internal social class differences in the French Canadian population, for an analysis of the voting patterns suggests that separatist candidates were elected in four east-Montreal French Canadian lower class ridings; ridings which had been characterized by conservative voting histories. Therefore, it would appear that there is an increasing correspondence between the traditionally divided French Canadian social classes.

With regard to these developments, it would seem that the double pluralism in Quebec is disappearing, and being replaced by a single dualism, based on French Canadian and English-speaking Canadian differences and conflicts. In other words, it would appear that the long-established French Canadian internal differentiations are increasingly being ameliorated by contemporary social and economic factors.

It would seem to me that such an assumption would be somewhat misleading in the face of the pervasiveness of the differences which have divided French Canadians historically. Some of these internal tensions continue to be of relevance to an analysis of the contemporary scene in Quebec. Before discussing these factors, I wish to refer to contemporary conditions which appear to be building a bridge between the French Canadian social classes.

The first factor is that of the massive educational explosion, especially the enormous increase in French Canadians exposed to higher education.

Many, if not most, of the French Canadians entering into institutions of higher learning are of lower social-class background. Dofny has estimated that approximately 37 per cent of the French Canadian students attending the University of Montreal are of lower class background, compared to about 17 per cent of English-speaking lower class background at McGill University.[62] Moreover, the newly founded but rapidly expanding system of C.E.G.E.P.S. (the equivalent of junior colleges, or university preparation programs) is catering to a predominantly French Canadian student population. The many branches of the University of Quebec are likewise designed essentially for French Canadian students.

Some of the ideological consequences of this French Canadian educational explosion appear obvious. Basically, it would appear that a conversion to new middle class values, including the ideology of separatism, is occurring among these upwardly mobile French Canadian students of lower class origins. There is some evidence that this conversion is taking place. Among the students at the University of Montreal, only the most conservative estimate would figure the pro-separatist sentiment at 90 per cent of the student population. Guindon, through a survey of first year students at *Ecole des Hautes Commerciales de Montréal* figures that 75 per cent of the students demonstrated a clear preference for *Le Parti Quebecois*.[63] It would be surprising if the magnitude of this French Canadian student support of new-middle class ideologies was not found also in the C.E.G.E.P.S. and University of Quebec, where staff are mostly graduates of the University of Montreal.

There are other indications of the relationship between the upward social mobility of the French Canadians and the conversion to separatism, thereby softening the middle class - lower class differences. Studies of the 1962 and 1966 provincial elections in Quebec have clearly shown the affinity between French Canadian youth and the separatist ideology[64]. There was shown to be a direct correlation between the percentage of young French Canadians in each of Montreal's 29 electoral districts and the strength of support for separatist candidates. Also, between both election years, the percentage of French Canadians in favour of separatism more than doubled, including almost half of a representative sample of young French Canadians from all income groups. The same studies also found that the more knowledgeable the French Canadian youth was about provincial politics, the more likely he was to support the separatist cause. If this latter finding is applied to the upward educational mobility among increasing numbers of lower class French Canadians, it would appear that conversion to the values of the French Canadian new middle class is very extensive.

---

[62] Jacques Dofny, *pers. comm.*
[63] Hubert Guindon, *pers. comm.*
[64] These studies, conducted by Pierre Guimond and Serge Carlos, both graduate students at the University of Montreal at the time, were reported in a number of newspapers, including *The Montreal Star,* July 26, 1966.

Have the increased educational opportunities for French Canadians correlated with increased occupational opportunities? While the exact nature of this relationship is difficult to assess, a recent study by Dofny[65] would indirectly suggest the existence of this relationship. In a comparison of upward social mobility patterns of English-speaking Quebeckers and French Canadians, Dofny found that the previously documented gap between the two groups was decreasing; that, indeed, the French Canadians were experiencing an unprecedented degree of upward occupational mobility. While Dofny attributed this upward mobility to basic structural changes in the Quebec economy, as opposed to the increasing competitive advantages of the French Canadians vis-à-vis the English-speaking Quebeckers, there can be no doubt that an increasing number of French Canadians are experiencing a "new middle class" way of life and are being at least exposed to, if not converted to, the separatist ideology resident in this group in recent years.

There is, however, evidence of the continuation of French Canadian pluralism, expressed in the historical internal social class differences. Whereas it is true that the proportion of lower class voters who supported *Le Parti Quebecois* increased, in comparison to their support for separatist candidates in previous elections, and thereby also apparently conforming to the middle-class pattern, it is also true that the majority of lower class French Canadians were anti-separatist. Expressions of hostility toward separatists and the French Canadian middle class generally, were very extensive during my daily visits to St. Henri, a lower class French Canadian area in Montreal where, over a period of three months in early 1970, I attempted to assess some aspects of social changes occurring there.

During my research visit to Montreal, it also became clear that the view of the French Canadian intelligentsia toward the French Canadian lower class was essentially a patronizing one, and consisted basically of the need to "politicize" the working and lower social classes; there was, however, little or no sense of social rapport or solidarity with the lower classes.

It is difficult to assess the role that the militant Confederation of National Trade Unions (C.N.T.U.) has played in bridging the gap between the French Canadian social classes. On the one hand, the massive support that its membership gave to Lévesque and his *Le Parti Quebecois* in the 1970 elections, would suggest that increasing organization among French Canadian workers would increase their sympathies for the aspirations of the new middle class. On the other hand, it has been suggested that most of the new members of the C.N.T.U. are affiliated with white collar occupations,[66] thereby making the argument somewhat redundant.

In any event, it does not appear that the C.N.T.U. has thus far provided the organizational vehicle for the problems and aspirations of the French Canadian lower classes. Its militant ideological basis, attempting to

---

[65] Dofny and Garon-Audy, "Mobilités Professionnelles".
[66] Hubert Guindon, *pers. comm.*

appeal to both middle and lower classes, is too diffuse and, I believe, too suspect to draw massive support from the lower classes.

What will be the future of internal French Canadian conflicts and their implications for Canadian confederation? The answer depends on social, economic, and political changes within Quebec, and on the reaction of Canadians elsewhere to these changes.

THEORETICAL CONSIDERATIONS OF ALTERNATIVES

One of the most penetrating analyses of internal social class conflicts among French Canadians has been provided by Pinard.[67] Pinard suggests that in the evolution of Quebec during the past forty years, the French Canadian lower classes and middle class have acted in contradiction to each other in terms of political behaviour. In some ways, the French Canadian middle classes over this period, including the recently emergent new middle class, have demonstrated more conservatism and self imposed cultural encapsulation, than have the French Canadian lower class who, in generally supporting economic reformist parties (as opposed to parties calling primarily for national unity), have demonstrated their own severe sense of economic deprivation and, coincidentally, suspicion of the French Canadian middle class.

Pinard's analysis is important in terms of the future evolution of Quebec. If a political movement in Quebec combines both the economic concerns predominant in the lower classes — with the aspirations for cultural identity, without over-emphasizing either of these components, an ideological merger between lower and middle class French Canadians would appear likely.

Perhaps Guindon's portrayal of Quebec's bureaucratic revolution[68] provides a key to the potential for such a merger to appear. Guindon suggests that the massive bureaucratic expansion of Quebec industry poses a dilemma for French Canadians. On the one hand, increasing participation of French Canadians in occupations associated with large bureaucratic organizations appears inevitable. On the other hand, bilingualism within these corporations is now being encouraged. Therefore, both the sheer impersonality of bureaucracy — its contractual, as opposed to cultural or traditional basis of operation, threaten to emasculate the cultural identity especially of middle class French Canadians. Moreover, and in adding to Guindon's thesis, the exclusive use of the French language within these bureaucratic organizations would be discouraged by the very nature of their associations with enterprise outside of Quebec, thereby further weakening French Canadian cultural identity which could better survive in the context of small-scale and localistic enterprise. Given such structural dilemmas, and their

---

[67] Pinard, "Working Class Politics".
[68] Hubert Guindon, "Language, Careers and Formal Organizations", research in progress.

inevitable dilusion of cultural traditions, it would appear that convergence between lower class and middle class French Canadians would increase, based essentially on common concerns of economic deprivation instead of cultural identity.

Extensive economic deprivation among French Canadians of all social classes could bring about a merger which would virtually guarantee a separatist government in Quebec within the next decade. On the other hand, the absence of such a sense of economic deprivation among the French Canadians generally would tend to perpetuate the double pluralism of Quebec which in many ways has been the most important factor in the preservation of Canadian confederation.

The reaction of the Federal Government and the English-speaking population to the manifestation of the social, economic, and political problems of the contemporary colony of Quebec will likely influence the interplay of these considerations and determine the fate of Confederation. French Canadians, similar to minority groups throughout the world, have attained temporary high levels of social solidarity and separatist sentiments in reaction to autocratic and symbolically racist policies and behaviour of the central government supported by majority ethnic groups. The use of arbitrary military force in reaction to the anti-conscription sentiments of the French Canadians during both World Wars and against the workers during the Asbestos Strike of 1949 has been typical of the entire history of French-English relations. But this policy has only contributed to the developing spirit of self-determination among French Canadians of all social classes. The use of the War Measures Act in response to the kidnappings and terrorism of the Front de Libération du Québec in October, 1970 can only accelerate the development of the separatist ideology among *les Québecois,* for it will remind them of their common heritage as victims of the double pluralism and elitist collusion which has marked their entire history.

6

EDITOR'S INTRODUCTION

Professor Carstens, in comparing the reservation systems of Canada and South Africa in the next article, shows one important way in which Canada can be considered similar to other societies which have developed a system of ethnic and social pluralism, as opposed to a system whereby the integration and assimilation of different social and ethnic groups is encouraged.

A plural society is a society which has become segmented in terms of diverse and discrete institutional systems including the family, religion, and at times political and economic systems. Canada is similar to many plural societies where the concept of the "mosaic" has been encouraged and perpetuated. Pluralism is a characteristic common to many of the former British colonies.

Arguments in favour of pluralism or against pluralism can be made without end. It is important to recognize that a system of cultural pluralism, such as that found in Canada, may have certain advantages over systems where ethnic and social differences tend to be leveled and obscured through the emphasis on conforming to standard norms (such as in the United States). However, pluralism also poses many social evils which, if not corrected, may contribute to the destruction of an entire society.

Professor Carstens discusses one of these evils — the reservation system, whereby members of indigenous groups (the Blacks and Coloureds in South Africa and the Indians in Canada) are refused entry into the main social stream. Reservation systems perpetuate ethnic injustices and inequalities and are certainly not "natural" developments which one expects to witness in any kind of society. An example of a different kind of development occurred in the former French colonies where a formal policy of "assimilation" or "direct rule" existed; this did not resolve gross inequalities but did decrease the social and political distance between conquerors and conquered.[1]

Carstens shows how the reservation system helps to maintain the status quo in favour of the white establishment in two countries which, on the surface, seem to be disparate, but in some fundamental ways are very much alike. His emphasis on the concept of "structural conditions" simply means that certain social arrangements result in similar consequences regardless of the individuals involved in those arrangements; thus, Reserve Coloureds in South Africa face the same problems of economic and social deprivation and powerlessness as those faced by Indians in Canada. The concept of structural similarities highlights the

[1] See, for example, Franklin Frazier, *Race and Culture Contacts In the Modern World* (New York: Alfred Knopf, 1957), p. 52, p. 185.

importance of avoiding a static racist interpretation of ethnic inequalities; i.e., the concept holds that regardless of the ethnic affiliation of a particular group, whether it be Anglo Saxon or non-Anglo Saxon, if they face similar structural conditions, they will find themselves in similar ways of life. Thus, in terms of structural conditions, the French-speaking population in Canada is in an inferior condition because of historical factors and colonial policy, along with obvious discrimination, while the French-speaking population in Belgium is the super-ordinate group because it has experienced some of the advantages that the Anglo Saxon population in Canada had.

Some observers might disagree with Professor Carstens' suggestion that it is the reservation system in itself that perpetuates inequalities between ethnic groups. They might suggest that the essence of apartheid and social separateness can be transmitted to even urban areas where social density exists but where apartheid can be maintained. It is well known, for example, that many Indians, who have migrated and settled in urban areas, have come face-to-face with the realities of discrimination and residential segregation for the first time — realities which were obscured because of the "separateness" involved in an exclusively reservation habitat.

However, it is quite proper to assume that over the long-run, urbanization and ethnic contact are essential to the break-down of group barriers. The reservation system, both in Canada and South Africa, serves as a real barrier to the accomplishment of this long-term ideal.

Carstens appears to agree with Professor Vallee that if any nativistic movements are occurring among the native populations of Canada, they are only in their early stages. Leaders of the "Red Power Movement" in Canada, however, would disagree with these assessments. Regardless of the interpretation that one makes about the extent to which nativistic or red power movements exist, it is clear that they are gathering momentum and the Pan-Indian-Eskimo-Métis movement will accelerate so long as conditions of apartheid generated by the traditional reservation system or its emergent urban counterpart are maintained.

Carstens also briefly discusses a tendency found within many lower status or minority ethnic groups — the tendency to vent hostility upon one another instead of the majority group. It is not surprising, therefore, to observe that deviant behavior occurring within minority groups often is ignored by white authorities; for as long as this deviant behavior exists, the establishment considers itself in a relatively safe position.

6

Coercion and Change

PETER CARSTENS

CONFERENCES AND COMMISSIONS

Early in September 1939, the day after the declaration of war in Europe, a Seminar Conference entitled "The North American Indian Today" was held at the University of Toronto. Its purpose was to discuss "the indisputable fact that the Indian has become a minority group, numerically overwhelmed by the preponderant White population".[1] There seem to be two significant features connected with this meeting. In the first place it was inspired by C.T. Loram, professor of race relations at Yale, who had spent several years in South Africa where he had worked closely with both liberal philosophers and anthropologists, and where he had been favourably regarded in government circles.[2] Moreover, the Loram-McIlwraith Conference took place two years after the publication by the South African Government of the *Report of the Cape Coloured Commission.*[3]

The second significant feature of the Conference were its contributors and their contributions. For example, anthropologist T.F. McIlwraith spoke on the "Basic Cultures of the Indians of Canada"; R.H.G. Bonnycastle from the Hudson's Bay Company's Fur Trade Department dealt with "The Role of the Trader in Indian Affairs"; Brother Memorian of St. Joseph's College, Alberta, and the Reverend T.B.R. Westgate, Secretary of the Church of England Indian and Eskimo Residential School Commission, spoke of the importance of Missions; R. A. Hoey and others of the Department of Mines and Resources (Indian Affairs Branch) dealt with land and economic problems. Other sections of the Conference were devoted to basic European cultural influence, arts and crafts of the Indian, and problems of government, law, health, and race tension. The Conference closed after the Reverend E.W. Wallace, President of Victoria University, Toronto had de-

---

[1] C. T. Loram and T. F. McIlwraith, eds., *The North American Indian Today: University of Toronto – Yale University Seminar Conference* (Toronto: University of Toronto Press, 1943), p. ix.

[2] See especially C. T. Loram, *The Education of the South African Native* (London: Longmans, 1917).

[3] *Report of the Commission of Inquiry regarding the Cape Coloured Population of the Union* (U.G. 54, 1937).

livered his valedictory address in which he argued amongst other things that the missionary and the scientist must work together.

These introductory remarks, which have deliberately been geared to the drama of a conference table, demonstrate very clearly the special position that persons of Indian heritage occupy in the composite society of Canada. The early occupiers of Canadian soil have become problem people in the minds of the settlers not only because they have caused problems for the invaders, but also because they possess problems as a result of their dying heritage. If the Indian people are a special category of minority group, what then are the main factors that have moulded their status?

Their problems and their status, I will argue, have nothing to do with "the frequent failure of Europeans to recognize the importance to the Indians of their psychological and emotional interests . . . ."[4] The social position of the Indian peoples of Canada, it will be asserted, has been created, often consciously, through time by an administrative design which culminated in the formulation of the Indian Act of 1876 and its subsequent amendments.[5] This colonial administrative design not only defined the boundaries of the land or territory (later called reserves) on which Indians should settle, but the legal concept whereby Indians were to be recognized, and, both directly and indirectly, the roles they could or should play. The effectiveness of The Indian Act from the point of view of the Government lay partly in the coercive nature of the treaties[6] and partly in the assistance received from missionaries, traders, and other culture agents from Europe. The term "acculturation"[7] could, therefore, in this context at least, be both unsatisfactory and misleading in explaining the processes of change whereby the administrative (legal) system together with its economic, religious, and educational concomitants have evolved. The culmination of this process of acculturation from among those involved in it has moreover been their encapsulation in closed communities. This social position has inevitably created a reduction of alternatives in decision-making processes at all levels within communities under the jurisdiction of the Indian Act.

Crucial to this argument is the contention that the essence of acculturation lies firmly embedded in the administration and power of the government. Thus the "missionary and the scientist" may set up alliances of friendship but they can not alter the status of Indian peoples. Traders,

---

[4] T. F. McIlwraith, "Basic Cultures of the Indians", in *The North American Indian Today*, eds. Loram and McIlwraith, p. 30.

[5] The 1876 Act was amended from time to time, but remained basically the same for about 75 years. A new Indian Act was passed in 1951 (R.S.C. c. 149). It has also been amended by 1952-53, c. 41; 1956, c. 40; 1958, c. 19; 1960, c. 8; 1960-61, c. 9.

[6] See *Canada: Indian Treaties and Surrenders from 1680 to 1890*, 2 vols. (Ottawa: Queen's Printer, 1905).

[7] For a brief but comprehensive statement of the term see "Acculturation", *Encyclopaedia Britannica* (1964), I, 83-84. In this statement, the author does, however, include the domination of the Canadian Indians under the sub-heading "Directed Change".

teachers, and the wives of the commercial elite may continue to co-operate with certain Indian groups to ensure that the Kamloops, Banff, or any other "Indian Days" are a continued success;[8] yet their action merely perpetuates and never undermines the administrative system.

The primacy of central government relations is borne out at all levels — notably by the willingness of the Government to establish joint committees on Indian affairs,[9] by the financing and publication of *A Survey of the Contemporary Indians of Canada*,[10] and by a general paternalistic concern to establish what will be "good for" the descendants of the indigenous population within the framework of the status quo. There are also the numerous reports and documents for public consumption issued by the Indian Affairs Branch.[11]

I would be misleading the reader if the impression was given that people of Indian (and Eskimo) origin had been silenced by Government command and prevented from expressing their grievances. The former have, on the contrary, been encouraged to put forward their views and state their grievances in briefs, public statements, the press, on radio, and on television. An analysis of these views also bears out the contention that the societal situation in which Indian and other persons with similar status live, is essentially oriented to the central authority. The views of Indian spokesmen in nearly every case, no matter how violent are their attacks on the Indian Affairs Branch, are always expressed within the framework and context of the federal political system in which they are encapsulated. Their ideological standpoint is in a very real sense a function of their predicament. In other words, the straight-jacket of law inevitably determines their actions to a large extent. Under the existing system there can be no other action because their stream of wills have been so conditioned. Moreover, as long as the system continues, the expression of Indian opinion in this manner will have a stultifying effect on the rate of change apart from coercive change, which is beyond their control.

The kind of responses expected from Indian peoples to royal requests brings out their dependent position on the Central Government very clearly. For example the following circular was sent to enfranchised Indians in 1887:

To the Indians: The Queen has always loved her dear, loyal subjects, the Indians. She wants them to be good men and women, and she

---

[8] See, for example, *The B.C. North American Brotherhood News*. (Published from June 1961.) The founding Associate Editor, Leonard Marchand, is at present Liberal M.P. for Kamloops. Also, see Conference of Indian Business Men, *Report of the Second Decennial Conference on Native Indian Affairs* (Victoria, B.C.: Indian Arts and Welfare Society, 1958).

[9] Joint Committee of the Senate and the House of Commons, *Indian Affairs Canada, Parliament* 1960-61 (Ottawa: Queen's Printer, 1961).

[10] H. B. Hawthorn, ed., *A Survey of the Contemporary Indians of Canada* 2 Parts (Ottawa: Queen's Printer, 1966, 1967).

[11] Perhaps the most useful of these for quick insight into government attitudes i *The Canadian Indian: A Reference Paper* (Ottawa: Indian Affairs Branch 1959).

wants them to live on the land they have, and she expects in a little while, if her great chief (sic), John A., gets into government again, to be very kind to the Indians and to make them very happy. She wants them to go and vote, and all vote for Dr. Montague, who is the Queen's agent. He is their friend and by voting for him every one of the Indians will please Queen Victoria.

Whether this document belongs to the paternalistic or coercive category is impossible to answer. There would appear, however, to be a strong suggestion that it was more of a governmental command than gentle persuasion from the Queen herself.[12]

The Indians of Canada who are under the Indian Act and live within the economic, social, and territorial confines of reserves are not wards of the Government as some have argued; they are members of little colonies within the borders of the dominating nation. A similar observation was made in a lecture by Peter Worsley regarding the peoples of Northern Saskatchewan in 1961,[13] and Leo Marquard and others[14] have drawn attention to the intra-territorial colonialism characteristic of South African reserves and of the neighbouring countries on which South Africa relies heavily for cheap labour.

Perhaps the notorious paucity of detailed anthropological and sociological studies of Canadian Indian Communities can be explained by the intellectual identification of Indians with the Central Government and its bureaucracy.[15] Thus any study of what Dunning has called "Indian status

[12] For an account of the personal qualities of administrators in an early period, see Oliver M. Spencer, *Indian Captivity* (New York: n.p., 1835). The author of this work was "rescued" from a group of Indians by a British Indian agent, Col. Elliot (p. 115ff). Elliot was described as a rough unpleasant man like many other agents. Of him, Spencer wrote: "...I well recollect [Governor Simcoe's] remark...that such conduct in a British Officer would subject him to trial before a court martial; but that he was obliged to overlook many improprieties in the agents who had such influence with the Indians, and were so necessary to his majesty in his intercourse with them." (pp. 146-47).

[13] This lecture was later revised and published as Chapter 22, "Bureaucracy and Decolonization: Democracy from the Top", in *The New Sociology Essays in Social Science and Social Theory in Honor of C. Wright Mills*, ed. I.L. Horowitz (New York: Oxford University Press, 1964).

[14] Leo Marquard, "South Africa's Colonial Policy" (presidential address to the South African Institute of Race Relations, 1957). W. Peter Carstens, *The Social Structure of a Cape Coloured Reserve* (Cape Town and New York: Oxford University Press, 1966), pp. 134-5.

[15] There would appear to be two categories of ethnographic community studies in Canada: (1) Those published by museums, notably the National Museum of Man, an institution of the Federal Government; and (2) those few published by university presses. The lack of interest among university social scientists in the museum publications is extremely marked and probably significant. For example, G. B. Inglis, a professor of anthropology, in a recent paper on reserve populations mentions only one (lesser known) "museum publication" and ignores all the important studies from the National Museum of Man. See G.B. Inglis, "An Approach to the Analysis of Reserve Populations as Partial Societies (paper presented at the 67th Meeting of the American Anthropological Association, 1968).

persons" unavoidably involves one in a study of the evolution and application of the Indian Act and of the network of bureaucrats who administer it. Most Canadian social scientists would appear to be reluctant to pursue this profitable research topic.[16]

Here my chief concern is to stress what might be called the importance of the process of "administrative determinism" in creating the lifeways of the contemporary Indian peoples. Little of my contribution is in any way "new" or for that matter original. At best, it will clarify what others have already said or implied;[17] and the introduction of parallels from the Republic of South Africa may help sharpen the focus of the argument. I realise that there are strong taboos against making comparisons between Canadian and South African institutions, but the disappearance of taboos is common when they are upheld only by the myths and the folk systems of an old and respectable elite. In other words, the reality of Canadian society is often blurred by the "Establishment" at the expense of minority groups. This mechanism takes many forms, ranging from the fear of comparative criticism to the aversion to American influence.

[16] Even H. B. Hawthorn and his co-authors of *The Indians of British Columbia* (Toronto: University of Toronto Press, 1958) admit the importance of looking into that part of the civil service of Canada involved in Indian affairs. But they did not further our knowledge of this distinguished body of officials. (See their reasons on p. 485 of their book.) Nor did the Hawthorn Report on the Contemporary Indians of Canada, published in 1966 take up this matter. Two important works dealing with closely related processes (one contemporary, the other historical) should be noted: R. W. Dunning, "Some Aspects of Governmental Indian Policy and Administration", *Anthropologica,* N.S. Vol. IV, No. 2 (1962) and Robert J. Surtees, "Indian Reserve Policy in Upper Canada, 1830-1845" (M.A. Thesis, Carlton University, 1966). See also H. E. Staata, "Some Aspects of the Legal Status of Canadian Indians", *Osgood Hall Law Journal,* April, 1964.
I am especially grateful to my colleague, Dr. S. Nagata, for drawing attention to de Tocqueville's discussion of the relevance of law in American transactions with Indians. See Alexis de Tocqueville, *Democracy in America* (Trans. Henry Reeve), I, 342-361, *et passim.*

[17] The best examples of this interpretation are: R. W. Dunning, "Some Implications of Economic Change in Northern Ojibwa Social Structure", *Canadian Journal of Economics and Political Science,* XXIV, No. 4, 1958; R.W. Dunning, *Social and Economic Change Among the Northern Ojibwa* (Toronto: University of Toronto Press, 1959); H.B. Hawthorn, C.S. Belshaw, and S.M. Jamieson, *The Indians of British Columbia* (Toronto: University of Toronto Press, 1958), esp. p. 485; Gordon K. Hirabayashi and Cecil L. French, "Poverty, Poor Acculturation and Apathy: Factors in the Social Status of Some Alberta Metis" (paper read at 33rd annual meeting of the Canadian Political Science Association in Montreal, 1961); R.W. Dunning, "Some Aspects of Governmental Indian Policy and Administration", *Anthropologica,* N.S. Vol. IV, No. 2; R.W. Dunning, "Some Problems of Reserve Indian Communities: A Case Study", *Anthropologica,* N.S. Vol. VI, No. 1; and Charles Hamori-Torok, "The Acculturation of the Mohawks of the Bay of Quinte" (Doctoral Thesis, University of Toronto, 1966).

TWO FRONTIERS COMPARED

The overall differences between the colonization of Canada and South Africa are obvious, yet when we turn to specific situational phenomena some helpful parallels facilitate the use of the historico-comparative method. In this context, we shall not be concerned with the chiefdoms and kingdoms of the Bantu-speaking peoples. Their great size, the density of their populations, as well as their complexity of social organization places these tribes in a different category from any peoples who used to inhabit that part of North America now known as Canada. By these same criteria they are not comparable with either the *San* hunter-gatherers, or the *Khoikhoi* herders of Southern Africa. We should note, moreover, that the Bantu-speaking peoples now numbering 12,750,000 have never been effectively conquered, either physically or psychologically. They have not retained their "traditional" way of life but at no time in their collective history can they be said to have been annihilated or had their ranks decimated by military conquest, disease, or famine. Bloodshed, sickness, and hunger were part of the price they paid, particularly in the nineteenth century. But they remain the largest category of people in present-day South Africa.[18]

Our comparison with South Africa is restricted therefore to those hunters and herders whom the Dutch (and later the British) encountered.[19] The initial interest in the indigenous population was their wealth in cattle which the colonists bartered for trade goods. In later years, as the colony grew, keen attention was paid to the acquisition of their land and their labour (especially their potential as shepherds, farm hands, traveller's guides, and members of the armed forces). From the earliest contact period numbers of Khoikhoi did join the ranks of the colonists and become fused with them through marriage and other alliances, but the majority remained members of dwindling tribes until they were engulfed by the renegade settlers (frontiersmen) and missionaries. As the frontier expanded, the Khoikhoi lost both their land and their tribal and cultural identity. Small portions of land were reserved for some by various "Tickets of Occupation" which guaranteed them certain rights. Later, in 1909, these areas were legally recognised as "reserves" by the Communal Reserves and Mission Stations Act (No. 29 of 1909).

During the eighteenth and nineteenth centuries, new communities formed on the north-west frontier. A few leaned towards the Khoikhoi

[18] In 1968, the total population of the Republic of South Africa was estimated to be 18,733,000. Of these 12,750,000 were classified as African (Bantu), 1,859,-000 as Coloured (mixed), 2,563,000 as White, and 561,000 as Asian.

[19] For different interpretations of the process of colonization among these people during various time periods, see E. Fischer, *Die Rehobother Bastards und des Bastardierungsproblem biem Menschen* (Jena: E. Fischer 1913); J.S. Marais, *The Cape Coloured People, 1652-1937* (London: Longmans, Green, 1939); I.D. MacCrone, *Race Attitudes in South Africa* (London: Oxford University Press, 1937); W. Peter Carstens, *The Social Structure of a Cape Coloured Reserve* (Cape Town, New York, Oxford University Press, 1966).

tradition but the majority developed a way of life that consisted of a blend-
ing of two main traditions, i.e. Khoikhoi and Dutch. Known as the *Basters*
(hybrids) these people became in many ways the parallels of the Canadian
Métis,[20] although the strong sense of community found amongst the Basters
seems absent among their Canadian counterparts.

I have drawn attention very briefly to these aspects of South African
history in order to suggest some of the obvious similarities between the
colonization processes in two different parts of the world that shared the
British imperial influence for a considerable number of years. During the
early years the parts played by the French and the Dutch as colonial
pioneers for the British should, however, not be underestimated.

With this common ethnological background the British Government
seems to have acted in a consistent manner in later years. The parallels
between the South African Coloured Reserves and the Canadian Indian
Reserves seem too similar to have been independent inventions. Whether
the same official placed the imprimatur of the British Empire on the
various acts of Parliament, which made them possible or not, is irrelevant.
What is of significance is that institutionalized segregation became a reality
through similar governmental channels, often for identical paternalistic
reasons, and that there are nowadays marked similarities between the two
systems.

THE ADMINISTRATION OF INDIANS

At the Toronto-Yale Conference to which I have referred earlier,
T.R.L. MacInnes, then Secretary of Indian Affairs, delivered an extremely
valuable paper.[21] Not only did it outline the early administration of
the indigenous peoples, but it expressed also the official attitudes and policy
towards "the Indian". These attitudes are significant because they arouse
similar emotions concerning non-Indian views of reform as did Part I
of *A Survey of the Contemporary Indians of Canada*[22] written more than
a quarter of a century later. For example, recommendation no. 4 of the
Survey states *inter alia* that the Indian Affairs Branch "should act as a
national conscience to see that social and economic equality is achieved
between Indians and Whites". Dunning, who is well-known as a scholar
and critic of Indian Affairs, reacts by asking: "In what better way could
paternalism be made permanent?"[23] Dunning may well have asked whether

[20] W.P. Carstens, "Basters", *Encyclopaedia of Southern Africa* (Cape Town,
1967); R. Douville and J.D. Casanova, *La Vie Quotidienne des Indiens du
Canada à l'Epoque de la Colonisation Française* (Paris: Hachette, 1967). See
pp. 197-239 for a short account of the contact between the French and the
Indians. And especially pp. 220-239 for a useful description of the early Métis
settlement and the whole question of inter-marriage and cohabitation.

[21] T.R.L. MacInnes, "The History and Policies of Indian Administration in Canada", in *The North American Indian Today*, eds. C.T. Loram and T.F. Mc-
Ilwraith (Toronto: University of Toronto Press, 1943), pp. 152-163. I have
drawn heavily on the work of MacInnes for the section that follows.

[22] Hawthorn, *A Survey of the Contemporary Indians of Canada*, Part I.

[23] R.W. Dunning, "The Hawthorn Report", *Canadian Forum*, June 1967, p. 52.

this well-intentioned recommendation reflects any change in attitude since MacInnes spoke in 1939. In his address, MacInnes boasted about the virtues inherent in the Indian Affairs Branch's complementary principles of *protection and advancement:* "The Indians from the earliest times have appreciated their treatment by the British Crown. Their loyalty has always been traditional [*sic*]."

The concept of paternalism is an extremely unsatisfactory sociological term since its meaning changes both through time and in the context in which it is used. Perhaps it would be more useful to consider the relationships implied by the term on a paternalistic-maternalistic oscillatory scale. The history of the administration of the Indian peoples of Canada would appear then to change according to the potential role of Indians in the wider society. For example, paternalism seems to have been greatest when the colonists were expanding their territory and consolidating coercive control. Maternalism may be seen to occur in periods when the rulers wish to maintain the status quo by permissiveness and generosity. The present period would appear to be of the maternalistic variety.

It would, I think, be difficult to link French colonial policy directly with the administration of the indigenous peoples of Canada. This assertion does not preclude French influence as a study of early Jesuit and other records shows.[24] Indian land was, however, recognised by the French Government in a peculiar way through the activities of the Catholic missionaries. It was only after the British began to control the destiny of the Indian people through its rigid colonial system that some of these institutions were incorporated within the bureaucratic framework. Thus the policy of Indian administration really began on North American soil during the reign of Charles II when the British began making treaties and agreements with certain Indian groups in New England, in about the year 1664. Yet it was not until the Treaty of Paris (1763) that the recognition of British administration in Canada became effective.

MacInnes describes the Indian Office as a "continuing administrative organization . . . for the protection and advancement of the Indian interests", and how the Royal Proclamation of 1763 crystalised the beginning of what later became known as the Indian Act. This Proclamation set forth with considerable and irreversable clarity the direction of future policy, stating *inter alia* by Sir William Johnson's proclamation that no Indian could be dispossessed of land without his (sic) consent — subject to the approval of the reigning Monarch (as in so many similar proclamations). Furthermore, the Proclamation made explicit that treaties would be drawn up from time to time with selected groups of Indians. These treaties provided for the "unsurpation" of native land in return for which the Government was to provide certain minimal services.[25]

---

[24] For a useful account of French influence, see R. Douville and J.D. Casonova, *La Vie Quotidienne.*
[25] In addition to *Canada: Indian Treaties and Surrenders,* see *The People of Indian Ancestry in Manitoba,* 3 vols. (Winnipeg: Department of Agriculture and Immigration, 1959), esp. Vol. I.

Few people, including government officials, will be in complete agreement with the belief held earlier by many benevolent liberals that the "government has more than fulfilled the letter of its obligations", nor for that matter will many agree with the contention that the Proclamation of 1763 was the bright side of aboriginal contact with western civilization, whereas the dark side was disease and degradation alleviated only by the missionary who was a sort of friend and helper as well as his enemy's keeper. Yet this was firmly stated in 1939, and there is evidence that these principles of paternalism are still present, though in the disguised form of maternalism. Sentiments such as these were frequently expressed too by South African liberals (especially in the 1930's) regarding the necessity of protecting African land from White intrusion, etc.[27] In both the Canadian and South African experience the sentiments were usually noble, but the implications of reserving land were never fully realised in terms of their long term effects, until it was too late to reverse the process.

For Canada and, to a certain extent, for parts of South Africa, additional concern regarding the degrading effects of firewater and brandy are also regarded by some as being among the main causes of poverty and its concomitants. The fur trade in Canada is also believed in some circles to be part of the nefarious process of "culture contact" which caused the disintegration of indigenous society as symbolised by the transition from the tepee to the cabin and shack. Here, however, it is contended that these and other cultural changes and exploitative events belong to a lesser order of importance than the inflexible codified power of the Indian Act of Canada that followed in their wake — geared to William Johnson's legislative machinery of an earlier era.

At the end of the eighteenth century, the Department of Indian Affairs evolved partly by a process of coercion and partly by one of segmentation. The former speaks for itself; the second may be observed within the Department itself whereby the office of Superintendent General of Indian Affairs and of the secretary of the department were located at Montreal, while the Deputy Superintendent and Assistant Secretary were both located at Niagara. This evolution was indicative of the positive expansion of the colonial powers toward the west with the full support of the military. For on May 13, 1816, the management of Indian Affairs was placed under the jurisdiction of the Commander of the Forces in what was then known as the British North American Provinces.

Various administrative changes occured during the next four decades, but for the purposes of this discussion it is relevant to remember only that it was the Imperial Government which was responsible for all aspects of Indian Affairs. However, in 1860, an act "respecting the management of the Indian lands and property" was effected, and "native affairs" now came under the control of the Provinces of Canada. What is perhaps most sig-

---

[26] MacInnes, "The History and Policies of Indian Administration", pp. 153-54.

[27] See for example: R.F.A. Hoernlé, *Race and Reason* (Johannesburg: Witwatersrand University Press, 1945), edited with a memoir by I.D. MacCrone; and E.H. Brookes, *The Colour Problems of South Africa* (Lovedale, South Africa: Lovedale Press, 1934).

nificant about this act was not so much the shift to the Canadian scene, but rather the fact that it became part of the Crown Lands Department This symbolised, I think, the new interest in the importance of acquiring land while the negotiations for Confederation were being discussed. (Indians living in other parts of the territory fell under the several provinces.)

With the advent of Confederation, the powers of the Dominion were defined by the British North America Act of 1867. Section 91, no. 24 reiterated the status of Indian persons by listing as one of the new powers of the Dominion the control of "Indians and Land Reserved for the Indians". Thus, unlike the status of Africans in what used to be Southern Rhodesia where all changes in administrative policy had first to be approved by the British Crown, in Canada the reserve population is now the prerogative of the Canadian Government only. As a consequence thereof, the Indian Act was first passed in 1867. This act in its various forms was a culmination of the early processes we have mentioned. It would appear also to be related historically to various reports and items of legislation found in the Cape Colony of Southern Africa.[28]

Confederation involved the Indians of Canada with a new department, soon after its inception — that of the Secretary of State — to which the Indian Affairs Branch was attached. This move revealed perhaps the determination of the new government to keep Indian Affairs at a highly centralised level of authority. In 1873, the Indian Affairs Branch was affiliated with the Department of Interior.

The expansion and growth of the Dominion of Canada soon created demands for the establishment of a separate Department of Indian Affairs, and in 1880 Sir John A. Macdonald became its first minister holding the title of Superintendent-General of Indian Affairs together with his office of Prime Minister — reflecting again the importance of centralising these duties in the affairs of the country.

In 1936, the same year that African men lost the franchise in the Cape Province, South Africa, the Department of Indian Affairs ceased to exist. I am not suggesting any direct relationship between these two events. At the most one could argue that the depression had manifested itself in two different ways. In South Africa, there was a fear that the growing economic and political competition with the natives, who were the hardest hit by the depression, would disrupt the existing distribution of power. In Canada the opposite was true; the battles over the status of the Indian and Métis people had been won. The problem now was to keep them as viable members of the labour force. It is not surprising to find therefore that the administrative successor to the Department of Indian Affairs was the Department of Mines and Resources. Following the era of depression

---

[28] J.S. Marais, *The Cape Coloured People, 1652-1937* (London: Longmans, 1939), pp. 74-84, gives a useful description of the Cape Coloured Reserves and their history. See also the Melvill Report (G. 60, 1890), pp. 4-5; *Votes and Proceedings of Parliament* (Cape of Good Hope, A. 7, 1896), Appendix 2, II, 1-4, *et passim;* and Carstens, *The Social Structure of a Cape Coloured Reserve,* esp. pp. 16-36.

and war the Indian Affairs Branch was placed under the Department of Citizenship and Immigration, a move which should require no comment.[29]

The discussion up to the present is well summed up in *A Survey of the Contemporary Indians of Canada:*

> Historically the Canadian Indian has had an especially strong link with the federal government and a weak and tenous relationship with provincial governments. The initial basis for this circumstance was the assigning of "Indians and Lands Reserved for the Indians", 19-24, to the federal government under the British North America Act. In response to this assignment of legislative authority, an Indian Act was passed, an administrative structure was created, and special policies were developed for a particular ethnic group, the indigenous inhabitants of Canada. The result of the preceding was that the federal government involved itself in the provision of a complex series of services for Indians which other Canadians received from provincial and local governments.
>
> This unique situation was justified and sanctioned by assumptions and attitudes which reflected the fact that while non-Indians lived in a federal system the Indians virtually lived in a unitary state. Up until 1945 the federal government uncritically accepted its special responsibilities for Indians on the grounds that they were wards of the Crown. Provincial governments, with no pressure to do otherwise, assumed that Indians were beyond the ambit of their responsibility. The Indians for their part, developed a special emotional bond with the federal government, and suspicious and hostile attitudes to the provincial governments.[30]

Whereas some writers, notably the authors of the Hawthorn Report, see the manifestations of significant change in central-local government and other relations since World War II, the evidence appears to be derived largely from the conference table. It is true that the qualifications of teachers have been improved, that welfare has been increased, that housing and economic development programmes have been established, that the budget of the Branch has been enlarged, etc. But none of these changes proves anything since far more extensive developments in all these areas are found in the mainstream of Canadian society — with the exception of the disproportionate growth of the overall size of the bureaucracy managing the Indian peoples. It would appear, therefore, that much of the debate over federal and provincial responsibility towards Indians is really an attempt, conscious or otherwise, to distract Indians and others from the fact that federal control is on the *increase.* Even *A Survey of the Contemporary Indians of Canada* makes it quite clear that:

---

[29] In South Africa, the Coloured Reserves were placed under the jurisdiction of the Department of Social Welfare in 1944, having been controlled by the Department of Native Affairs from 1913 to 1944. In 1952 a Department of Coloured Affairs was created for the first time.

[30] Hawthorn, *A Survey of Contemporary Indians of Canada,* Part I, p. 199.

The Indian responsibilities assumed by the federal government are significantly greater than what is required under treaties or the British North America Act.[31]

In spite of this statement, the report disagrees with Laskin's contention "that Parliament alone has authority to regulate the lives and affairs of Indians on a reservation and, indeed to control the administration of a reservation . . . ."[32] It is of course perfectly accurate to state that there has been attention from the federal government in developing "self-government" and Indian participation in decision-making; but this trend merely confirms my thesis that the policy of the government towards Indian communities is one of mature segregation similar to that found in parts of South Africa. Thus the removal from the Indian Act in 1951 of restrictions relating to potlatches,[33] Indian festivals, stampedes, and the like, can also be interpreted as part of a centrally-directed retribalization process. In a similar light, much of the incentive for the revival of the traditional artistic culture — arts and crafts — appears to be based outside of Indian communities while the "internal participation ratio" in the operation is extremely low.

THE CONSEQUENCE OF RESERVE SYSTEMS

As I have already implied, the establishment of Reserves for the native people in Canada and in parts of the Cape Province, South Africa, was not motivated only by exploitation. There were also strong liberal feelings of paternalism which helped promote the "success" of these minority enclaves and alleviated some of the guilt from the shoulders of their architects. At the level of an "intellectualist" interpretation, we would wish to argue that the reserve system, as a concept, embodies all the ideas concomitant with the processes of contact and change. Thus it is maintained that much of the "folk lore" and differences in attitude towards reserve life, both from within and without, makes sense when seen in the context of a multiplex ideological tradition.

It is, however, to the more general social characteristics (and manifestations) of the typical contemporary reserve that I wish now to turn. Nearly all reserves belong to that intermediate societal species which has in recent years received recognition by social scientists — peasantry. Most reserve communities have all the characteristics of peasant communities according to Kroeber's definition of peasants as rural people living in relation to market towns, provided we see them (as Kroeber did) as consisting of class segments of a population that contains urban centres. One

---

[31] *Ibid.,* p. 251.
[32] *Canadian Constitutional Law,* p. 550 as quoted in *ibid.,* pp. 251-252.
[33] For a convenient collection of articles on various aspects the institution known as *The Potlatch,* see Tom McFeat, ed., *Indians of the North Pacific Coast* (Toronto: McClelland and Stewart, 1966), Part III.

significant difference, however, between reserve and peasant communities needs to be noted. Reserves are social systems which have been ossified by the economic and political systems on which they are dependent. Some may argue that reserves in both South Africa and North America cannot be peasant communities because migratory labour and other forms of exploitation have created relations with the "great tradition" of industrialism that invalidates the comparison. But if we see migratory labour and temporary "off reservation" residence within the framework of a market economy the justification for the comparison is strengthened.[34]

This leads me to a brief discussion of the key concept of peasantry, i.e. dependence.[35] These societal sub-species, it has been argued, are dependent on the wealthier and more powerful dimension of their world network for survival and for the maintenance of those demands dictated in diverse ways by the dominant external system. It would appear, then, that the problems of peasantry and reserve dwellers are similar. The members of both community types are involved in these relations of dependence coupled with a strong element of conflict. Both are, moreover, what Marx, Weber, and Ossowski would consider social classes. In his *Poverty of Philosophy,* Marx expresses very clearly the conflict inherent in class systems

---

[34] In Hawthorn, *A Survey of the Contemporary Indians of Canada,* Part I, p. 10, it is asserted that: " ... their numbers are growing faster than any sectional rate of increase in Canada, and many of them are accustomed to living in regions and latitudes that are seeing vital new industrial development". Perhaps the potential of Indians in the labour force of Canada should not be underestimated; nor should the possibility of their exploitation especially in the North. *The Globe and Mail,* May 15, 1969, reported that:

> Canada's registered Indian population increased in 1968 to 237,490 from 230,902 [in 1967], the Indian Affairs Department said yesterday. In a news release the department noted that 120,412 Indians are under 17 and that the biggest single age group — 40,073 — is four and under. The department also said that the infant mortality among Indians is 51 per 1,000 live births compared to the all-Canada rate of 22 per 1,000. It is said life expectancy among Indian men is 60, compared to the national male life expectancy of 68.
> Population by province and territory with 1967 figures in brackets: Prince Edward Island 418 (409), Nova Scotia 4,411 (4,287), New Brunswick 4,156 (4,039), Quebec 26,302 (26,650), Ontario 52,981 (51,731), Manitoba 33,358 (32,579), Saskatchewan 33,852 (32,579), Alberta 27,-322 (26,440), British Columbia 46,046 (45,152), Yukon 2,562 (2,477), Northwest Territories 6,482 (5,911).

[35] Dependency relationships are of course universal. The nature and degree of these relationships in any group, class, or community are, I believe, amenable to measurement, ranking, and classification if we analyse them in terms of the major institutions that link these internal social systems (groups, classes, communities) to the external or wider social system. For example, political and legal dependence in an Indian Reserve can be discovered by analysing the decision-making and processes; the religious dependence of a community of Cape Coloured reserve dwellers can be determined by the nature of the office of missionary and the structure of the Church government of the denomination that wields religious power; similarly dependence in formal education can be deduced from the roles of teachers and the type of school administration; economic dependence needs no example, and military dependence is well exemplified in most feudal systems.

between the dominating and the dominated, the entrepreneur and the worker, the rulers and the ruled. It is the techniques of coping with this situation and the reaction to it that is of concern to us here. As far as the general model is concerned, however, we need to state the following contention or hypothesis simply but formally: *Peasants, the working class, and people who live in reserves belong to the same social genus in terms of the relationship in which they stand to the dominant segment of their social milieux.* They are all "class segments" of society, as both Kroeber and Ossowski would agree.

To return specifically to the concept of reserves within the general framework of the above hypothesis, this does not seem to be the place to provide the South African evidence[36] — should such evidence be necessary. But the fact that the significant work of Canadian scholars in this area during the past two decades has been largely ignored or misunderstood by both the government and the social sciences calls for an evaluation of their contribution, especially as it is crucial to my argument.

The observation needs to be repeated again that there has been an almost complete disregard in recent works on contemporary Canadian society, of Indian and Eskimo peoples.[37] It is as though the authors of these works regard only Europeans as members of Canadian society; in many ways I suppose they are correct.

At the end of the 1950's and early 1960's, Dunning published the results of his extensive field work on specific groups of Indian peoples in Canada.[38] In his well-known work, he demonstrated to the government and social sciences alike the way in which dependence on welfare and wages (migratory labour) together with permanent legal (political) attachment to Ottawa had produced "lower-class behavioural patterns in the nation society". Dunning's conclusions were supported by the findings of Hawthorn, Belshaw, and Jamieson.[39] Hirabayashi and French, moreover, in an unpublished paper on Métis groups with some reference to certain Indian groups also state:

> It would appear that the acceptance of disease and other unpleasant life situations which these people show might indicate an internalization of a lower-class set of norms and values which would include

---

[36] For a general background to the socio-economic position of reserve dwellers in South Africa, see *Keiskammahoek Rural Survey,* 4 vols. (Pietermaritzburg: Shuter and Shooter, 1952); Union of South Africa, *The Tomlinson Commission* (Pretoria, U.G. 61, 1955); and Carstens, *The Social Structure of a Cape Coloured Reserve.*

[37] For example, Bernard R. Blishen *et al,* eds., *Canadian Society: Sociological Perspectives* (Toronto: Macmillan of Canada, 1968); W.E. Mann, ed., *Canada: A Sociological Profile,* (Toronto: The Copp Clark Publishing Company, 1968); B.Y. Card, *Trends and Change in Canadian Society: Their Challenge to Canadian Youth* (Toronto: Macmillan, 1968).

[38] See footnote 16.

[39] H.B. Hawthorn, C.S. Belshaw, and S.M. Jamieson, *The Indians of British Columbia: A Study of Contemporary Social Adjustment* (Toronto: University of Toronto Press, 1958).

poor self images, feelings of unworthiness and apathy towards the environment.[40]

Elsewhere the authors tend to see this "lower class" norm and value orientation as less binding on Indians than Métis. On the whole, however, all the evidence which these authors present agree with those hypotheses I have already mentioned. The points of disagreement inherent in these studies seem to border on the problem of the nature of stratification in general and the concept of dependence in particular.

STRATIFICATION AND DEPENDENCE

The dependence relations of the Indian people can be seen in almost all the major areas of social life. Dunning and others have stressed the importance of economic and political dependence, but we should not fail to recognise the fact that formal education, religion (with some notable exceptions), medical services, and even entertainment tend to be fed into the community from outside. This is, of course, inherent in the nature of reserves, regardless of minor changes that have occurred since policy was first formulated. It is, in fact my contention that moves toward integration are usually accompanied by countermoves towards segregation. Expressed in different terms, it can be argued that whereas reserves as structural systems appear to change, they do not and cannot. Thus an apparent centrifugal move (e.g. school integration off the reserve) tends to be accompanied by a centripetal one (e.g. an increase in qualified self-government). At first glance it would appear that comparison with South African reserves breaks down if we apply this generalization (derived from the Canadian material). A closer look at the data, however, suggests that in South Africa, too, the extension of educational "facilities" and economic opportunities to all non-Whites has also been accompanied by attempts to grant greater qualified internal autonomy.[41] The inequalities of the South African system are well-known but the parallels found in Canada in certain respects are too seldom acknowledged.

If dependency is one of the concomitants of reserve systems, it may well be asked what are the consequences of dependence relations. This has in part been answered, and I have mentioned some of the psycho-social affects on those individuals who have been "trapped" or encapsulated in a societal position which offers few rewards or opportunities in itself — a societal position in which there are few alternatives. For the Canadian scene, I cannot ignore the phenomenon of discrimination against Indian persons any more than I can pretend that race prejudice does not exist

---

[40] Gordon K. Hirabayashi and Cecil L. French, "Poverty, Poor Acculturation and Apathy: Factors in the Social Status of Some Alberta Metis" (paper read at 33rd Annual Meeting of the Canadian Political Science Association, Montreal, 1961).

[41] In other words, the granting of "special" privileges to people who do not possess power is an index of a reconsolidation of the ruling group's strength over them.

in South Africa. Thus, to begin with, there are strong external factors which inhibit their desire to join the open society. But whether discrimination be disguised or overt, it is not the only factor that contributes to a relatively low rate of permanent out-migration. There is ample evidence to demonstrate that a process of positive conditioning takes place in reserve communities. This process may be regarded as the socializing mechanism that creates the pull to remain in a social refuge area. As Dunning would argue for his Type B reserves,[42] this phenomenon is essentially a structural one, having nothing to do with any cultural differences relating to an earlier period, should such cultural differences exist at all. Even in the northern trapping regions, the effects of external structural factors imposed through culture agents (and the reserve or incipient reserve system itself) on Indian communities is noted. Dunning appears to perceive the major cause of the process in terms of welfare and relief, but it is quite apparent from his and other data that the primary initial and major cause is that of "administrative determinism".

CONFLICT IN INTERPERSONAL RELATIONS

Although there is no accurate way of measuring co-operation and conflict as basic forms of sociation, there are times and situations, when one form can be said to predominate. As is so frequently the case in peasant communities, interpersonal relations in Canadian reserves are characterized by a greater degree of conflict than in other Canadian communities. This phenomenon appears to be related to two factors: (1) the marginal or dual life-situation to which Indians are attempting to adjust and (2) the shortage of land. I shall discuss the first of these only since the other subject has been clarified in another context elsewhere.[43] Moreover, the whole question of land and land shrinkage on reserves is well-known.

Canadian Indians and Cape Coloureds, in relation to Whites, occupy what may conveniently be described as a *marginal* status. In other words, their attitudes, values, and sentiments are determined for them largely by the position which they occupy in their respective societies. The concept of marginal men and women, as used here, characterizes those who are forced by circumstances to live in two or more major different social situations or groups at the same time. All of us, of course, are in some way or other marginal men, but none are so marginal as minority groups, notably those who live in reserves.

The problem, in effect, is that both Indians and Coloured people are faced with the conflict of trying to adapt themselves to a dual life-situation; but in so far as this situation is structurally determined, it has no ultimate solution. The members of both groups are too closely interwoven

[42] R.W. Dunning, "Some Problems of Reserve Indian Communities", *Anthropologica*, N.S. VI, No. 1 (1964), 3-38.
[43] E.g. George M. Foster, "Interpersonal Relations in Peasant Society", *Human Organization*, XIX, No. 4 (1960-61), 174-84.

with, and dependent on the Whites to become separate from them, and yet the factors already stated inhibit or prevent the process of complete integration.

How does this dilemma manifest itself? And if we accept the proposition that frustration tends to lead to some form of aggression, how does this aggression manifest itself?

The dominant reaction among both Coloureds and Indians seems to be that of avoidance and acceptance. When we inquire more deeply into these reactions we find that they are frequently tinged with aggression or that the frustration is translated into aggression which is not always recognised.

In South Africa, the reserve Coloureds (and some other categories of Coloureds too) usually give the impression in their behaviour that they are merely accepting their low and dependent status; they display a fawning attitude towards Whites when greeting, begging, offering to do a job of work, bidding farewell, etc. In practice, however, they are doing two things. On the one hand, they are being servile, submissive, timid, and sensitive (implying acceptance); at the same time, they are expressing humorous aggression in their gestures and speech tones, a type of coping behaviour often described by the term "joking relationship".[44] Joking relationships constitute a peculiar combination of friendliness and antagonism occurring in many societies in situations in which tension is likely to arise. And Canadians will surely recognise the parallels in many Indian-White relationships. In these situations the joking relationship fulfills an additional function by enabling members of the minority groups (and the Whites) to express aggression in an institutionalised and hence approved manner. Joking relationships are the safety valves which help to let off steam in situations of social disjunction; but often the valves get clogged.

The tendency among Indians and Coloureds to express direct aggression against Whites is to a large extent curbed partly to avoid White counter-aggression,[45] but also, I believe, because of the strong emotional ties of dependence which they have with Whites in general. Thus the aggression manifestations of the ambivalent attitudes of Indians and Coloureds are not obvious, but take a variety of indirect forms, as writers about other minority groups have noted. These include the wasting of time and materials at work (inefficiency), petty thieving of materials by workmen (and in South Africa of food by domestics), leaving a job at short notice, failing to turn up at a new job, and malicious gossip among themselves and with certain Whites about Whites. It is interesting also to record that in South African towns Coloured hawkers vacillate between obsequiousness and aggression to their dealing with Whites. They "command" Whites using the term "master" to buy their goods and they resent

[44] A.R. Radcliffe-Brown, *Structure and Function in Primitive Society* (London: Cohen and West, 1952) Chap. iv and v.

[45] For South Africa, see Sheila Patterson, *Colour and Culture in South Africa* (London: Routledge and Kegan Paul, 1953), pp. 181-93, *et passim*. See also N.W. Braroe, "Reciprocal Exploitation in an Indian-White Community", *Southwestern Journal of Anthropology*, XXI, No. 2 (1965), 166-78.

any refusal. Coloured chars "attack" the house noisily and firmly, polish the floors and windows unnecessarily vigorously; and tell the housewife how to run her home, although they tactfully use "we" when they mean "I", and "our" when they mean "my".

Overt aggression against Whites by Indians and Coloureds, however, is often displaced onto the members of the minority group itself, because the consequence of such action then tend to become less serious, or perhaps because of hidden taboos which keep such "deviance" internal. Thus among both Indians and Coloureds (especially among the latter) crimes or personal violence of this kind do not involve legal action and tend to be settled at a personal level. They include wife-beating, fist-fighting, and the like. Much of this kind of violence takes place while the parties concerned are under the influence of liquor, yet it would be utterly erroneous to attribute to drinking the cause of the violence. The effect of alcohol merely facilitates the escape of inhibitions, which allow aggressive impulses related to those other factors we have mentioned to assert themselves.[46]

Another form of displaced aggression is that of vandalism — the destruction of or damage to White-owned property, notably public property. This form of displaced aggression appears to be symbolic of the rejection of White institutions. The acts provide an emotional outlet and, hence, personal gain for the individual participants themselves. Such acts strongly suggest that Indian and Coloured aggression is not directed against Whites as persons but rather against their institutions. Vandalism in its many forms is a rather crude way of expressing disapproval of the status quo. An example given by Hawthorn and his co-authors clarifies the point. The intoxicated Indian, they report, may curse and strike the White officer who arrests him, but he is more likely "to content himself with urinating in the patrol car and doing his cursing later in conversation with Indian friends".[47]

In one Canadian reserve where I worked, police records reflected a very high incidence of crimes against property, including destruction of telephones, tearing down of official notices, house-breaking without theft, deflating patrol car tires, etc. The story goes that Indians captured a patrol car, removed the wheels, hacked the car to pieces, stripped the two police officers of their uniforms which were burnt, and sent the officers home in their underclothes. Whether the details of this account are entirely accurate, I do not know, but the legend illustrates the suggestion made earlier — that it is not the White man who is disliked, but the institutions which he represents and enforces.[48] This is particularly evident in parts of Canada where many Indian status persons have the physical characteristics of non-Indians. It is the "office" of white man which carries a stigma.

---

[46] Hawthorn, *et al, The Indians of British Columbia*, pp. 323-29.
[47] *Ibid.*, p. 327.
[48] Hawthorn and his co-authors present this point of view very well in *The Indians of British Columbia*. Those unfamiliar with the South African material will find it dramatically told by Harry Bloom in his novel *Episode* (London: Collins, 1956).

SUMMARY AND CONCLUSIONS

In this chapter, I have been able to touch only briefly and super-ficially on the main processes that have moulded the social position and lifeways of the Indians of Canada. References to South African parallels have been made not merely because they are obvious, but because the comparative method is crucial in the development of a science of society. The comparative method is, however, more appropriately termed historico-comparative, for without its temporal dimension, neither the present nor the past can be understood. And if predictions are ever to be made about the future, static "functionalist" orientations tend not to be helpful. My concern in these pages has been to demonstrate *inter alia* how the lack of attention to forces that have operated through time has tended to inhibit various analyses of the Indians of Canada. Most important of these forces has been that of the continuing coercive power of the central government. If this hypothesis is accepted then the contemporary Indians of Canada and the manner in which they have changed can never fully be understood un-til the evolution of the civil service for Indians has been unravelled.

The lack of predictive sophistication in sociology and social anthro-pology is well known, notably when dealing with data of this order. At best, I can draw attention to the increase in the number of socio-political movements among the Indians of Canada — a trend which owes its origin to isolation from the mainstream of Canadian society.[49] In South Africa, this trend has declined since legislation was introduced to discourage or prevent it. For the Canadian scene some would wish to find significance in the phenomena of "Red Power" and "nativistic" movements, but these seem no more than the dramatization of those minor socio-political move-ments to which I have already referred. In short, the "Indian question" will continue in its present form for several generations as a problem of class — not of culture.

A RECENT DEVELOPMENT

A Government White Paper has recently been issued outlining a new policy for the Indians of Canada. The policy sketched is simple: it calls for the repeal of the *Indian Act* and eventually "winding up that part of the Department of Indian Affairs and Northern Development which deals with Indian Affairs". The statement indicates, moreover, that Parliament will propose to the provinces that they take over the same responsibility for Indians that they have for other citizens in their provinces. The Gov-ernment will also appoint a Commissioner to consult with the Indians over various matters. And it is noted that Indian lands will require special atten-tion for some time.

[49] See, for example, the various briefs submitted to the *Joint Committee of the Senate and the House of Commons on Indian Affairs, 1960-61* (Ottawa: Queen's Printer, 1961).

These proposals by the Canadian Government do not alter any of my hypotheses or my "predictions" about the future of the Indian people. In the first place, legislation has still to be passed; in the second place the proposals to appoint a Commissioner (of Indian Affairs?) and to establish an Indian Lands Act which would enable the band members to manage their own affairs seem to be moves in the direction of "parallel development" — to use a synonym for apartheid. The Indian "Red Paper", written by Harold Cardinal in collaboration with both Indians and Whites, in response and in opposition to the "White Paper" suggests the perpetuation of the status quo for some time to come.[50]

[50] See Harold Cardinal, *The Unjust Society* (Edmonton: Hurtig, 1970).

7

EDITOR'S INTRODUCTION

In discussing social change and social conflicts, social scientists frequently concentrate on industrial-urban populations. As Carstens has pointed out in the previous article, the indigenous populations of Canada have been largely ignored and considered as virtually irrelevant.

Professor Vallee, in the following article, provides a comprehensive historical and contemporary portrayal of Canada's native populations in the North, including Eskimos, Indians, and Métis. These peoples have experienced and continue to face massive and rapid changes as a consequence of contact with various exploiters, both governmental and private, of Canada's huge area north of the Tree-line.

The contemporary dilemma of Canada's indigenous populations generally can be seen all the more clearly through examination of the historical evolution of some of these groups as portrayed by Vallee. His discussion fills a wide gap in our knowledge about the social dynamics of subordinate populations. Most of the studies of Indians, Eskimos and Métis in Canada have been restricted because they are highly specific and confined to isolated locales. The sum total of these studies has not added up to a coherent and general portrait of major and strategic social changes occurring among these groups.

By discussing some aspects of change that are common to all three major groups of the native population, Vallee presents a general overview which indicates the peculiar problems that are common to them as a consequence of contacts with Whites over the years.

Similar to other indigenous groups throughout Canada, the Eskimos, Indians, and Métis of Canada's North, find themselves within the delicate and transitional stage of extreme marginality between their own customs and traditions, which have been drastically altered through contacts with Whites, and the largely imposed customs and mores of the newly emerging northern white society. Cultural survival is only one of the issues; equally important is economic survival which at least in recent decades, has depended heavily on participation in the white-dominated economy.

The ambiguity of this situation, as Vallee points out, has been partly reflected by the difficulty of the indigenous groups in reconciling their own participation in or dependence on the newly developed northern economic activities with their developing aspirations for economic self-sufficiency and self-determination. Increasing problems of role-ambiguity and alienation, especially among the younger generation, have greatly stimulated the proliferation of native-dominated and controlled individual co-operatives which are beginning to develop coordinated activities between them. While it would be a considerable distortion to compare this particular development with the emergence of cooperatives in agrarian Saskatchewan (as discussed by McCrorie in another chapter), it cannot be denied that the sense of alienation and need for self-determination were common to both movements.

The development of native cooperatives in the North is both reflective of and catalytic to the process of cultural homogenization of which the author speaks; historical differences and cleavages between the various Eskimo, Indian, and Métis groups are decreasing at a time when the cultural and economic penetrations of the Northland, both private and governmental, are increasing. In a sense, solidarity is enhanced because of the various native groups facing "the common enemy". This process has been witnessed in many social and economic contexts where subordinate groups which differ in many respects tend to unite in opposition to a common superordinate group. Taken to its extreme, this process has often resulted in "nativistic" movements, whereby indigenous groups revitalize lost customs and rituals and often engage in militant opposition to "the outsiders". Although the possible early stages of this process can be seen in his discussion, Vallee cautions the reader that it appears unlikely that a pan-Eskimo-Indian-Métis movement will develop fully in the near future.

The contemporary developing conflict in the North is largely the consequence of historical contacts between Eskimos, particularly, and various outside exploiters. In discussing these contacts, Vallee shows that only selected and restricted economic and social changes occurred as a consequence of contact with whalers during the early nineteenth century. These contacts were sporadic and there were no apparent intentions on the part of the whalers to affect significant changes among the Eskimos.

Later contacts, however, had more impact; the fur traders and missionaries, directly or indirectly, drastically altered the geographical distribution and social life of the Eskimos and rendered them vulnerable to periods during which economic subsidy and activities by the outsiders tended to slacken. However, even these changes were minor compared to the massive contemporary onslaughts resulting from the newly evolved policy of integration, a drastic departure from the past policies of pluralism. Integration may have "worked" over the long-run and at an earlier stage, but the social and economic distances between the native populations and the outsiders were never greatly altered; consequently, forced integration inevitably produced conflict.[1]

Another dynamic dimension of the emerging northern mosaic is discussed; the increasing differentiation, competition, and perhaps even conflict between the "New-Northerners" (who have migrated with a view to a permanent stake and settlement) and the mobile civil servants and entrepreneurs. This development not only suggests the rapidly

[1] Similar conflicts have occurred in other societies, such as Indo-China, where forced integration was encouraged between the greatly disparate French colonists and the Indo-Chinese.

increasing importance of Canada's Northland but also raises the intriguing possibility of at least a loose kind of alliance between the native populations and the "New Northerners".

Among other things, the following discussion shows clearly that complexity and dynamic change are not exclusive to urban-industrial communities.

7

The Emerging Northern Mosaic[1]

FRANK G. VALLEE

This article is an overview of the drastic social and cultural changes underway in that vast region beyond the Tree-line in Canada's North, in the jurisdiction of the Northwest Territories Government and that of Arctic Quebec. Our attention is focussed on the native peoples, by which I mean those of Eskimo and Indian origin, as well as those of mixed origin, often called Métis, who identify to some extent with Eskimos and Indians but who are not legally regarded as such.

Because I confine my remarks to the region beyond the Tree-line, most of my references to native people are applicable only to Eskimos, for this is their area of concentration. At the edges of the Tree-line, a few thousand Indians and Métis share regional and community space with the Eskimos. Examples are Aklavik and Inuvik in the Mackenzie Delta and Great Whale River in Arctic Quebec. There are important differences between Eskimos, Indians, and Métis, but it would weigh down the text unduly to keep spelling out the significance of these differences. Furthermore, recent studies show that, at least for the Mackenzie Delta, there is a kind of merging for many purposes into a category of "native", a merging of groups which were formerly distinguished from each other.[2]

Change among the native people is viewed in the contexts of their relationships with non-native people. At the risk of sounding trite, it is worth noting that one cannot understand situations and trends among the native people without taking into account the non-native people who form part of the social environment. Even where there is little direct and meaningful contact between native and non-native people in a community, as is the case in many northern places, it is necessary to look closely at both populations in order to assess what is likely to happen to either. Indeed, it is imperative to look at both populations, native and non-native, as parts of one system of relationships for some purposes, especially where there is little direct and meaningful contact between them. I say this because we

[1] The author's discussion is based on data derived through his extensive field-work among peoples of Canada's Northland.
[2] See e.g. Donald Clairmont, *Deviance Among Indians and Eskimos in Aklavik* (Ottawa: Department of Northern Affairs and National Resources, NCRC-63-9, 1963); Richard Slobodin, *Métis of the Mackenzie District* (Ottawa: Canadian Research Centre for Anthropology, St. Paul's University, 1966), pp. 162ff.

know that the keeping of distance and avoidance of one another do not imply the absence of a relationship. On the contrary, avoidance is a kind of relationship of considerable significance.

Another introductory remark has to do with perspective. In this article, social and cultural change is portrayed in two perspectives. At the local community or regional level, the perspective is that of the "little picture", in contrast to that of the "big picture", perspective in which the changing patterns are viewed in the context of a predominantly industrialized ethnically-plural society, the so-called "Canadian Mosaic".

An ethnically-plural society is one in which ethnic origin is used as an important principle of social organization. In Canada, ethnic origin is and always has been used to sort people out for social purposes. As Porter and others have shown, there is inequality in the distribution of prestige, power, and resources among Canada's ethnic groups.[3] On just about every index of prestige, power, and command over valued resources, the native peoples of Canada are the least advantaged.

Even where they form a numerical majority, the native people occupy a minority status, a rural non-agricultural proletariat. To amplify this point I cite a formulation of Bierstedt which I used in previous publications to put the native people's minority status into perspective:

> As Bierstedt points out, there are three sources of social power for groups: numbers, organization, and access to valued resources [and facilities]. All other things equal, the numerical majority is more powerful than the minority. Where two or more groups are equal in number, the one with the most control over crucial resources is more powerful than the other ... In the context of Canada as a whole the [native people] are a small [feebly organized] minority with very limited access to significant resources. In the context of the local region and community in the Arctic, the [native people] out-number the non-native, but they are comparatively unorganized and, by and large, have access to little more than subsistence resources. There is little which they can withhold which would cause the non-native people much discomfort, except their services and their co-operation in helping the non-natives achieve their goals.[4]

One consequence of the imbalance between natives and non-natives in access to facilities and resources is the emergence of a kind of disestablishment". In this respect, the situation in Canada's North is a special case of a more general, if not universal, feature of modern society. With rapid advances in technology, thousands become unemployable because the skills they have are obsolete. Should they live in economic backwaters

---

[3] John Porter, *The Vertical Mosaic* (Toronto: University of Toronto Press 1965).

[4] Frank G. Vallee, *Kabloona and Eskimo in the Central Keewatin* (Ottawa: Canadian Research Centre for Anthropology, St. Paul's University, 1967) pp. 196ff.; the formulation in question will be found in Robert Bierstedt, "An Analysis of Social Power," *American Sociological Review*, No. 15 (1950), pp. 730-738.

they become alienated from the mainstream of social and economic life. Those who guide the system attempt in different ways to prevent the dis-established from remaining outside, by giving them a "stake" inside. These ways vary from grass-roots community development to large-scale retrain-ing programmes. The native population of Canada's North is not unique in being served with such programmes, but a special feature of that population is that it is differentiated racially from the Establishment minority in its midst. This physical factor accentuates the social and economic distinctions, based on a coincidence of class and ethnicity, between groups enjoying different levels of prestige, power, and material well-being in the society.

A final aspect of the "big picture" perspective to consider in this intro-duction has to do with ideology. A content analysis of public statements by official spokesmen for governmental and other agencies with an interest in native affairs reveals an espousal of two ideals: that of *cultural pluralism,* the recognition of a group's right to cultural distinctiveness; and that of *participation of native people in decisions affecting them.*[5] It is one purpose of this paper to assess the extent to which these perhaps incompatible ideo-logical goals are being translated into social action. Recent research in the Canadian North provides the basis for this assessment.

Because of the peculiar demographic situation with the people of native ancestry in the numerical majority, the Canadian North beyond the Tree-line is a setting in which the ideals of cultural pluralism and participa-tion are being put to the test. The outcome of that test has serious implica-tions for Canada as a whole.

THE ANCIEN REGIME

To study changes in intergroup relations in Canada's far North in any detail would require following the history of specific contact between the various types of outsider — explorer, whaler, trader, missionary, and so on — and the different sub-groups of native peoples in this or that region. Such a task is far beyond our scope which is limited to overviews of group re-lationships, internal and external, with the focus on the contemporary per-iod. However, one cannot make sense of the contemporary period without at least a sketch of the historical dimension.[6]

Archaeologists have demonstrated that change among the native peoples in the Canadian Arctic is not something which began to occur only after contact with outsiders of European or North American origin. Funda-mental changes in ways of getting a living, in material culture and in resi-dence patterns can be traced in some detail for the thousands of years that

---

[5] In connection with a research project the results of which are yet to be pub-lished, the author examined policy statements by cabinet ministers and leading officials in government departments concerned with Indian and Eskimo affairs in Canada. The period covered in the study is 1958-1967. Statements were analyzed in terms of cultural goals and means of achieving these goals.

[6] Much relevant material on the historical background will be found in Diamond Jenness, *Eskimo Administration: II. Canada* (Montreal: Arctic Institute Tech-nical Paper, No. 14, 1964), pp. 186ff.

preceded the opening of the historic period in the eighteenth century.[7] These prehistoric changes are usually interpreted as adaptive ones, adaptation in most cases occurring in response to pressures from, or interaction with, "outside" human groups. During the historic period, however, changes in the Arctic way of life are almost always presented by writers as native adaptations to the socio-economic environment created and shaped by outsiders who moved into the North.

Historical accounts of Arctic groups in Canada are often cast in terms of three major economic stages. The earliest was that of hunting and gathering and extends from the earliest times into the latter part of the nineteenth century. The second stage is that of trapping combined with hunting and gathering. Finally, the most recent stage is that in which these activities are combined with wage labour in service occupations, dependence on statutory grants, and relief.

In the present section, the focus is on the later period of the second stage, when trapping was a vital pursuit and scores of small settlements had appeared in the Arctic. This stage came to a close in most places during the 1950's and brings us to the beginning of the contemporary period, the topic of the next section.

Certain changes in technology and ecology of great significance will not get the attention they deserve, for we wish to concentrate on social relationships. For instance, before they acquired the rifle in the late eighteenth century, the Eskimos hunted caribou with bow and arrow, spears, and other short-range missiles. The technology limited the magnitude of the kill and required that much of the hunting be done collectively. The use of the rifle resulted in a vastly larger kill per hunter and contributed to the decline in caribou herds. The new hunting technique did not require that large groups work collectively and thus had an effect on patterns of interdependence and of residence. Unfortunately we must sacrifice discussion of chain reactions to technological and ecological innovation in order to concentrate on changes more directly connected to social contact between outsider and native.

A striking feature of contact between the native and outside groups in all stages is the asymmetrical shape of the relationships between them, with the outside group in the dominant, patronising position, and the native group in the subordinate position. To some extent this inequality was a direct reflection of the historical *zeitgeist* of imperialism, with its assumption of white, Christian moral superiority. Of course, this ideological view could only be sustained upon a foundation of real superiority in economic and political power in the embracing society.

Because the natives were "there" and the outsiders came in deliberately for purposes which can be specified, a useful starting point for studying native-outsider relations is to examine the manifest purposes of the out-

---

[7] For a recent survey and interpretation, see William E. Taylor, Jr., " An Archaeological Overview of Eskimo Economy", in *Eskimo of the Canadian Arctic,* ed. Victor F. Valentine and Frank G. Vallee (Toronto: McClelland & Stewart, 1968), pp. 3-17.

siders in their northern invasions. This is a one-sided and oversimplified view but a useful one in considering the comparative significance among types of outsiders for the development of northern society. It should be kept in mind that this approach deliberately underplays the manifest goals of the native peoples and how they manipulated situations. However, a corrective to this initial bias will be applied later in the paper in the discussion of the contemporary period.

The range and depth of effect on native peoples of contact with outsiders depended to a large extent on the particular self or group-interests of the outsiders on their goals vis-à-vis the native peoples. The primary goals were those required by the institutions which the outsiders represented: trading company, church, police force, government, mining company, and so on. To see things in this way does not imply that we look only at the "intended" consequences of the actions of the outsiders. Indeed, it is the "unintended" consequences of these actions which are the most telling and which get most attention later in this paper.

Apart from sporadic contact with a few explorers, the most sustained of the earliest contact the native people had in northern Canada was with whalers, in the early nineteenth century. This contact was mostly limited to Eskimos who inhabited coastal regions and did not link them into strong chains of interdependence. Eskimos were not needed so very much as producers, for the crews caught their own whales. The chief influence of the whalers was in the things they introduced, such as firearms, dancing and clothing styles, diseases, and, in some places, liquor. Their influence was most felt in the Western Arctic. Another result of these contacts was the mixed progeny derived from male crew members and Eskimo women. However, in terms of basic economy and social organization, the whaler influence was comparatively slight.

The influence of the fur traders was of broader range and went deeper than that of the whalers. The traders needed the native peoples to solve their problems of economics and logistics. The value of the natives to the traders was in terms of various roles: producers of furs, consumers of trade goods, and for a small but ultimately influential segment, intermediaries, guides, and servants. Some traders also saw themselves as bearers of the Christian message, but the evidence suggests that traders had no consuming interest in changing the basic way of life of the native people. After trapping became the established economic base, it was in the trader's interest to fight whatever policy kept the native people away from trapping and its associated activities. This was the situation until the influx of other sources of income — wages, transfer payments and relief, originating from the south — made the native people valuable as consumers independent of their role as producers. The process of the changing relevance of the native people as consumers went on at the same time as the process of decline in significance of wild fur as a commodity.

If the intentions of the whalers and traders were not to change the way of life in a deliberate fashion, the same cannot be said of the missionaries whose very *raison d'être* was the selective personal and social transformation of the native people. The conversion program was selective in the sense that only those aspects of the way of life which were judged as inimical to Christianity were to be transformed. The remainder of the way of life was to be maintained. In terms of ideology, the traders and missionaries were more conservative than radical, seeking to alter only those ideas and practices which militated against their particular mandate.

The same may be said for the third element in the familiar triumvirate of non-native settlers in the North, the Royal Canadian Mounted Police. The purpose of the police was not only to maintain law and order by checking the few deviant customs which went against the codes they imported with them. More important was the purpose of representing the government of Canada as living symbols of that country's sovereign rights to Arctic regions. The police had no explicit program of planned change for the native peoples.

So far, I have dwelt on the manifest purposes of the outsiders who made up the first non-native settlers in the Canadian Arctic. The intended consequences of their efforts should be reviewed briefly. As for the traders, in most regions the native people did indeed become producers of fur and consumers of imported products, adapting certain of their living habits and attitudes in the process. The native response to the missionary was to become adherents to a denomination and to publicly abandon those practices which were forbidden by Church rules, although many such traditional practices survived in a kind of underground. The missions also introduced literacy in the Eskimo and some Indian languages through the translation of scriptures. Furthermore, a number of natives accepted the very much limited formal education which the churches offered in the absence of government schools. As for the police, whatever minimal demands they made on the way of life were usually accommodated by the native people.

These are "big picture" generalizations which require much amending and refining in any given local situation. For instance, individual outsiders had personal intentions concerning the native people which were not actually required of them by the institutions they represented. Thus, some undertook to socialize, heal, and act in *loco parentis,* even though they were not, strictly speaking, required to do so. The important thing to note is that there was general compliance with the wishes of the outsiders and certainly no organized opposition to them on the part of the native people.

During the first quarter of the twentieth century, there emerged patterns of residence in the Canadian Arctic which would become stabilized and would characterize the human scene in the Arctic for up to fifty years. During that period there developed what during the 1960's became regarded as the *ancien régime.* Dotting the coastal areas and barren lands were scores of tiny settlements, most of them dominated by the trading post. In some of these tiny posts, the trader would be joined in permanent residence by the missionary and policeman.

Reflected in the location of these settlements was the growing significance of the outside world for the native people. Previous to the fur trade period, the location of living sites was determined by whatever animals the people were exploiting at a given time. The most important factor in the placing of the trading posts was access to the outside world, places which ships could visit to deliver their goods and to pick up furs.

Actually, only a small number of native people, those who served the outside agencies were encouraged to settle in these places; the trader's post-servant, the policeman's assistant or special constable, the missionary's catechist. The remainder of the population continued a nomadic life in scattered camps, from which regular but widely-spaced visits would be made to the posts. Some of these land camps would be visited by traders, missionaries, and policemen on their occasional tours between posts.

The trading system introduced an element of structuring into native groupings, such as extended families and camp groups, because the traders preferred to deal with one or a few natives whom they regarded as representatives or leaders of the nomadic people who lived on the land. Some missionaries, policemen, and, later, government administrators reinforced this tendency.

Because the Canadian government had scant interest in the Arctic regions until after the second World War, the matter of native affairs was left to the agencies with personnel resident in the Arctic, namely the churches, the Hudson's Bay Company and the Royal Canadian Mounted Police. Except for the latter who represented the federal government, and many of whose policemen were Canadian citizens, the outsiders among the Eskimos were mostly from Britain, Newfoundland, and French-speaking parts of Western Europe, with a handful from Scandinavia. They can hardly be said to have been strongly oriented to the Canadian polity. Indeed, the bulk of the Arctic population, Eskimos and outsiders, were Canadian in only the technical sense of inhabiting geographical space to which Canada laid claim. Each of the communities and sub-regions of the Arctic was a self-contained little world whose frail and tenuous connections with the centres of the Canadian polity only highlighted its isolation and autonomy.

In this situation, the outsiders interacted directly and personally with the natives in their midst. From this interaction there developed sets of relationships between the settlers from outside and selected natives and their families. The latter became intermediaries, the forerunners of a kind of elite of native settlement dwellers about whom more will be said later. During the *ancien régime,* these intermediaries broke from their camp and band networks to move from post to post, in some cases ending up in regions distant from their original homelands. This mobility was, in a sense, sponsored by the agencies with which the intermediaries were affiliated, thus enhancing the dependence of the intermediaries on their agencies or, more specifically, on the local representatives of the agencies. They were more oriented to the agencies they served than to the communities in which they happened to reside at a given time. They were the first native cosmopolitans in the Canadian Arctic.

This category of persons we loosely call intermediaries was by no means homogeneous. Some traced their descent exclusively to native ancestors. Our impression is that most were of mixed origin. The latter may be further differentiated into families whose biological progenitor had not married and settled in the Arctic and those whose biological progenitor had done so. In the latter connection, we refer to a handful of non-native trappers and private traders who married native women and founded lines of descent which were the first in the Arctic to use surnames. Only a few of these surnamed families inhabit the Eastern Arctic, most of them having settled in the Mackenzie Delta region of the Western Arctic. These were the most acculturated of the intermediaries between native and non-native.

During the period under review, this category of persons we call intermediaries never formed a solidary grouping. Because they were neither completely native nor completely non-native, we may regard them as marginal persons or families, but they did not form a marginal group covering the Arctic or substantial regions within the Arctic. It is only with the growth of sizeable settlements that incipient marginal groups emerged. But this takes us to the contemporary period, the topic of the next section.

To summarize this section, the typical communities of Arctic Canada until the early 1950's were isolated and tiny, with only a few natives sharing living space with the outsiders over most of the year. Each place was dominated by one or two male persons representing outside agencies. Usually these outsiders were linked to the native people through intermediaries who were themselves identified as permanent Arctic dwellers, although many were of mixed origin. Settlement organization was simple. The small population and lack of a complex division of labour required little in the way of coordination and structure.

THE CONTEMPORARY SCENE

The contemporary scene stands in dramatic contrast to the one just portrayed. The decade from about 1955 to 1965 witnessed revolution in way of life which saw the previously peripheral folk drawn into the massive embrace of modern society. The reasons for the rather sudden surge in significance of its Arctic for the Canadian people need not be detailed here as there is ample documentation available.[8] Suffice it to say that for military, political, and economic resource reasons, the Canadian Arctic and its people have become the focus of concern and attention in the Canadian polity.

Government involvement in human affairs, previously minimal and indirect, suddenly bore directly on just about every person in the Arctic, its facilities and services touching on every aspect of life. It was on the Central and Eastern Arctic Eskimo people that the sudden intrusion of the outside world made the strongest impact. For the people of the Mackenzie Delta region — Eskimos, Indians and Métis — the intrusion had begun earlier and was more gradual.

The provision of educational, health, welfare, and other services entailed the spread throughout the Arctic of new types of community of which the most common is the administrative or service centre type. Many of the small posts described earlier have been abandoned; a number of others have been adapted by the addition of schools and nursing stations

[8] See e.g. Jenness, *Eskimo Administration*.

to the requirements of the new service-based system. Several new settlements have been established, some of them planned by experts.[9] There has been a spectacular drain of people from land camps and abandoned trading posts into these centres. In former days, a settlement with 150 permanent inhabitants would have been regarded as "urban". In the mid-1960's, most people beyond the Tree-line lived in settlements of from 200 to 500 population. There are four communities with between 500 and 1,000 and two, Inuvik in the West and Frobisher in the East, with more than 1,500 each.

While the population of about 12,000 beyond the Tree-line seems minute, it is large considering the traditional economic resource base and it is growing at an even rate higher for the country as a whole. Population growth among the native people is a direct result of the massive health programme which began in the early 1950's, cutting sharply into the previously very high death rate. Income required to sustain the growing population with its constantly rising level of needs is derived from a multiplicity of sources of which wild life harvesting constitutes a dwindling portion. Only a small minority of native settlement dwellers depend on traditional wildlife harvesting for the most of their livelihood; another small minority is employed full-time for wages. In between are the majority who engage in very mixed pursuits, none of which can be regarded as a full-time occupational role. Income from those pursuits has to be supplemented by statutory grants and welfare in order to reach the minimal level required to keep a household going. The total average income for native peoples is far below the national average. This is in contrast to the non-natives in Arctic communities, the majority of whom are employed by some level of government and enjoy a standard of living higher than the average for the country as a whole.

As we have seen, during the *ancien régime,* there was no deliberate plan to alter the total way of life of native people, although missionaries and others sought to bring about changes in those ways of behaving which made their mandate difficult to accomplish. In contrast, much of the change underway since the 1950's has been aimed at a global transformation of native culture and society. Statements of government spokesmen about respecting native cultures notwithstanding, the evidence shows that *cultural replacement* is the goal of the most important programmes which have been introduced by government.[10]

The health programme, for instance, aims at changing customary practices and attitudes towards foodways, bodily care, housing, mental illness

[9] For a discussion of various types of Arctic settlement, see Jacob Fried, "Settlement Types and Community Organization in Northern Canada", *Arctic,* June 1963, pp. 93-100. A detailed account of Eskimo adjustment to living in a large settlement will be found in John and Irma Honigmann, *Eskimo Townsmen* (Ottawa: Canadian Research Centre for Anthropology, St. Paul's University, 1965), esp. pp. 157-227.

[10] Charles S. Brant and Charles W. Hobart, "Eskimo Education, Danish and Canadian: A Comparison", *The Canadian Review of Sociology and Anthropology,* No. 2 (May, 1966), pp. 47-66; Jenness, *Eskimo Administration,* esp. p. 123ff.

and sanitation. The sweeping educational programme has hardly any relevance to traditional culture and quite deliberately excludes adult generations in order to transform the youngsters. The attempt to short-circuit the socialization process by concentrating on the younger generation is quite explicit. Where programmes of preparation for local government have been implemented, these follow parliamentary and electoral models which have no precedent in traditional culture. The only programmes which pointedly seek some continuity with the past are those aimed at local economic development, almost always in the form of cooperatives, about which comments will be made later.

Some material objects with a primarily symbolic or expressive function — such as carvings, prints, handicrafts — continue to serve as symbols of native culture and identity, but most of the material culture of the people has been consigned to museums. Non-material expressive features of native culture, such as lore, dance, song, ritual, have been widely abandoned. Revival of traditional performances, such as drum-dances, appears to be primarily for tourist gratification. Certain practices and beliefs associated with the past, such as shamanism,[11] continue in a kind of subterranean existence, carefully shielded from outsiders. Briefly, it can be said that those manifest features of a culture which serve as reference points for identification as a distinctive group are dwindling rapidly. Apart from physical characteristics, standard of living, and style of living, it is only language which continues to mark off unmistakably those who are native from those who are not. No programme recognizes the native languages as an important component.[12]

So far, I have mentioned those visible and audible aspects of culture which lend themselves to *performance,* those aspects which serve as reference points for *identification.* However, significant aspects of culture in the anthropological sense are not of this order. I have in mind those aspects which have their locus in the internalized value system and in ways of comprehending reality — sometimes referred to as cognitive mapping. It is generally agreed that these aspects are most resistant to change. As for native cultures in the Arctic, some claim that these internalized patterns show strong persistence despite the obvious changes in life styles and despite the pressures to abandon traditional attitudes and values.

To summarize, the trend among native peoples, particularly in the burgeoning settlements, is toward cultural uniformity. Traditional differences between various Eskimo groups and among Eskimos, Indians and Métis become blurred. Reasons for this blurring among previously different groups are the sharing of a similar social and economic position vis-à-vis the outsiders and exposure to the non-native way of life in schools and in the spreading mass media. Lip service is paid to highly selected

---

[11] The Shaman (Eskimo: *angakoq*) is a person who has special powers of communication with the supernatural and who used these powers to discover the reasons for various misfortunes and to restore conditions of good fortune.

[12] An exception should be noted. The Province of Quebec in 1960 announced its intention to use Eskimo as the language of instruction for at least the first few grades when the provincial responsibility for Eskimo schooling would be taken over from the federal government.

aspects of traditional cultures, such as forms of artistic expression, but the evidence is that traditional value orientations and ways of viewing reality are discouraged by the non-native ideological elite.

If large numbers of native people are adopting the cultural styles of the mass society, this does not mean that they are being assimilated socially. All observers consulted agree that in the new Arctic, social distance between native and non-native is still quite pronounced. Before discussing the reasons for this, let us look at the social structure of contemporary Arctic communities as compared with those of the *ancien régime*. Needless to say there are variations among communities, but we ignore these in the interest of describing typical situations in those places with a few hundred or more inhabitants.

One characteristic of many modern Arctic communities is the heterogeneity of the native element. In the traditional settlement the natives were mostly from the one cultural group, sharing customs, language or dialect of a language and band or tribal membership. Now we find differentiation within the native group on several dimensions: sub-culture of origin, religious denomination, occupation, orientation to urban settlement living or to hinterland camp living, and the like.[13]

In some places the abrupt change in way of life has given rise to divisions between generations. Despite the complexities internal to the native group, in the overall structure of communities they tend to form a sub-system clearly distinguishable from the non-native. Networks of sociability and areas of residence tend to divide along the native and non-native line.

This does not mean that the natives in a community present a united front of solidarity and togetherness. There are exceptions to be noted later, but the general rule is that the native element in an Arctic community is weak in capacity to act in concert and to effectively influence local or regional affairs. In modern society, such influence is usually wielded through voluntary and governmental organization for which there were no native precedents. Living in small, egalitarian, nomadic groups, the Eskimos and Indians of the North had no need of formal organization. The process of formal debate, of voting, of majority rule, which many outsiders take for granted, was unknown until it was imposed from outside. The native style was that of concensus in decision-making. It might take a long time to achieve that consensus on particular issues, but that time would be so invested and what we would regard as highly developed human relations skills brought into play to achieve consensus. In modern settlements, the imported practice of formal debate and resolution by voting leaves many natives unenthusiastic. Their silence is sometimes mistaken for assent by the outsiders.

Another reason for the relative passivity of native people is that much community decision-making has been vested in local representatives of remotely located government centres. Besides these representatives there

---

[13] Frank G. Vallee, "Differentiation Among the Eskimo in Some Canadian Arctic Settlements", in *Eskimo of the Canadian Arctic,* eds. Victor F. Valentine and Frank G. Vallee (Toronto: McClelland & Stewart, 1968), pp. 109-126.

have always been other outsiders eager to take an active hand in community affairs. As we shall see in a moment, the number of these outsiders is growing substantially.

There is some meaningful participation of native people in large places like Frobisher and Inuvik and in those few places where community development programmes thrive, although even in these communities the natives are much overshadowed by the non-natives in local and regional affairs. Those identified as native who have a voice in the affairs of larger communities are mostly what we have called intermediaries, people with long experience of settlement living and of contact with outsiders.

It is from the younger generation in this category, confronted with problems arising from status ambiguity and incongruence, that we hear more and more protest about the condition of native people. They do not confine their concern to the local setting, but generalize to include Eskimos, Indians, and Métis everywhere in the North. Such protest is sporadic and infrequent and cannot be regarded as representing a movement, although the protest could become channelled and linked with movements originating outside the Arctic.

Native people are beginning to gain access to group resources such as associations concerned with human relations — the Indian-Eskimo Association is an example — and mass media which foster the exchange of information and ideas across community boundaries. Native exploitation of such group's resources, hitherto the exclusive preserve of non-natives, is so recent and experimental that one hesitates to comment on implications for group relations in the Arctic.

I have observed elsewhere that one organizational vehicle which could carry a movement concerned chiefly with native interests and sentiments of solidarity is the cooperative.[14] In a few communities where cooperatives are multi-functional, they have become the key integrative bodies in community organization and are not unlike local governments. Although cooperatives are legally non-ethnic, in the Arctic their composition is about 95 per cent Eskimo, Indian, and Métis. This ethnic component looms large in the cooperative group identity. The emergence among cooperatives of links which transcend community boundaries has been documented in recent studies in which it has been shown that bonds of ethnic solidarity, especially among the Eskimos, are being forged through the cooperative movement.

The significance of this movement, as well as that of the sporadic protest mentioned earlier, should not be magnified to the extent that we anticipate an early confrontation between native and non-native. The trends in native organization and collective feeling which are noted here are new and exceptional. In most communities and in the Arctic as a whole, there

---

[14] Frank G. Valee, "Notes on the Cooperative Movement and Community Organization in the Canadian Arctic", *Arctic Anthropology*, No. 2 (1964), pp. 45-49. See also by the same author, *Povungnetuk and Its Cooperative: A Case Study in Community Change* (Ottawa: Department of Northern Affairs and National Resources, NCRC-67-2, 1967), p. 57.

is not even passive resistance to the dominance of non-natives. There is hardly any public formulation of problems in terms of the different interests of native and non-native.

Ethnic group consciousness, like class consciousness, is not an automatic correlate of the "objective" existence of given ethnic groups. Fostering such consciousness for a given group is the presence of a conspicuous outgroup. A crucial feature of the contemporary Arctic community scene compared with that of the past is the much larger number and variety of non-native residents who share community space with Eskimos, Indians, and Métis. As long as native people lived in residential contact with only a few outsiders, their ethnic and racial distinctiveness was of little or no significance to them. But that distinctiveness grows in salience and is thrust into one's awareness where there are large numbers and a variety of resident outsiders and where the outsiders are mostly defined as responsible for the affairs of the native residents, a definition which highlights the distinction between native and non-native.

The majority of non-native residents who have moved into the Arctic since the early 1950's have been government employees. Administrators, nurses, teachers, technicians and others, as well as the families of some of these, dominate the new communities in the Arctic. To these government-sponsored residents are being added private entrepreneurs, small businessmen, insurance agents, merchants, and the like. The latter are not so numerous in the Eastern Arctic communities but are coming to form a sizeable segment of a few Western Arctic communities. It is common for this element to refer to themselves by some term which denotes a commitment to the North, the most common one being "New Northerner".

Community studies have shown that the non-native element is not a homogeneous bloc. It is differentiated in terms of government department, class, occupation, commitment to the North, and so on. The most significant emerging differentiation is between people, most of whom spend only a few years in the Arctic in the service of government and big industry, and those who have made a personal commitment to long-term or permanent residence in the Arctic. Most of these are not supported by corporate agencies, governmental or otherwise. These are the New Northerners mentioned above. This is not to say that commitment to the North by outsiders is an entirely new phenomenon. Scores of traders, trappers, and missionaries made this commitment in the past, some marrying native women and raising families. What distinguishes the Old from the New Northerners is that the latter have at hand a government apparatus to manipulate.

Without going into detail about politico-administrative trends in the Arctic, let us just note that, after a period during which Arctic affairs were almost exclusively in federal government hands, there is a move towards greater autonomy and control over these affairs on the part of provincial and territorial governments. It is likely that many of the decision-making vacuums left behind by the federal government will be filled at local and regional levels by New Northerners, many of whom have agitated for removal of federal government control and the location of politico-administrative power centres in the North.

The New Northerners have been particularly critical of the special treatment received by those in the employ of government; the privileges which include special financial allowances, the superior housing at low rents, and the more or less exclusive use of such services as sewers and electrical power. On issues like these, the New Northerners at times ally with the native people or at least try to see issues through the eyes of the latter. On the other hand, there is the possibility that many of the New Northerners, because of their head start as controllers of local government and local economies, will discourage native participation, inadvertently perpetuating a kind of settler-native imbalance common in colonial situations.

In the power equation outlined on page 150, we noted that the only advantage enjoyed by the native people in the Arctic has been numerical dominance. With the prospective development of mineral resources and the resulting influx of outsiders, even this advantage would lose the potential significance it has. If the native cultures continue to be downgraded and their participation in community decision-making lingers at the current level, the Arctic society will remain a vertical mosaic, a totem pole with the native peoples at the bottom. According to the perspective used in this paper, the direction of change in the Arctic, whether toward the ideological goals presented on page 151 or toward the "totem pole" mosaic, will be determined not only by what the native people do as native people, but what they do in interaction with other elements in the population, in particular with those who settle there permanently.

The
Mass
Media:

Distortions and Reflections

8-9

EDITOR'S INTRODUCTION

In the following two articles, social changes occurring in the mass media in North America are discussed by James M. Minifie and Frederick Elkin. Minifie is broadly concerned with the uses and abuses of power in the control of the mass media in North America, especially in the United States but in relation to recent developments in Canada. Elkin deals with changes occurring in the style and content of the mass media in Quebec during the dramatic emergence and continuation of the Quiet Revolution.

Both approaches are important in the analysis of the relationships between the mass media and the "audience". An analysis of the power behind the mass media, largely the concern of Minifie, is crucial to an understanding of the influence of the mass media in bringing about changes in attitudes, opinions, and, even perhaps, deeply held values within a given population. Emphasizing a somewhat different aspect, Elkin shows quite clearly the extent to which major social changes are reflected directly in the style and content of the mass media, thus suggesting the vital link between the two, a link which has remained obscure in most other studies of mass media by social scientists.

There are a myriad of concepts and interpretations of the control over and consequences of the mass media of communications. To go into each of these perspectives in detail would take up an entire volume. In essence, all of the perspectives, whether they have emerged among the lay public at large or among professional analysts, may be boiled down to two major and often conflicting categories of thought. One category, which I will refer to as the *European model*, emphasizes the actual or potential manipulative power of the mass media in bringing about massive and significant changes in the thinking of the audience; the other category, which I will refer to as the *North American model*, emphasizes the reflective aspect of the mass media whereby the mass media are perceived as merely reflecting or, at most, reinforcing the predispositions of a given community or nation.

Proponents of the first model have attempted to emphasize the important role that propaganda has played in swaying a population toward or away from particular political activities or parties or movements. Advocates of the North American model, on the other hand, have tended to stress the extent to which the content of the mass media is actually a mere reflection of the actual behavior or aspirations of a given population.

There can be little doubt that the survey research approach which has become so dominant in the social sciences, especially sociology, has been applied extensively to the analysis of the content and influence of the mass media by researchers who generally tend to begin from the perspective of the American model, and they generally claim (as to be expected) that the mass media are no more than reflectors or rein- forcers. It is far more difficult to test the validity, in a systematic sense, of the European model. How does one measure the relationship be- tween mass media content, especially in propaganda, and the extent to which political attitudes and behavior change because of that content? Even so dramatic a work as Vance Packard's *The Hidden Persuaders*[1] concentrates more on the techniques rather than the specific influences of gimmicks used to sway the tastes of the public. But the difficulty in applying systematic and "objective" research techniques to the evalua- tion of the European model does not by any means deny its potential or actual validity. When all is said and done, it cannot be denied that many research perspectives of methodology applied to human behavior are tinged to an extent by the time, place, and ideological restrictions placed upon the observer. Thus, Wertham's *Seduction of the Innocent*[2] abounds in dramatic cases of the effects of the mass media in produc- ing violence among the audience; but, upon scrutiny, the rare excep- tions rather than the general rule are revealed. This is, of course, an extreme example of the application of what I referred to as a European model interpretation of the mass media. On the other hand, a relatively recent collection of articles on the mass media edited by one of the proponents of the North American model contained a section which suggested that governmental intervention in the mass media would be disastrous. This conclusion becomes rather suspect and ludicrous when it is discovered that the sponsors of the book were a group of private broadcasters.

It is fruitless to speculate about the specific question relating to which of the approaches contains the greater validity. It is far more useful to examine each of the approaches and to discuss the kinds of social situations which might be relevant to them. According to much of the research dealing with the mass media, there is little doubt that a direct relationship between the broadcaster and members of the audience is virtually non-existent. There are all kinds of variables that intervene between them and modify, distort, or completely negate the message as it was intended by the broadcaster to be understood by the receiver. One of these variables is *selective perception.* Selective per- ception is a generic term which subsumes a myriad of factors, ranging from the tendency among advocates of a political party to follow only the party's message as conveyed by the mass media and to negate or ignore the messages conveyed by the party in competition, to the well known but frequently obscure tendency among members of different social class, ethnic, age, and religious groupings to absorb and retain only those messages that are favourable to their own sense of propriety and self-images. While these tendencies have been well documented, and tend to lend credence to the reflective consequences of the mass media, they must be seen in terms of time and place and the quality of

[1] Vance Packard, *The Hidden Persuaders* (New York: D. McKay Co., 1957).
[2] Benjamin Wertham, *Seduction of the Innocent* (New York: Rinehart, 1954).

group and inter-group relations. So long as groups distinguish themselves through peculiar qualities from other groups, the phenomenon of selective perception will inevitably occur. However, should those distinctions break down or become obscured, as so many observers of "mass society" have suggested, it seems reasonable to assume that there would be potential for the mass media to manipulate individuals, shorn of group identification, into positions that are compatible with and conform to the propagandists' intentions.

Research into the effects of the mass media has proliferated especially in North America during the last several decades. As in so many other respects, Canada has tended to lag behind the United States where elaborate studies were initiated as early as the late 1930's (at that time, dealing with the influence of movie films on the audience). In Canada, the audience relations research branch of the Canadian Broadcasting Corporation has accelerated the pace of mass media research in Canada within the last decade, but there has been relatively little coordination of these efforts and a generalized social science profile of the mass media is yet to emerge.

While all aspects of the mass media in Canada cannot be explored in this volume, the major dimensions dealing with both methodology and topics are covered by both Minifie and Elkin. The major changes, on a comparative basis, are clearly indicated and many here-to-fore obscured aspects of the mass media in Canada and the United States are revealed.

Mr. Minifie outlines and details the facts of concentration of power in the control of a mass media, especially in the United States. This aspect in the study of the mass media is often ignored by social scientists who do recognize the development of elaborate bureaucracies supporting the various mass media, but too often fail to examine the powerful individuals or groups that are represented by these bureaucracies.

Mr. Minifie also suggests the increase of the "credibility gap" in both the United States and Canada with a special emphasis on this communications barrier occurring in the United States. It should be noted, however, that whatever credibility gap is established with respect to the events in the United States, it is mirrored to a large extent in Canada because of the great dependence of Canada on the mass media of the United States. The relationship between "private" broadcasting and the influence that successful private broadcasters have within government is discussed at some length by Mr. Minifie. The danger of increasing monopoly over reporting of political and racial events and the danger of misleading the public either through errors of omission or commission are also stressed.

Mr. Minifie's suggestions that the role of "herald" be established to serve as an intermediary between broadcasters and the audience is an intriguing idea in view of the immense complexity involved in broadcasting views and events which, if broadcast prematurely, might distort the entire context of the situation.

Professor Elkin discusses the distinctive aspects of the mass media in Canada, generally, through comparison to the mass media in the United States, emphasizing the extent to which the U.S. influence is indeed pervasive. The geographical and political background of Canada is summarized and demonstrates more clearly the distinctive factors at work in bringing about the peculiar features of the past and emerging trends in the mass media of Canada.

In discussing the Quiet Revolution in Quebec and the changes occurring in the mass media during this period, Professor Elkin clearly demonstrates the relationship between the mass media and social change. As the idea of separatism developed in Quebec, so did separatism in the content of the mass media in that province.

Professor Elkin's discussion also demonstrates very clearly the effects of selective perception, especially in the extent to which the same events are reported differently by the French- and English-speaking media. His article should serve as a considerable enlightenment to those who advocate the notion that "the news is the news", and caution those who rely almost exclusively on the social and political proclivities of their respective provinces and communities.

Professor Elkin's portrayal of the changes in advertising content before, during, and after the Quiet Revolution is but an indication of the great extent to which social events are mirrored in the mass media. This is not to say, however, that the mass media content followed social events, for it is clear in Elkin's discussion that each tends to reinforce the other.

It is my opinion that the existence of social and ethnic pluralism in Canada tends to strengthen the effects of selective perception more than in the United States. The encouragement of the "mosaic", each group with its vested interests and peculiar traditions, presents a significant and perhaps formidable problem of a national dialogue. On the other hand, these differences may have the advantage of more clearly identifying the significant and pervasive issues which individuals and groups must face, instead of obscuring these differences through a standard message. The recent proliferation of various ethnic modes of communication, particularly the press, seems to be a distinctively Canadian phenomenon, and may indeed signify the principle that Canada is integrated through conflict and not through conformity to some national and majestic norm. It is thus paradoxical that the Canadian Broadcasting Corporation was developed to promote national unity and may now have to achieve this through accommodation to regional and provincial preferences.

8

Mass Media and Their Control

JAMES MacDONALD MINIFIE

PRIVATE AND PUBLIC CONTROL: SOME ISSUES

Early in the 1920's, Herbert Hoover, then U.S. Secretary of Commerce declared that it was unthinkable that broadcasting, this marvellous new medium of communication and instruction, should be delivered into the hands of advertisers, to be used for the monetary advancement of certain individuals rather than to inform or divert the public, to whom the air waves theoretically belonged.

As often happens, failure to think about "the unthinkable" insured its advent. Despite Mr. Hoover's warning, private ownership of broadcasting was acceptable to the American public for several reasons:

(1) Traditional antipathy to "government interference" in business works for private broadcasters;

(2) Assurances that the private networks would be policed by the Federal Control Commission were taken at face value;

(3) Constitutional guarantees of freedom of press were extended to prohibit governmental regulation of any other mass medium;

(4) Vague charges of communist infiltration of government made it politically difficult to establish control of such a powerful propaganda instrument.

In Canada, other factors were at work to produce a very different result to that which obtained in the United States. A Crown corporation was charged with providing the Canadian people, particularly those in remote areas, with quality programs of Canadian content, designed to foster national unity and consciousness. There were several supporting factors, the most important of which were:

(1) Canadian experience of governmental operation in the private sector was generally good; e.g. the Canadian National Railways, Polymer, Trans-Canada Air Lines (Air Canada), the Canadian Wheat Board, and others.

(2) Experience with newspapers and magazines indicated that private owners of broadcasting stations would find the profit motive stronger than patriotism and consequently would prefer inexpensive American shows over more costly Canadian productions.

(3) Vast thinly-populated territories made coverage of outlying areas in Canada economically unattractive to private enterprise.

(4) Special Canadian problems of finding unity through two languages and cultures demanded special direction and control removed from the immediate profit motive.

These influences were not present in the United States, where, historically, all factors made for private operation of the mass media.

It has, therefore, been all the more surprising and exciting to find a recent American tide flowing the other way. In 1967, former President Lyndon B. Johnson sent to Congress a bill to establish a public broadcasting body. It was originally drawn as a measure to establish a public television corporation. Radio was ignored at first but later added to cover all broadcasting. Support came from two powerful foundations, and from congressmen sensitive to their constituents' outrage at the fare offered by the commercial networks. Members of the Congressional Committee to which the bill was referred also complained of the violence, commercials and rubbish put out by the private stations. Their sense of outrage to some extent offset their distrust of what they feared might become a "government propaganda agency".

The Ford Foundation had a proposal to put aloft synchronous satellites to serve as communications distribution centers which would route programs directly from the production center to local broadcasting stations, thereby avoiding the enormous land-line tolls which networks currently have to pay. The Ford plan would have distributed this saving — estimated at $100,000,000 annually — half to the broadcasting stations and half to a public broadcasting corporation as its major source of revenue, to be supplemented, however, by Foundation monies. They were talking in terms, for the first four years, of an investment of some $150,000,000. This was probably an underestimate.

The Carnegie Institute had another proposal for financing by means of an excise tax on the sale of sets supplemented by monies from the general tax fund plus private Foundation money. Carnegie did not contemplate the immediate use of satellites and would have used local educational TV and other network products as the building blocks for their program. Ford would have centralized production and would have fed it to the periphery. Reaction of the private networks to these proposals varied. The American Broadcasting Company (ABC) opposed the Ford project; it hoped to merge with International Telephone and Telegraph and did not want to see I.T.T.'s revenues slashed by the direct communications satellite.

There was surprising support from both the National Broadcasting Company (NBC) and the Columbia Broadcasting System (CBS). Dr Gillian, president of Massachusetts Institute of Technology, supported the idea of a public broadcasting corporation; so did Hoving, the director of the Metropolitan Museum of Art. McGeorge Bundy, closely connected with the Ford Foundation, supported the project; so did Fred Friendly whose independent presentation of news had brought him acclaim.

This broad support was in part a significant result of the resentment that commercialized broadcasting had created over the preceding genera tion or two. This also came out in derogatory comments from members of the committee. Congressmen learned that some of the best shows produced by the British Broadcasting Corporation (BBC) and the Canadian Broadcasting Corporation (CBC) were available but rarely used by the American commercial nets. For instance CBC's remarkable production, "Eight Hundred Million Chinese," was offered to NBC. But the American network insisted on rewriting the script with the object of pointing out how terrible conditions were in the mainland of China, thus making the show more acceptable to a public nourished on the official line that no good could come from dealings with "the atheistic red Chinese", to use a term favoured by John Foster Dulles. The film ultimately went to the more limited audience of the educational network; but it was also viewed by Senator Fulbright and members of his Foreign Relations Committee. Sen. Fulbright expressed regret that the film was not available to a wider audience.

A curious argument in favour of publicly owned broadcasting was put before the committee. In effect the head of one major network said: "We get hell from these goddamned commercial people. We have to take them because we have to keep up the level of profits or otherwise our shareholders raise hell with us. But if we had a really good competitive system, then we'd be able to put it to the shareholders that we've done it in order to meet this running competition."

Effective competition is theoretically the essence of private enterprise. But the situation has been reached in the American communications media, where the traditional ideal of competitive private enterprise can only be realized if a public corporation can and will supply appropriate competition. This duplicates conditions in the utilities, where the yard-stick for power costs has been supplied by state-owned hydro-electric systems, of which Ontario Hydro and the Tennessee Valley Authority are notable examples. The problem with publicly owned industry is to keep research and development ahead of revolutionary advances in technology. This means taking risks which public servants are reluctant to assume.

The problem before a broadcasting corporation, whether publicly or privately owned, is also to insure revolutionary quality which adequately reflects a revolutionary age such as this, despite pressure from the Establishment to conform. The problem of maintaining non-Establishment revolutionary drive is formidable. But it is reasonable to assume that if a public broadcasting corporation can maintain itself for a decade, or, hopefully, for a generation before being absorbed by the Establishment amoeba, then it will have trained two or three generations of viewers whose level of culture, information, and intellectual vigor will have been substantially raised.

I suggest that a public broadcasting corporation which is really fulfilling its educational mission in the United States would be enormously attractive to the Canadian public, and would be a much greater threat to Canadian identity than the flow of American money into Canadian oilfields or industries. Ideas are far more potent than money or bullets; the day this truth sinks home in the United States will be the day for Canada to sit up and take notice. It is in the nature of Americans, when they have painted themselves into a corner, to make a great leap forward, across the area of paint to the door and out into the open. Educationally, they did this with the land-grant colleges more than one hundred years ago. They may soon make a comparable break-through in the area of public education (in the widest sense) through broadcasting. The potential of a dissent-minded public broadcasting system in the United States is electrifying. Its effect on the Canadian scene would be either the irremediable subordination of Canadian to American culture, with the side-effect of the elimination of Quebec as a significant factor in the new amalgam, or a competitive stimulus which would support the Canadian Broadcasting Corporation in doing the job intended by its founding fathers.

In cleaving to this hope, one should not ignore the difficulty of maintaining a dissent-minded broadcasting system in the United States.

THE MASS MEDIA AND SOCIAL DISSENT

The great American free press has failed sadly to meet the challenge of reporting dissent. I remember how difficult it was, even on so great and liberal a paper as *The New York Herald Tribune,* to get into print stories which dissented from the then-accepted military view that fantastically expensive early warning systems would enable the population of great cities to be evacuated into safety from bomber-borne nuclear attack. The military arranged a splendid exercise in which at the sound of the sirens former President Eisenhower and his Cabinet were whisked away from the White House bomb shelter (which for security reasons could not be mentioned, although every passer-by could see the surface indications of the huge excavation) and transported to some equally secret and obvious destination in Maryland from which the ashes of Washington could be governed. I checked with the weather bureau and found that wind conditions at optimum explosion height would have drenched the super-secret refuge area with lethally radio-active fall-out just at the moment when the President and his cabinet were arriving; thirty seconds exposure — the time to dash from their car to the shelter — would have been fatal. The story was not printed.

To this day the fact has never been printed, as far as I know, that all the major highways leading out of Washington have notices warning that in the event of bombing attack those roads would be closed. The apparent governmental attitude toward a possible exposé of such a blatant contradiction appeared to be: This will not do; dissent is dangerous; we must keep up our illusory guard, and not let either the enemy or our own people know the facts.

I was just as unsuccessful at reporting the arrangements made at U.S.A.F. bases in Newfoundland for compensating civilians for a variety of indignities at the hands of U.S. soldiery. Dissent could not be tolerated from the concept of the benevolent, rich uncle, dutifully defending his poor but greatful allies against any and all comers. There was no room either for suggestion that Denmark was less than enthusiastic about NATO and would willingly have exchanged membership in this rag-bag alliance for return of her authority over her lawful territory of Greenland.

Dr. Blumberg's study of the reporting of dissent in the American press points out that dissent from the war policies of the U.S. Government came to be regarded as a threat to the existing order because it moved out of Congress and into the streets, where it became linked with yet another threat to the political power structure — the drive of the Black American for his fair share of political and economic rights.

Elmer Davis, who was so acutely aware of dissent that he left his broadcasting station immediately after his newscasts — before the abusive phone calls began to pour in — remained hopeful that a public broadcasting corporation could reflect dissent. But he feared that a revolutionary drive which had collapsed before the impact of the Establishment would be absorbed into a reformed Establishment which would then become more dogmatic than its predecessor. He recognized that the problem of maintaining a non-Establishment revolutionary drive would be formidable. The answer does not lie with imposed rules. J.K. Galbraith has pointed out that after ten or fifteen years a regulatory board tends to identify with those it regulates and to become "either an arm of the industry or senile". In short, it joins the Establishment.

The effort to impose controls on broadcasting in the United States illustrates some of the hazards. The Federal Control Commission holds hearings to allocate broadcasting channels, which are extremely valuable properties. It hears promises of good behaviour from a number of applicants; there is little to choose between them and the commissioners are under no illusions about the validity of these pledges. But they are political appointees and they award the channel — not wholly on a basis of political pressure which might be exerted by interested congressmen, but certainly not without some glances in that direction. Stations in which members of Congress have some holding have an advantage. It has consequently become sound practice to capture a Congressman before submitting an application to F.C.C. for a channel. Nobody was surprised when important franchises for radio and television stations in Texas went to the Johnson family, although at the time Mr. Johnson was only a Texas Congressman with a future. Neither was anyone surprised when a show which ridiculed Johnson was taken off the air.

Efforts have been made from time to time to flush station-owning Congressmen into the open, but no firm figures are available as to just how many Congressmen or Senators owns bits of their local broadcasting stations. There are enough, however, to make F.C.C. control a myth to which many give lip-service but few give belief. There is no effective check by F.C.C. on commercialism in broadcasting. Public outrage has not been very effective either, partly because, on the whole, the public has come to accept with a shrug a plethora of objectionable commercials as the price of "free" broadcasting. There is also some public recognition that in the matter of reporting dissent the broadcasters have done better than the press. Television editors have boldly challenged the Establishment; their reporters have not flinched at the risk to life and limb which close reporting of war or civil violence demands and their editors faced inrepidly the risks to sponsors, jobs, and future attendant on frank presentation of data inconsistent with received views and the political status quo.

These achievements invalidate much of the criticism of private broadcasting in the United States and make even more surprising the congressional support which appeared for public broadcasting.

Where broadcasters failed, as in coverage of preparations for the disastrous Bay of Pigs descent on Cuba, the press was equally remiss. Even the stately *New York Times* suppressed stories from its correspondents, which clearly indicated that trouble was brewing. Former President Kennedy is said to have held in retrospect that this cautious regard for security was no asset for security, since some hint beforehand of what was afoot might have prevented a disastrous error which had repercussions in all policy theatres, including Vietnam. An instinctive feeling for national security prevented reporters or their editors both in press and broadcasting, from revealing the massive military concentrations which marked the final phase of the Cuban missile crisis. A *Newsweek* reporter who had assembled accurate details of military moves and had drawn logical conclusions from them withdrew his story after receiving a flat denial from a Pentagon officer whose word he trusted. The obvious pleas that this revelation might have triggered a Russian preclusive strike and a general conflagration, emphasizes the barrier to dissent produced by the critical tensions of the cold war. It should be noted however that this crisis was resolved on the authority of a radio broadcast by former Chairman Nikita Krushchev from Moscow. The settlement was agreed to by President Kennedy before the actual text of the Russian proposals had been decoded and sent to the White House.

The threat posed by military security to the reporting of dissent has been paralleled on the civil side by the growth of racial and student violence. There is evidence that civil disturbances feed on the radio and television publicity they receive at the outset. A small fracas appearing on the screen calls sympathizers into the street to take part. What might have been no more than a minor encounter between police and demonstrators swells into mob action as reinforcements flock to the scene. Close-ups of police roughing up demonstrators does nothing either for police morale or prestige; police become "the enemy pigs". Their conduct becomes a new excuse for destructive violence. Recognizing their responsibility to the public in the matter of keeping the peace, broadcasters worked out an informal understanding with police officials whereby incidents are not reported until police on the spot have given up hope of containing the trouble. This "Chicago compact" has been adopted in major cities across the United States where tension is high. It is a voluntary censorship in the interests of law and order, but it tends to conceal tensions until they become explosive, which makes it a moot question whether such controls do not increase the danger they are supposed to off-set. "Voluntary" censor ship is more restrictive than an imposed check, for doubtful cases tend to be decided negatively; there is missing the stimulus to evade which imposed censorship provides. Negro frustration can only be intensified by such measures as the Chicago compact. Removal of a vent for these frustrations lends color to the complaint of the activists that non-violence does not get the message across, and that the only way of getting attention from the White Establishment is through violence, and the more outrageous, the better. This conclusion was implicit in the study of recent outbreaks of Negro violence conducted by the Lemberg Center for the study of violence at Brandeis University in Massachusetts.

Dr. John P. Spiegal, who conducted the study, reported that "the contemporary ghetto riots grow out of the failure of the civil rights movement in its attempt to achieve normative adjustment for black people through non-violent protest". Lemberg Center researchers concluded that only rioting and violence seem to spur the white community to act on the problems of the ghetto. The extent to which broadcasting checks violence by censoring it at the outbreak inhibits action on the problems of the ghetto, and builds up the tension to the point at which moderate leadership is rejected. Concern with the problems of security adds up to greater insecurity, followed by stricter regulation, in a vicious spiral of restriction — tension and violence, and more restrictions.

The implications of this spiral for the continuance of the democratic process in North America are so grave as to deserve intensive study and to demand early and drastic action. The Lemberg Center undertook a survey of racial relations in six northern U.S. cities in the hope of learning how to control or prevent the spread of violence. The Lemberg Center for the Study of Violence was established at Brandeis University in September 1966. For its study of race relations, it chose three cities which experienced riots in the summer of 1966 — Cleveland, Dayton, and Boston — and three matching cities which escaped — Pittsburgh, Akron, Ohio, and San Francisco. The latter was paired with Boston since both are large coastal cities, cultural and educational centers, well out of the Southern tradition, and neither is heavily industrialized. Both have enduring racial problems. In a preliminary report, subject to possible qualification later, the Center found that a riot was a product of the interaction of two factors: "the level of dissatisfaction within the Negro population of a city, and an inflammatory incident which triggers a disturbance. The relation between the two factors is reciprocal. The higher the level of dissatisfaction, the lower need be the inflammatory power of the precipitating incident, and vice versa."

The report notes that an inflammatory incident is "usually an act committed by Whites which is perceived by Negroes as grossly unjust and insulting to their race or their community".

The enquiry did not study the role of broadcasting in reporting the inflammatory incident" in feeding the developing disturbance, but the evidence suggests that failure to communicate is at the root of much of the discontent. The report notes indeed that "high levels of Negro dissatisfaction are correlated with high levels of feelings that the city government has done too little to encourage integration. Therefore the perceived attitude toward integration and increased opportunities for Negroes seems to be the key factor in determining the riot potential of a city."

Failure of the media to inform both sides is implicitly recognized in two conclusions drawn by the report:

(1) If city governments were to take more active steps to increase opportunities for Negroes and to relieve their sense of injustice, the riot potential within the ghetto would be reduced.

(2) If white populations generally had a fuller appreciation of the just grievances and overwhelming problems of Negroes in the ghetto, they would give stronger support to their city governments to promote change and to correct the circumstances which give rise to the strong feelings of resentment now characteristic of ghetto populations.

The media, however, have failed in their duty to inform the white population. The question now arises whether they will reform and try to cope with conditions which create unrest, or continue along the path of least resistance, applying controls which only intensify pressures until the inevitable explosion sweeps away controls, media, and the Establishment with them.

In this respect, Canada has a great advantage. Racism is not as acute as in the United States;[1] not because of any Canadian merit, so much as because there are fewer Negroes and no long tradition of a slave society. Negroes are the American problem; they will not go away; they show no signs of dying off, as the Indians nearly did, and they refuse either to conform to the rules of the Establishment or to accept the consequences of non-conformity.

The mass media have not informed the American masses about the hard core of the problem, which is that the Negro is not assimilable in terms of the imposed norms of the American Establishment. His views on work and play, crime and punishment, are irreconcilable with those of the Affluent Society, which is intolerant of non-conformists who do not adhere to the "Protestant Ethic". Beneath the surface differences are sexual taboos. White and black may mate, as in the past they obviously did. But if they marry, they cease to be members of the Establishment in good standing. Neither miscegenation nor apartheid, its alternative, is acceptable for public discussion, and this makes dialogue on race tensions an exercise in futility. It is impossible to reach an agreed solution to a problem which cannot be publicly discussed. The American media must be faulted for lending themselves to this contradiction. Canadian media saddled with no such domestic pressures, have been no more resolute in making known the fundamental nature of the problem.

Can the dilemma of the media be relieved? It took more than 20,000 men to ease one Negro into Ol' Miss. It would take more than that to guard the stations of any Southern network which tried to tell the Negro story like it is. One CBC crew was refused studio facilities in Birmingham

[1] Editor's note: The highly emotionally charged English Canadian backlash in support of the War Measures Act legislated in October 1970, in response to terrorism in Quebec, might modify Mr. Minifie's optimism about the lack of racism in Canada.

Alabama, for a very modest effort to present both sides. The crew was given clearly to understand that Negroes could not be brought into the show, the studio managers asserting that "they did not want their cable blown again", as apparently it had been after an earlier adventure into liberalism. Communication bowed to security, for which the demand is increasing as real or imaginary threats to it multiply.

EMERGENT TRENDS AND ISSUES

What will the concern for security, internal and external, mean for the mass media in the United States and Canada? It could lead to a drive for controls, imposed or voluntary, despite growing evidence that tamping down resentments only increases the violence of the explosion. Opposition to controls gains strength from their demonstrated incapacity to improve the quality of programming. There is no future for controls; but if they reject them, can the media get to the heart of current resentments persuasively enough to remove them? The answer is probably no. Negro resentments go back too far and too deeply into the fabric of the White Establishment. They reflect the fact that Whites do not regard Negro culture, traditions or outlook on life as compatible with their own, or as values which could assimilate or be assimilated by their own. Against this bedrock obstacle, the media are powerless. Can the media tell this story in all its nakedness, or will they try to dress it up in conventional acceptable rainment? On the way this question is answered depends the future of the "American Way of Life". The mass media have tried to gloss over the problem with such fairy-tale solutions as "Guess Who's Coming to Dinner", but they have shied away from the horrid truth, which is that the Negro is not assimilable through integration into the American Establishment.

The media may not touch this basic truth; this taboo makes discussion of race tensions an exercise in futility. It is impossible to reach an agreed solution to a problem which does not admit public mention. The media must be faulted for lending themselves to this contradiction. Canadian media, which for reasons possibly of international courtesy have been no more resolute, are not making a solution any easier. While the media temporize, events have moved.

They have moved in a very disturbing direction, towards less discussion, and more violence, and this trend makes the task of the mass media much more difficult. The violence born of racial frustrations has been joined by violence fostered by student frustration; the impatience of the Black with the White Establishment has been wedded to the impatience of youth with the Academic Establishment or any Establishment. Both youth and the Blacks have formed nihilistic revolts against all order and discipline.

One wintry evening in 1924, I walked towards a bonfire blazing in a little square on the outskirts of Florence, a middle-class square of bourgeois home-owners. I was attracted to the firelight and the noise. My curiosity was not without danger; broken furniture, including tablelegs and smashed chairs was flying out of second storey windows, followed by bundles of papers and pamphlets. I picked one up. I had only time to notice the emblem of the Freemasons when the leaflet was snatched from my hands and thrown on the bonfire. A tough-looking young man in a black shirt warned me to have nothing to do with such rubbish. It was dangerous, he said, and vile.

I moved away from this scene as the police moved in. There was no room for discussion or compromise. The air was filled with meaningless slogans: Freemasonry must go; Basta! We have had enough! Mussolini is always right.

Modern slogans shouted by students seem just as pointless. Modern youth goes further: It indulges in a nihilistic passion for destruction for its own sake, as a good in itself, bound to be followed by something better. Christians in the latter days of the Roman Empire were no more perverse in their determination to destroy; they at least were animated by the vision of a heavenly kingdom to come. Students today lack even this excuse for denying allegiance to the Establishment. Ostensibly, radical modern youths are generally sympathetic to communism, although it is hard to see why except as a weapon to destroy the Establishment.

This possibility makes more urgent the task of the mass media to warn the masses of the peril facing their society, and it adds significance to the establishment by the Canadian Senate in March, 1969, of a special committee to examine and report on the extent and nature of the mass media's impact and influence on the Canadian public. The committee is also empowered to consider and report on the ownership and control of the major means of mass public communication in Canada. Sen. Grattan O'Leary injected nationalism into the issue. He was reported as saying that only Canadian citizens should be given authority to publish in Canada. An imprimatur authority however is a dangerous weapon to give the Establishment. The earlier experience of the 1960 Royal Commission of Publications, which was chaired by Sen. O'Leary, does not encourage optimism. Publication "cum priviligio" does not inspire confidence in the reader.

Media which, for whatever reason, have lost the confidence of the reader, listener, or viewer cannot expect to find believers among young people, whose scepticism, natural or cultivated, feeds on mass media's fatuities. This scepticism, finds its outlet in nihilism.

Western youths have lacked the discipline of poverty and fear; the have been denied the spiritual excitement of church and university leader who believed in the faith they were trying to inculcate. Reaping the inevitable harvest of frustration and violence, the leaders of the North American Establishment have looked about for scapegoats. The mass medi among others appeared ideal for the role. Unfortunately, by discreditin them, the Establishment will have destroyed one of the few remainin instruments by which the conditions it deplored might be remedied.

The campaign got off to a fast start when Sen. John Pastore (R., R.I., chairman of the communications subcommittee of the Senate Commerc committee, began hearings on television violence. It followed a standar pattern, with Sen. Pastore calling on broadcasters to "clean up the dirt", and network presidents demanding scientific data to substantiate alleged harmful side effects on children of television violence. Some of the more literate pointed out that children were required to spend years in study of Shakespeare, Euripides and Homer, whose addiction to violence, they said, far surpassed anything a family network would dare to show, while the language of Aristophanes was better left in the original Greek.

This did not discourage Sen. Pastore from proposing to control or censor broadcasting output. The difficulties and dangers of this course so appalled Frank Stanton, president of Columbia Broadcasting System, that he told the committee: "I would rather spread the responsibility and fix it at the local level, rather than try regulation from above or from outside. I get very nervous when I see a medium that has the power and reach of television passing through one or two or three men to make a judgment on it."

Unfortunately for this position, Mr. Stanton's own network had just displayed its intolerance of criticism by cancelling a magnificently humourous show which had had the audacity to take a round-house swing at President Johnson. It was the sort of thing which Louis XIV did not tolerate from Molière. I was disappointed but not surprised when CBS bowed to the former autocrat of the White House to emphasize that if you want to stay on the air in "the Land of the Free", it is a good idea to respect "Sacred Cows" and "Fat Cats". The incident did nothing to inspire the youth of the nation with confidence in the Establishment. CBS explained that the show had not been taped in time to be shown to the affiliates, who are held legally responsible for the shows they air. The Smothers Brothers argued that the network censors' cuts had been so extensive that they had not had time to fill the holes.

This exchange made the point that *lèse-majesté* is still a sin in the United States, and that the head of the Establishment must not be ridiculed. As long as this principle is unchallenged, it makes an important difference whether the media are locally controlled by a monopoly or are competitively owned, which was the next point to which the Pastore subcommittee applied itself.

Reporting the story, *Newsweek* alleged that "29 U. S. communities have a single commercial TV station and a single daily (newspaper) with an ownership interest in the station, and perhaps a score of other cities have a degree of joint newspaper-TV control that is only somewhat less concentrated."

The Federal Communications Commission took notice of the situation by transferring the TV license of Boston's WHDF from the Herald-Traveller Corporation to a citizen's group. It also voted four to two to withhold renewal of KRON-TV's license pending a hearing on charges that the station managed news to benefit the Chronicle Publishing Company. Congressional attacks on the integrity of broadcasting made an inauspicious background for proposals to televise proceedings in Congress. Present American practice is to restrict television coverage to joint meetings of the House and Senate in the House chamber since it is commodious and wired for sound. Joint sessions are convened irregularly to hear a message from the President or an address by some distinguished visitor.

Otherwise, television is limited to covering Senate committee hearings at the discretion of the chairman. By decision of former Speaker Sam Rayburn, no House hearings may be televised. The system worked effectively at the height of the McCarthy furore by exposing the malevolent nature of his campaign. With this distinguished contribution to national sanity to its credit, its subsequent tremors over *lèse-majesté* are the more regrettable since they make honest coverage of the White House and State Department almost impossible. The viewer must be very alert to detect the misleading nature of former President Johnson's statement on the Gulf of Tonkin incident, which he used as an excuse to initiate aerial bombing of North Vietnam. The mass media made no attempt to point out the contradictions and gaps in the story, and senatorial attempts to do so were scored by Pentagon brass as giving aid and comfort to Hanoi. The President himself briefed the Senate Foreign Relations leaders in such a way that Sen. Fulbright, the chairman, reproached himself for his gullibility. "I should have been more cautious," he told the Senate. "I should have been more suspicious. I am to blame." But even Fulbright hesitated to charge openly that he had been misled, although he made this fairly obvious.

His *mea culpa* changed nothing. The Foreign Relations Committee of which he was chairman suppressed the only available coherent account of the Tonkin episode. The account was drawn up by the committee staff and printed as a committee print from information supplied by the Pentagon and State Department. It was mentioned briefly in a story by the New York Times Washington Bureau as throwing a new and disturbing doubt on official claims that an unwarranted attack by North Vietnamese PT boats had been made on a U. S. warship innocently patrolling international waters. The doubt was never cleared up, for that brief reference was all the public learned. The committee print was never made public and attempts to obtain it ran up against a blank wall. Strict orders had come down to the committee not to allow either leaks or explanations. Even the irreverent Drew Pearson and I.F. Stone, usually infallible sources of material the Establishment would like to keep secret, drew blanks. I was never able to find out where the order to suppress came from. Bits and pieces, highly contradictory, came out little by little in testimony before various Senate committees, but no coherent story was ever pieced together by the mass media on a matter of major importance to the security of the nation. Historians might profitably investigate the mystery of this report on the Tonkin incident.

The task which the mass media and the Senate could have carried out with relative impunity was left to rebellious students, who could only perform this duty at the peril of their careers. They laid their future on the line to perform a duty which the mass media shirked.

This dereliction coincided with a growing need to report more vividly and honestly the growing interference of government in every phase of national life. This is not a totally bad development, but it makes more urgent the establishment of a clear and credible two-way channel communications between rulers and the ruled. The mass media have vacated this role.

What has been developed to replace them? An interesting experiment is under way in Canada. It is a limited attempt to fill the information vacuum; it may have significant results. The Federal Government created in 1962 an agency styled the Canadian Council of Resource Ministers. It was composed of one federal member and one member from each of the ten provinces. They were instructed to discuss and report on problems relating to the management of Canadian natural resources. A limited secretariat was created which kept members supplied with source material and liaised between the Council and the media, in order to give the public a coherent account of what the Council was doing. The Council early decided that water resource management would best repay in-depth study, owing to the complex local, regional, national, and international aspects of water and the urgency of formulating policy for the use of Canadian water resources. The Council held a seminar in which water workshops were set up. Some seventy members at the ministerial and senior civil servant level attended; background papers were also commissioned from authoritatives on water management. To permit candid and uninhibited exchange of views, the seminars and workshops were closed to press and public. The press commented on the contradiction between the Council's desire to be a channel of information between the government and the public and the secrecy with which it wished to cloak its proceedings. How can the mass media inform the masses, if it is not allowed access to material?

At this point, the media came up against the difficulty, noted by Einstein, that phenomena change under observation, or are changed by the very fact of observation. This scientific quandary — how to record without modifying the phenomena being recorded — applies exactly to such a sensitive apparatus as a water workshop. To be effective, members must be assured that their expressions are confidential. Ministers and civil servants could not risk their political or professional careers by honestly voicing opinions which differed in the slightest from orthodox generalities. Indeed, they would hardly know what their views were until these had been modified, polished, and justified by uninhibited exchanges with their colleagues. For the media to have used early, rough material would have given the public an erroneous impression of conflict before viewpoints were compromised plus a suggestion of surrender if they were compromised.

Since the media deal chiefly in these over-simplified terms of conflict, they would inevitably single out and thus magnify possibilities of conflict, thus distorting the phenomena they observed. Thus, the cherished freedom of the press to observe at first-hand is in fact an obstacle of factual reporting, since observation by the media modifies the phenomena under study. Basically, this is an inhibiting defect of the media, largely a factor its tendency to see news only in terms of conflict, victory, or defeat.

If the public is to be informed, therefore, other means must be found secure public comprehension of and participation in the management natural resources. There must be an intermediary who has the confidence of both sides, who can be present at discussions without inhibiting their spontaneity, and can report their trend and outcome discreetly but objectively, without imperilling the position and future of the participants but also without withholding from the mass media details essential to a comprehensive report on what happened. This calls for an individual of skill, experience, and integrity. He is usually referred to as a public relations officer, or for short a "P.R.". It is a poor term, for he is not dealing with the public but with media representatives, who in turn must also be possessed of intelligence, experience, and a readiness to forego "scoops" and sensationalism in the interests of sober presentation of the issues. They in turn must be backed up by editors who would sooner have the news straight than first. A better title for the P.R. might be "Herald", for that is his function: to convey precisely the proposals and reactions of both sides one to the other.

Reporters must also be convinced that the Herald is capable and honest, and that they are obtaining a more reliable and complete account of what went on than they could have obtained through open sessions. Breach of confidence by either side is fateful to the relationship. The Herald principle has been adopted by the C.C.R.M., so far successfully It could be a long step forward in continuing consultation among rulers and with the ruled.

There are obvious dangers in spoon-feeding the media, but it canno be avoided in face of the increasing complexity and ubiquity of govern mental intervention in "private" business and the supreme importance o obtaining public understanding and assent, or modification of government' plans. The water workshops of the C.C.R.M. for instance stressed the im portance of a continuing dialogue with the public, instead of contentiou issues like pollution, pricing, and sale of water being reserved for th scramble of an election campaign. The secrecy necessary for unhampere discussion could easily be used to cloak dissent. This cannot be ignorec Official sources tend to identify with the Establishment. Not if they ca help it, will any "Fat Cat" be singed nor the milk of any "Sacred Cow be soured.

For practical reasons, however, information of a complicated natur must be given to the media in advance in order to have it intelligibl presented. For example, the U.S. Treasury delivers to accredited newsme printed copies of the budget and ancillary documents along with a sho ping bag to carry them in, several days before they are sent up to Congres Not even the greenest cub would dream of breaking the embargo on pr mature publication.

Use of the embargo, which makes the reporter a confidential age of government, is increasing with the volume and complexity of informatic the reporter has to handle. To assist him, the role of Herald must I perfected and accepted and the reluctance of media to use his servic must be overcome. The Water Workshop Seminar of the Canadian Coun of Resource Ministers was a prophetic glance in the direction which loo most promising for progress, particularly in Canada where regional cc ditions are so diverse and the difficulty of conducting a significant dialog is so great. The Council agreed that other resources could usefully be examined. Forest products, mining, and environmental contamination will also come under scrutiny.

This method of conducting public business is limited however by the contradiction between the need for secrecy to permit through discussion of problems at a high level and the need for publicity to make the complexity of the problems and the consequences of alternative solutions known to the public who will suffer or benefit from the consequences. The role of the Herald becomes more vital and more urgent. It is perhaps significant that the need for a new officer in media communications becomes recognized coincidentally with the need for a new officer in justice — the ombudsman. The trend of the age demands new machinery to deal with its complex problems. The Herald should be the ombudsman of the media.

9

Mass Media, Advertising, and the Quiet Revolution

FREDERICK ELKIN

This article includes a discussion of two seemingly unrelated topics — the mass media in Canada and advertising during the Quiet Revolution in Quebec. In various ways, however, these topics are linked. The mass media as we know them in both English and French Canada serve as the context for advertising. Over the years, in newspapers, magazines, radio, and television, patterns of organization and style have developed in which advertising plays a crucial role. Without advertising, the patterns would surely be different — perhaps the mass media would be directed by government agencies or powerful private associations or limited to the well-to-do who could pay the cost. Mass media owners and directors currently take for granted their dependence on advertising for support.

More obviously, and again in both English and French Canada, the advertisements and commercials are part and parcel of mass media content. Advertising, through the intermediary of the mass media owners, also influences the non-advertising content, sometimes indirectly and sometimes quite directly, especially in radio and television. In the western world, the public accepts such advertising as a normal and proper component of the mass media. Certain intellectuals and consumer associations continually condemn advertising for its deception and irrational appeals, but these criticisms have not been taken up by the mass of people to whom advertising is directed, nor have the intellectuals, themselves, had much effect on the media.

Advertising and the mass media, it is evident, are inextricably entwined; but wherein does the Quiet Revolution enter the picture? The Quiet Revolution was the popular name given to the nationalist social movement in Quebec beginning in 1960 which sought to modernize the province and assert the parity and rights of the French Canadians vis-à-vis the superordinate English Canadians. The precipitating event was the death in 1959 of Premier Duplessis, the leader of the National Union Party, and the election victory the following year of the Quebec Liberals. The new government, supported by youth, labour, and significant segments of the church, business, and professional community, led the movement to reform the social and political structure, revive French language culture, and become *maîtres chez nous*. Many accounts give details of this movement.[1]

In English Canada, one effect of the Quiet Revolution on the mass media was the establishment of French language stations, for example CJBC in Toronto; another was the furnishing of grist to journalists for news and editorial comment. In French Canada, the mass media had a more direct and instrumental part to play. Many prominent mass media figures were in the vanguard of the movement; but more important, the mass media in various ways gave enormous publicity to all facets of the movement, and often strong and direct editorial support.

French-Canadian advertising personnel also played their part. They were among the members of the new middle class, the group recognized as the primary carrier of the movement;[2] and also, they sought as best they could to carry out specific aims of the Quiet Revolution within their own occupational sphere of influence. The links between the mass media, advertising, and the Quiet Revolution will be more readily evident in the last part of this paper; but first, in part for its own value and in part as a backdrop, we review the distinctive features of the mass media in Canada.

MASS MEDIA IN CANADA

The mass media in any country are integral parts of their political, economic, and social contexts. Technologically, they may be simple or complex; esthetics may or may not be a relevant concern; the organization may be highly or loosely structured; the content may be serious or lighthearted; and change may be slow or rapid. In Canada, the mass media serve in the context of a highly urbanized, industrialized and rapidly changing world. Canada, except perhaps in film and the organization of its radio-television network, has not pioneered in the establishment of

[1] Among the reports discussing the Quiet Revolution are: R. Jones, *Community In Crisis* (Toronto: McClelland and Stewart, 1967); P. Desbarats, *The State of Quebec* (Toronto: McClelland and Stewart, 1965); T. Sloan, *Quebec: The Not-so-quiet-Revolution* (Toronto: The Ryerson Press, 1965); H. Guindon, "Two Cultures: An Essay on Nationalism, Class, and Ethnic Tension", in *Contemporary Canada,* ed. R.H. Leach (Toronto: University of Toronto Press, 1968); and F. Scott and M. Oliver, eds., *Quebec States Her Case* (Toronto: Macmillan of Canada, 1964). For a statement of some French-Canadian positions, see J. Cotnam, *Faut-il inventer un nouveau Canada?* (Montréal: Fides, 1967); P. Garigue, *L'Option politique du Canada français* (Montréal: Editions du Lévrier, 1963); M. Chaput, *Pourquoi je suis séparatiste* (Montréal: Editions du Jour, 1961); and R. Barbeau, *J'ai choisi l'indépendance* (Montréal: Editions de l'Homme, 1961).
[2] For a discussion of the role of the "New middle class" in the Quiet Revolution, see J. Brazeau, "Quebec's Emerging Middle Class", *Canadian Business,* XXXVI, No. 3 (1963), 38-40 and H. Guindon, "Social Unrest, Social Class and Quebec's Bureaucratic Revolution," *Queen's Quarterly,* LXXI. 1964, 150-162.

the mass media; but once developments did begin elsewhere, Canada soon followed.[3] England's first newspaper appeared in 1665, the United States' first newspaper in 1704, and Canada's the *Halifax Gazette* in 1752. Canada's radio and television operations — which began in 1918 and 1953 respectively — followed much closer with just a few years between the early stations or channels elsewhere and their introduction here.

The patterns of organization and control of mass media in Canada are common to those of the western world.[4] The newspapers, magazines, and most of the radio and television stations are privately owned and organized for profit; at the same time they are expected to manifest — and they generally do — a sense of public responsibility; all media to a greater or lesser degree are overviewed by government, ranging from minimum legal controls of libel and drug advertising to the licensing of radio and television stations which may be renewed or withdrawn. The content of the mass media is directed to a literate, relatively well-educated public and appeals to a wide range of social levels and interested groups.

In certain specific aspects, however, the mass media of Canada are unique to this nation. These unique aspects stem in great part from three distinctive features of the Canadian scene — its physical geography, its proximity to the United States, and its bicultural setting.[5]

Physical Geography

Canada has the second largest land mass of any nation in the world, yet its population is but 21 million. Some 80 per cent of this number live in a relatively narrow strip within a hundred miles or so of the United States border, but the rest are scattered far and wide through the country. Between the limited number of heavily populated sections lie wide expanses of sparsely inhabited land. With such a diffuse distribution of its population, Canada can have no national centre such as London or Paris from which all major lines of communication radiate.

Nor are there natural geographic and ecological lines that run through the country as a whole. Major lines in fact, those that would naturally derive from the lay of the mountains, plains and rivers, run north and south cutting into the United States. Such contours likewise, along with the variety of accompanying resources, tend to divide the country into regions and explain in part the oft-mentioned strong sense of regionalism.

Such geographic factors have their effects on the mass media — an effect evident above all in equipment and distribution costs. The cost is

[3] If we look for a positive function, we may say that Canada in this way, like other secondarily developing countries, has saved the expense of developing new techniques.

[4] For an excellent discussion of the ownership of the mass media in Canada, see Chapter 15 in John Porter, *The Vertical Mosaic* (Toronto: University of Toronto Press, 1965).

[5] J.A. Irving, "The Problems of the Mass Media", in *Mass Media in Canada*, ed. J.A. Irving (Toronto: Ryerson Press, 1962), p. 223.

great for establishing the lines and cables required for national radio and television networks, especially when the equipment must be put through bleak and difficult terrain. And since the costs are little different whether the population be twenty or fifty-million, the per capita cost for Canadians is exceedingly high. The distribution of printed media points up the same problem. Compared to countries of similar population, the cost — for example of distributing a national magazine throughout Canada — is enormous, especially when the distribution includes isolated distant points. Advertising represents still another example of the price of Canada's geography. One television commercial in the United States, costing no more to produce than in Canada, has a potential audience ten times as great. The greater New York area alone has a population almost as large as Canada's.

One result of the high costs entailed by such geographic factors has been a greater role on the part of the Federal Government in establishing national radio and television communication networks. A national mass communication system, it was generally agreed, was essential to encourage national unity, and since this was not a primary concern of private industry, the responsibility fell to the Federal Government. In seeking to bind the country together through communication, the Government was not without its precedents; the same rationale, generations back, had underlain the assistance given the Canadian Pacific and Canadian National Railroads in establishing cross-country railway systems and later the Trans-Canada Airlines. Each was a pioneering effort, costly and not without opposition, but accepted by the Nation's leaders as a necessary device for creating a sense of national unity and purpose; so, too, in electronic communications. Today, radio, public and private, with approximately 300 stations and 180 relay transmitters reaches over 99 per cent of the population. In the North, where small isolated groups may be hundreds of miles apart, radio also serves as a means of local communication. Television with approximately 80 stations, along with special rebroadcast points for remote areas, reaches 96 per cent. Considering the size of Canada and the distribution of its population, these figures represent no mean achievement. Private industry too, when it has established cross-country communication lines — by wire, radio, and television — has also had to undergo the high expense of adapting to Canada's physical geography and here, too, of course, the costs, if not the decisions, are ultimately met by the consuming public.

Proximity to the United States.

Closely overlapping the geographical problems are those stemming from the proximity to the United States. The United States is our large, wealthy, powerful, and problem-ridden neighbour to the south, and we cannot help but be interested and enmeshed in its affairs, be these affairs of race relations, explorations in space, movie star marriages, student riots, or political elections. Our economic dependence on United States companies established in Canada and on the American market for our products, along with implications regarding our political vulnerability, is a never-ending subject of discussion and manifests itself in our constant fear of being overwhelmed and our nagging concern with Canadian identity.

How does the proximity to the United States affect our mass media? Perhaps foremost and underlying any other influence is the model the United States presents of mass popular appeal and of private ownership of mass media. Newspapers, magazines, radio, and television in the United States in various ways set the pace for us. In style and organization, for example, our newspapers — and also our magazines, few though they may be — are very much like those south of the border. Our private commercial radio programming with its popular songs, advertising jingles, quiz programs, and "hot lines" would be difficult — except for the news and weather — to distinguish from that of many American stations. Our television style, likewise, with some notable exceptions in the programmes of English and French CBC, often appear to be a local variation of U.S. channels rather than an expression of any Canadian uniqueness. We might also see something of an American model in the development of Canadian newspaper chains (which control about half of our newspapers), a news gathering agency such as Canadian Press, business magazines, radio networks, and film distribution, and in the arguments put forward by private radio and television broadcasters and certain advertising personnel against strong government regulation or the CBC. Models in modern societies are difficult to trace because those with similar values may well or their own develop similar patterns; but who is to gainsay some strong U.S. influence on Canadian mass media institutions?

The most obvious effect of our proximity to the United States is our exposure to media content. Much of the exposure comes about from the constant travel of Canadians to the United States. Much more comes about through American originated news reports, newspaper syndicated columns magazines, and television programs — all of which we have come to take for granted. Some exposure to U.S. media cannot be avoided unless - and this is difficult to conceive in Canada — we would accept jamming of U.S. radio and television stations. Almost all Canadians, at least a night time, can hear U.S. radio, and probably one-half of Canadian families can receive good television reception from U.S. channels.[6]

Some exposure to printed U.S. media could presumably be avoided through legislation, but we choose, for a variety of reasons, not to be very restrictive. In 1966, following a Royal Commission Report on publications,[7] legislation was enacted to protect the Canadian magazine industry by refusing business tax deductions to Canadian corporations that advertised in non-Canadian publications where such advertising was directe

[6] E. Hallman, "Television," in Irving, *Mass Media* reports in 1962 that 37% of Canadian viewers receive good to excellent reception of American television the percentage is certainly much higher today. Statistics on the number of stations, public and private, and size of audience may be found in *Canada Year Book*, (Ottawa: Queen's Printer, 1968).

[7] Royal Commission on Publications, *Report* (Ottawa: Queen's Printer, 1961

to Canadian markets. However the main culprits, *Time* and *Readers'
Digest*, which receive over half the advertising money invested in Canadian
magazines, were spared, ostensibly because they were printed in Canada.
Undoubtedly behind the limited action, lay a fear of reprisal, but it is also
true that many influential Canadians with their interests, values, and traditions do not wish to feel that they are opposing free and easy communication. Such magazines as *Time, Readers' Digest, Life, Look, Woman's Day*
and others published in the United States, it is believed, should be available
to those who want them at low cost, notwithstanding any competitive advantage they have over Canadian published magazines.

We have also deliberately put some limited barriers in the way of
competitive U.S. radio and television. In order that Canadian radio and
television station owners not just plug in to U.S. networks and intrude
local commercials, which would be the simplest and most profitable way of
running their stations, they have had to meet minimum percentage requirements for Canadian content; for a long time this was 55 per cent and the
rulings of the C.R.T.C. in 1970 have perpetuated the emphasis on Canadian
content. However, although such a limitation surely does encourage our
own artists, it is no easy task to define Canadian content (the World Series
in baseball, along with Commonwealth programmes were considered
Canadian content) and limiting the percentage of foreign programmes in
itself does not help to achieve another of our values, programme quality.

Thus some American mass media content we cannot help but admit
into the country and others with certain limits we choose to admit; still
others we actively speak out against. Our newspapers, partly because of
the relatively low cost, subscribe to such syndicated U.S. columnists as
Ann Landers, Art Buchwald, and Dr. W.C. Alvarez, and sometimes re-
print articles of James Reston, Walter Lippman, and others. Dozens of
U.S. originated comic strips, for example, Blondie, Pogo, Peanuts, Rex
Morgan, and Mary Worth, are just assumed to be part of the Canadian
scene. The Royal Commission Report observed that 90 per cent of the
magazines which sell more than 10,000 copies a year in Canada are
American. Some of our private radio stations have mostly local programming (although some of the content, especially popular songs, is American) but others, for many hours, are hooked into American stations:

> Our radio, particularly private broadcasting, speaks with an American
> vocabulary, expounds American philosophies, and stimulates 'the
> great American dream' . . . private commercial radio is only one
> expression of the North American free enterprise economy, which
> Canada shares with the United States . . .[8]

On television, the percentage of American content, especially on prime
evening time, and even allowing for the regulations, has always been high,
especially for popular entertainment and drama. Furthermore, these programmes invariably receive the highest audience ratings — which of course
why the Canadian stations choose to show them in the first place.

---

[8] Bruce Raymond, "Radio," in Irving, *Mass Media*, p. 107.

Canadian stations justify showing such programmes in part by affirming that they thereby hold the audiences for the Canadian programmes which follow. Feature length films, still another mass media in Canada, also tend to be produced primarily in the United States; the audience that sees non-American produced films is relatively small.

Even French Canadians are exposed to considerable U.S. mass media content in translation. Comic strips, sometimes the American columnist, baseball games on radio, and even television programmes (one of the most prominent for some years was *Papa a Raison, Father Knows Best*) are read, heard, and seen in French-language media. Before the Quiet Revolution, perhaps no radio day-time program was more popular than *Le hit parade américain*.

To obtain precise data on American originated advertisements and commercials is not feasible because of the complications of adaptations. American ads, however, cut through all our mass media. Some we know by virtue of a "spill over" effect; that is, we see the advertisements in American magazines, or we hear the television commercials telecast by U.S. stations. Others we know in Canadian media because they are placed directly therein by American advertising agencies, or more often because the advertising agencies in Canada, in their work for U.S. subsidiaries, merely repeat or adapt the ads or commercials prepared for the American market

That we accept with little question a heavy exposure to U.S. media of course is understandable. Our way of life, at least in English Canada is very much like that in the United States. We have some national popular culture interests that set us apart — the Grey Cup Game, the hockey complex, certain popular entertainers, and our political figures, but they make up a relatively small proportion of our cultural life. We seek out that content of mass media which is available and which we consider the best of its type. This means in effect the U.S. media which can afford to produce a weekly Ed Sullivan or daily Merv Griffin Show on television or a *Life* magazine, or the Sunday *New York Times*. Why should we no view U.S. prepared television shows or read U.S. magazines if we conside them better?[9] Similarly, for advertising, those responsible for informing and selling to the Canadian market often consider it both sensible an efficient to use an expensively produced television commercial made i the United States. We buy the same cars, so it seems plausible to assume that we respond to the same advertising appeals with any necessar adaptations into English- or French-Canadian usage.

Proximity to the wealthier United States, strengthened by the sim larity of our cultures, further means that we lose Canadian develope mass media stars to the more lucrative U.S. market. Many a singer, acto and writer, as we might expect, prefers to perform for the larger audienc and greater income and glory that accompanies success in the Unite States. Many a budding film or television producer in Canada too, it

---

[9] By the same token, we avoid the less attractive aspects of the mass med in the United States, the worst of the scandal sheets, and the most ad-ridden popular radio programmes.

said, seeks only to build a file of good productions, looking forward to the day when he might try his luck in New York. Even in print, the Canadian author who writes a good short story may be paid several times more by an American than a Canadian magazine — so as would be expected, he sends his story to the former.

France instead of the United States serves as the counterpart for the French-Canadian writer, entertainer, artist, or producer. In both English and French Canada, the lore also affirms that success in one's own country is more likely to follow success first achieved elsewhere.

Mass Media in French Canada.

Crucial in the consideration of any significant problem in Canadian life, including the problems of the mass media, is the nation's bilingual and bicultural character. Canada has two charter groups — the French Canadians who first settled the country and the English Canadians who, following the battle of Quebec, came to supersede the French Canadians in number, authority, and power. The French Canadians however, as we know, did survive as French Canadians and did maintain their language and certain distinctive aspects of their culture. The ethnic groups who succeeded the French Canadians, important though they may be in Canada today, are relative newcomers.

As in English Canada, in the early days of French Canada's development, the mass media played a very minor role. With literacy limited, the circulation of newspapers and magazines was small. To a great degree, public information was passed on through inter-personal communication, with priests, teachers and other professional people serving as opinion leaders. In recent years, the development of mass media in French Canada has followed the pattern found elsewhere in the western world. Practically everyone is literate; newspapers and magazines are read throughout the province (although circulation is less per capita than in English Canada); radio and television are almost universal. In 1966, there were in the French language approximately 12 daily newspapers, 175 weekly newspapers, 47 radio stations, and 13 television channels.

Thus two languages and cultures in Canada have meant in effect two parallel communication systems with each group expecting to receive communications in its own language. Relationships exist, of course, between the two systems. Organizationally, for example, many French Canadians have important advisory roles in such privately owned groups as Canadian Press and Maclean-Hunter and more equal representation in such groups as the CBC and National Film Board which represent the official federal position. And in content, English language reports and publications are often translated into French and vice-versa, though less often.

Leaving aside any implications regarding national unity, such a parallel system adds additional expense. To translate material into two languages is in itself costly; the expense of duplicate organizations and independent operations add millions more. The splitting of the Canadian audience into English- and French-speaking means, too, that particular programmes have small audiences — the highest potential audience for an English language television show, for example, may be 16 or 17 million, and for a French programme about four-million.

Underlying any unique development of the mass media in Canada is the fact of language difference. Without a distinctive language, the French-Canadian group would not have such a strong feeling of separateness and would not, at least as we know it today, have survived. Language lay at the basis of the separate culture and informal communication network of the French Canadians and, through limiting contact with outside groups, served as a barrier to the diffusion of ideas.

The distinctive language likewise underlay the development and success of French-language media. Few in the general public wish to expend much intellectual effort in order to be informed about public affairs or to be entertained. This, at minimum, means that communicators in the mass media must approach French Canadians in their own language. Thus developed the opportunity for the French-language journalists, writers, producers, entertainers, as well as managers and entrepreneurs.

The English Canadians had no such problem. Except for local items and certain distinctive Canadian events, political and otherwise, most English Canadians undoubtedly would be quite satisfied with the mass media of the U.S. The pressure, therefore, for a distinctive English-Canadian mass media has come not from the public, but from nationally oriented officials and intellectuals. For the French Canadians on the contrary, the basic interest in French-language media stemmed from the people themselves and they were strongly supported by the protectors and proponents of a French-Canadian identity and culture.

The two parallel systems have certain basic similarities. Except for magazines, which by virtue of their range and polish in English language media have no counterpart in French Canada, the mass media have the same basic style. The place and format of ads and commercials, the tone of radio announcers, the sectioning of newspapers and programming of radio and television are all very much the same. So too is the major part of the content even though the local news events, sports and entertainment stories may be written and reported independently.

But the differences are also significant. First of all, certain aspects of style, especially since the Quiet Revolution, are not always the same. In advertising language, Elkin and Hill have shown that French language ad writers and translators avoid slang and dramatic phrasing and anything that smacks of an anglicism.[10] Of greater significance, the mass media in French Canada are more likely to express strong opinions in editorial and public affairs columns. In the English newspapers, editorials are unsigned and present the considered opinions of the editorial board. In the French-language newspapers, on the contrary, editorials are often written

---

[10] F. Elkin and M.B. Hill, "Bicultural and Bilingual Adaptations in French Canada: The Example of Retail Advertising", *Canadian Review of Sociology and Anthropology*, No. 2 (1965), pp. 132-148.

and signed by individuals. Thus since the newspaper as such does not commit itself, more leeway is permitted. Even radio and television are identified with strong expressions of opinion, in recent years often nationalist opinion. Particular public affairs programmes allow speakers to present their individual points of view and even the light entertainers are not without their strongly expressed and identifiable positions. Singer Pauline Julien is a notable example.

Closely associated with such expressions of opinion in French Canada is the general awareness and importance of "personalities" in the mass media especially on television. The French-language actors, entertainers, announcers, and masters of ceremony have in the course of the years become popular heroes and heroines, known and acclaimed by French Canadians throughout the province. What seems especially significant is that such stars remain almost completely unknown among English Canadians, demonstrating once again the different cultural and symbolic worlds of the two groups. To illustrate, how many English Canadians know of Roger Baulu, Michèle Tisseyre, Jean-Pierre Masson, Gilles Pelletier, Jean Duceppe, Dominique Michel and Denise Filiatrault?

The media in French and English Canada are also different in content. The French-Canadian media give much more attention to matters of interest only, or primarily, to French Canadians — their social clubs, local politics, entertainment, church activities, developments in France and French-speaking countries, talks by Quebec intellectuals, labour activities, French-language theater and provincial matters. Similarly of course the English media give more attention to events of interest to English Canadians, including relatively greater emphasis to national and commonwealth events.

Not only is the amount of space given to particular topics different, the very selection from common source material also varies depending on the interests and concerns of the reporters and the respective audiences. Two reports, one in English and one in French, of a talk by ardent French-Canadian nationalist and former government minister, René Lévesque aptly illustrates this point. On April 5, 1964, Lévesque addressed *La Ligue l'Action Nationale* at a Montreal hotel. The following morning the major headline on the front page of the English-language *Montreal Gazette* read: *LEVESQUE DEFENDS RIGHTS OF NON-FRENCH MINORITIES STRESSES EQUALITY OF ONE-FIFTH PEOPLE,* and the first sentence began: "No matter what happens in the Quebec of the future, French Canadians would only 'destroy themselves' if they sought to destroy the non-French-speaking population, Natural Resources Minister René Lévesque warned last night." The general tenor of the article was in the same vein.

In the French language *La Presse* of the same day, the talk was reported, with two rather large headlines on page 15. The major headline quoted from Lévesque's talk: *NOUS VOULONS METTRE FIN AU DOUBLE COLONIALISME ECONOMIQUE DU QUEBEC* — We want to put an end to the double economic colonialism of Quebec — and the article that followed stressed the government's awareness of the role of

Quebec in the national economy. Lévesque was quoted: "Quebec must cease being the appendage of the American economy". The second headline, almost as large, read: *LEVESQUE CROIT ECONOMIQUEMENT VIABLE UN QUEBEC INDEPENDANT* — Lévesque believes an independent Quebec is economically viable — and this served as the main theme for the second article. Mentioned almost incidentally in this article is the statement cited in the *GAZETTE*. The English and French then, even in the reporting of a public address and leaving aside any differences of interpretation, are not exposed to the same content.

We may view the French language mass media in Quebec as having two principal functions, both necessary for the success of the Quiet Revolution. On the one hand, the mass media played a major role in introducing and bringing French Canada into the contemporary world. The media, in general, were organized and directed by educated, intelligent, and alert French Canadians eager to erase the regressive aspects of the traditional French-Canadian way of life and to encourage active steps towards modernization and reform. In innumerable ways, the journalists, editorial writers, and commentators of the mass media sought to extend the horizons of the French Canadians, to change their self-conceptions, and to motivate them to act in what they considered progressive directions. They gave considerable attention to educational needs and developments, to the necessity of reforming dishonest and inefficient institutions, to the lack of French-Canadian owned, efficiently run secondary industry, to the extension of women's rights and opportunities, to the value of professional training in such French-Canadian under-represented areas as technology and finance, and to problems of under-developed areas in other parts of the world. Such discussions in the mass media were all in line with the demand that French Canadians move forward as rapidly as possible into the modern western industrializing world.

But in themselves, such developments and aspirations, even if successful, would not create a Quiet Revolution; they could, in fact, well lead to assimilation into the surrounding English-language world. What was needed in order to survive this movement as French Canadians was the counterweight of the old appeal — in a broad sense and with some novel twists — of nationalism. The mass media, through editorial comment and the attention given to current developments and popular speakers, served this function as well. They defended the French language and sought to rid it of its perversions and anglicisms;[11] they applauded the takeover of an English-Canadian owned power company because it gave the Quebec government greater control of its economy; they spoke of the 150 million French-speaking people in the world, the 33 countries in which French is spoken and the consequent cultural benefits available through the French language; they harped constantly on the inferior position of the French Canadians vis-à-vis the English Canadians in government, business

---

[11] Jean-Paul Desbiens *Les Insolences du Frère Untel* (Montréal: Les Editions de l'Homme, 1960) which sold some 125,000 copies, was the forerunner of many reports that sought to upgrade the language, both spoken and written

and social life. They told French Canadians that with appropriate training and an end to discrimination — which was a battle in itself — they were capable of competing for positions of economic power. Such appeals to French-Canadian interests, identity, and nationalism were necessary, they implied, lest French Canada be absorbed by the English-language world.

We have been discussing only the major factors which determine the distinctive character of the mass media in Canada. In minor ways, other factors have also left their mark. The ties with Britain, for example, manifest themselves in newspaper reports of football and cricket scores, broadcasts of the BBC news, British comedy programmes, televised stories of the Queen and British government officials, and the attention given the Commonwealth.

The 30 per cent or so of the Canadian population which is neither English nor French in origin is likewise very much in evidence in the mass media. Some 80 ethnic newspapers in a few dozen languages, with a circulation of some 500 thousand and an estimated readership of two million, emphasize ethnic group activities. Radio stations, to a lesser degree television, in such ethnic centres as Edmonton, Winnipeg, Montreal, and Toronto, direct dozens of programmes to minority ethnic groups.

The principle of provincial rights, of which the provincial governments are notoriously jealous, has also influenced the mass media in Canada. No review which considers educational broadcasts, political content, or even jurisdictional problems could omit this provincial role.

The mass media in Canada therefore, although basically akin to those of the western world, have their unique characteristics. Advertising, although it remains very strongly influenced by developments in the United States, also partakes of this uniqueness, especially regarding French-English relations. In the next section, particular problems raised in this specific area of French-language advertising by the nationalism of the Quiet Revolution will be discussed.

ADVERTISING AND THE QUIET REVOLUTION

Advertising is closely linked to many segments of Quebec society. Its ties are close with industry, popular culture, problems of U.S. economic power, new occupational areas, English-French relationships, consumer and professional associations, and the symbolic aspects of language as well as mass media. As such, advertising serves as an excellent key to social change. In the review to follow of advertising content and the Quiet Revolution, the links concerning English-French relationships and language symbolism are especially noteworthy.

Advertising before the Quiet Revolution.

National advertising in Quebec, like other industry, was introduced primarily by English Canadians and Americans. The general policy was to take an English ad which had been very carefully developed by an advertising agency and turn it over to a translator for a quick more or less literal French translation. The ads were then placed in French media selected by not very knowledgeable English Canadians. Translation was not considered a difficult matter. A French-Canadian reminisces:

> The French specialist in an advertising agency was a young chap who knew English well and who came from Quebec. They gave him a little corner with a typewriter on his knees and a pile of texts to translate. They said to him; "My boy, translate that, translate that, and translate that." This fellow couldn't be himself at all. On the contrary if ever he tried to interpret instead of doing a foolish translation, he was in danger of losing his job.[12]

Over the years, many French-Canadian translators and clerks, through working in media and advertising agencies, learned the advertising business and moved into supervisory and executive positions. In the 1950's, these French Canadians who were making their way began to argue that French Canada had a distinctive culture and that the translated ads were not effectively communicating the message. Minor changes were sometimes made in translating English ads: A girl at a typewriter, identified in an English ad as Betty, became Blanche in the French; an ad for coffee included in the French version, *préparé à Québec;* an automobile ad that gave the total price in English referred to a time payment plan in French. But on the whole, few such changes touched on basic themes, styles, or personality differences.[13] The French Canadians now argued that new original ads should be developed, directed to the values, interests, and dispositions of the French-Canadian public.

The first such significant opportunity came during the Korean War in 1951 when the Department of Defence sought an increasing number of French-Canadian volunteers. A small group of French-Canadian advertising men were permitted to develop a series of ads associated with traditional French-Canadian culture and values. In selecting the themes, the director of the group, Yves Bourassa, observed:

> The French-Canadian people are proud of two things. Proud that they have survived and not been assimilated like the people in Louisiana . . . and proud of their ancient ancestry in this country.[14]

The ads therefore "turned back to the heroes of the past", to the heroic explorers, settlers and pioneers of New France. Separate campaigns were developed for the navy, army, and air force all of which associated the traditional and patriotic values of French Canada with modern-day military services. To attract recruits to the navy, the ads referred to the

---

[12] F. Elkin, "Advertising in French Canada: Innovations and Deviations in the context of a Changing Society", in *Explorations in Social Change,* eds. G. Zollschan and W. Hirsch (New York: Houghton Mifflin, 1964), p. 529.

[13] F. Elkin, "A Study of Advertisements in Montreal Newspapers", *Canadian Communications,* No. 1 (1961), pp. 15-22 and 30.

[14] *Marketing,* October 18, 1952.

sailors and fishermen of Britanny and Normandy who founded Canada. One ad headed with "Partons . . . la mer est belle" was illustrated by the drawing of a ship and a famed ship captain Salaberry who commanded several ships in New France from 1735-60. Said the ad in part,

> Several of our ancestors were brave men of the sea. It is not surprising that so many *Canadiens* have an inherent taste for a life at sea and adapt to it as easily as fish . . . The life of the sailor is the true life of a man!

The ads for the army above all emphasized the pride in and necessity of defending the French-Canadian home and heritage. In one ad, a mother was smiling at her baby in a crib; in the background, a cross was seen hanging on the wall. The heading "Béni fut son berceau" — Blessed was his cradle — was followed by:

> The Canadian home, temple of the family, crucible of future generations that we wish to be healthy, strong and free. This family, and everyone within it whom we cherish — wife, sister, mother, grandparents and children — are today threatened by the greatest affliction of the century, the godless, an enemy as cruel as he is insidious.

The theme of the air force ads sought to establish a link between the old *coureurs des bois,* the early French explorers of the forest, and the modern men who fly and handle the planes. In both instances, the men were courageous pathfinders, each appropriate to his time. One ad referred to an explorer Nicolas Perrot and showed a group of canoes shooting the rapids. The heading quotes a line from a well known French-Canadian romantic poet Louis Frechette: "Que d'exploits étonnants, que d'immortels héros" — Such astonishing feats, such immortal heroes.

This entire campaign, it is reported, was an outstanding success; it led to an increase in the number of French-Canadian volunteers and was well received by influential French-Canadians. To the French Canadian in advertising, the campaign was a veritable milestone.

The next step for the French Canadians was to carry the principle over to the marketing of commercial products. Labatt's Brewery took the lead. During 1957, Labatt developed a new campaign for an anniversary "50 ale", known in French as "Bière 50". The English campaign stressed the "modern" touch with scenes of golf, social activities, etc.; the campaign in French featured a short stocky French-Canadian lumberjack, Monsieur Cinquante, wearing a checkered shirt partially covered with a large number 50. Monsieur Cinquante became the symbol of "Bière 50". A few French Canadians appropriately dressed walked the streets giving out fifty-cent pieces. A Monsieur Cinquante also appeared on television commercials discussing such topics as hunting and fishing in Quebec. In advertisements in the French language edition of *Readers Digest,* Monsieur Cinquante was shown in cartoon fashion scoring a spectacular hockey goal and rescuing a drowning skater while holding on to a cliff with one bare hand. The copy likewise sought a French-Canadian identification referring to the beer "brassé dans le Québec au goût du Québec". Company executives reported that the campaign was a great commercial success.

While the Monsieur Cinquante campaign was in full swing, Labatt was developing still another with a unique French-Canadian touch on a subject of popular and fascinating interest to French Canadians — genealogy. We may, with certain qualifications, trace back the 5 million French Canadians in Canada today to the 10,000 or so French settlers who arrived in New France in the sixteenth century. Thus the same family name, following the male line, is likely to be held by thousands of families today; in some instances it is estimated 35,000 or more.

The interest in genealogy among French Canadians has always been linked to the glory of French Canada's early history. The popular historians portrayed the early settlers as courageous, valiant, and hardy pioneers who, under great hardship, cleared the forest, hunted wild animals, fought the Indians and the English, and tilled the land. The French Canadian was taught almost from the cradle to feel pride and honour in his ancestors.

Labatt, taking advantage of its French-sounding name and the fact that a Labat (sic) was a settler in New France, launched a campaign entitled "Vieux noms du Québec". A genealogist traced back the ancestry of those French Canadians whose names are most common in Quebec today, obtaining for each original settler information on the region of origin in France, the occupation and place of settlement in New France, the partner and date of marriage, and number of children. A brief biographical sketch along with a pen-line drawing depicting the man at his task, for example fighting Indians or sailing a ship, was prepared, then placed as an institutional ad in Quebec newspapers and offered to anyone who had the same name.

The copy almost always referred to the settlers' numerous illustrious descendants and, like the campaign of the armed forces, appealed to the tradition and heroic glory of the French-Canadian past. The style of the biographies was invariably flowery and embellished. For example:

> The name of Morin known throughout the province calls forth the courage and qualities of the soul so well illustrated by the original settler. Through the devotion they give to their tasks, the many descendants of Noël Morin continue to enrich the social world of Quebec.

Labatt considered the campaign to be an enormous success. A spokesman reported:

> Believe it or not the letters arrived by the thousands. The first year we received 10,000 letters for the names Tremblay and Bouchard and to my great surprise while visiting relatives I would see the page from Labatt's framed and hung in the kitchen in the place of honour besides the Sacré-Coeur. . . . it was an extraordinary publicity for us.

Other French Canadians in advertising looked to French Canada's folk heritage for distinctive themes. One series of radio commercials for a breakfast cereal employed a jingle to the tune of "Cadet Rousselle". Others in the late 1950's were adapted from traditional folk songs. For example the following skit, sung to the tune of "Mon père m'y marie" concerned a husband reluctant to get out of bed:

FEMME: Jérôme! . . . mais lève-toi donc, Jérôme!
                Ma mère me l'avait dit
                C'est le plus paresseux des hommes.
                Pour le sortir du lit
                Te faudra du Chase & Sanborn.
HOMME: Quel est ce bon arôme?
FEMME: En s'éveillant cria mon Jérôme.
HOMME: Chase & Sanborn, ça c'est du café.
FEMME: C'est le café des bons déjeuners!

Another radio commercial to the tune of a folk song "Boum Bodiboum" went as follows:

A woman sings: J'ai un marie fidèle
                     Qui ne voudrait pas me quitter d'une semelle.
                     Mais quand vient la vaisselle
                     Finie la lune de miel!
                     Mon chéri s'envole à tire-d'ailes.
                     Ah, s'il connaissait le Surf Bleu
                     Il me reviendrait tout joyeux.
                     C'est si gentil, faire la vaisselle à deux
                     Avec le nouveau Surf Bleu.
                     Un petit trempage.
                     Un petit rinçage,
                     Et tout brille,
                     Tout scintille.
                     Y a rien de mieux pour laver la vaisselle
                     Y a rien de mieux
                     Que Surf Bleu!

Thus French Canadians in advertising even before the Quiet Revolution were sometimes allowed by their English superiors to develop their own campaigns. What is striking, however, in all those campaigns is that the content harks back to the French-Canadian past and traditional values. The heroes were the explorers and pioneers of two centuries ago; the lumberjack was an admired folk figure; the songs stemmed from childhood or an idealized rural past. These were the themes learned in the schools and around the hearth. None in the slightest way suggested any threats to the powers that were in French Canada or to the superordinate English. The military advertisements for example did not mention the fate of the French language or culture once recruits were accepted into the armed forces and the lumberjack ad did not observe that he was an unskilled manual worker in the employ of the English. The ads were all backward looking, pre-revolutionary and non-threatening.

Advertising during the Quiet Revolution.

Like other French Canadians, those in advertising were deeply emotionally involved in the Quiet Revolution. They were eager to make whatever contribution they could which, within their own particular sphere, meant fighting for more French-language advertising, more attention to the quality of the language itself, and more original campaigns. But while thus fighting for the Revolution, they did not wish to endanger their chances for successful careers in English-controlled companies. Herein lay a dilemma. If they fought too vigorously on behalf of the Quiet Revolution with its anti-English overtones, they jeopardized their chances for successful careers; on the other hand, if they did not, they were not contributing to the Revolution or receiving the sought-for recognition from fellow French Canadians. Ideologically, the French Canadians in advertising agencies resolved this dilemma by continuing to fight for French-language advertising and at the same time stressing their "expertise" and their acceptance of the English Canadian's advertising ideology. Practically, they promoted ideas which presumably were both appropriate to the spirit of the Quiet Revolution and effective in increasing sales.

Such themes were found above all in references to nationalism and ethnic identity. To French Canadians, such ads presumably demonstrated a respect for their sentiments and loyalties; to English Canadians, they were appropriate techniques for attracting emotionally involved consumers. Dozens of English-controlled companies in one way or another tried to identify their products or companies with something French-Canadian. In some cases, this meant only minor modifications of English ads; in others, it meant new ads written specifically for French-language audiences. These advertisements with a French-Canadian ethnic identification may be classified under six general headings.

Language Idiom. Since language above all manifestly distinguishes the French from the English Canadian, any ad in French may suggest an ethnic identification. However, over the years, French Canadians have become accustomed to reading and hearing mass media, including advertisements, in their own language; thus French, in itself, is taken for granted. But ethnic identification through language can still be expressed by slogans and twists of common expressions which suggest membership in the group. Old Type Syrup adopted the idiomatic "c'est bon en sirop"; Paarl wines advertised "je paarl, tu paarl, il paarl", a twist of the conjugation of the verb *parler;* Jello turned, "J'ai l'eau à la bouche", meaning my mouth waters to "Jello à la bouche"; Coca Cola adopted "Il y'a de la joie", the title of a popular song to accompany an advertising theme of light hearted happiness; and Dupuis Frères department store pulled no punches in calling itself, "le plus grand magasin du Canada . . . à l'accent français". Some companies sought an ethnic identification by replacing English names of products with their French translations: "Mr. Clean" became "M. Net"; "Red Kettle" soup became "Chaudron rouge"; and "Mr. Salty Pretzel" became "Capitaine Bonsel Bretzel".

Adopting French-language slogans, however, can have its dangers. Pepsi Cola translated its English "Think young, think Pepsi" to "pense 'jeune', pense pepsi". In French grammar, as in English, a verb should be modified not by an adjective but by an adverb. So "pense 'jeune' " violates grammatical rules. In English, advertisers are allowed a certain license (Few objected to "Winston tastes good like a cigarette should"), but such license in French, especially in the context of the Quiet Revolution, shocked many French language purists and intellectuals. To some, the continued use of "pense 'jeune' " served as a prime example of the disdainful attitude of English companies.

Association with the Province. To French Canadians, the Province of Quebec is more than a geographical and political jurisdiction; it is a symbol. For generations, they have identified with the Province and have spoken of themselves as *Les Québecois*. The Quiet Revolution reaffirmed this identification both politically and culturally — politically in the demands of the Separatists and strong nationalists for political and economic power and culturally in the support given to French-Canadian education, cultural developments, and the improvement of the language.

Even before the Quiet Revolution, some English-controlled companies suggested an identification with French Canadians by referring to Quebec on their labels or in their advertising. Thus we observed that Labatt's beer was "brassé dans le Québec", and Maxwell House coffee was "préparé au Québec". Following the Quiet Revolution such references became more common. On radio, Maxwell House coffee was "fait ici même dans notre belle province"; O'Keefe's ale was more and more popular "au pays du Québec"; Schenley's OFC whiskey was "distillé au Québec"; Molson's ale was "la préferés du Québec", and their Laurentide beer was "un produit de chez nous"; and "les 'gars' du Quebec" buy more Bols gin than all others put together. Products everywhere were popular "chez nous" or in "la belle province".

Association with Traditional and Popular Culture. During the Quiet Revolution, some companies still referred back to traditional folk characters and tunes to establish an ethnic link. But the general context was so different that the symbols did not have the meaning or implications of earlier decades.

Nescafé, for example, adapted a French-Canadian folk tune, "I Go to the Market", for a television skit. In the skit, a storekeeper and customer dance around and sang, even including certain English words of the original song. But the manner of the characters and music was such that no subordinate status or backward look could be inferred; rather the skit was affirming a traditional theme in a modern context. The commercial was so well viewed in fact that in December 1960 it won an award from the French-Canadian Publicité Club.

Molson's, in advertising its Laurentide Beer, employed a traditional symbol of French Canada — a rooster — and other companies at various times displayed the *fleur-de-lis* emblem. But such symbols were accepted during the Quiet Revolution as legitimate images of a distinctive and active French Canada; they were not symbols that French Canadians were seeking to hide or forget.

Themes associated with traditional culture were used less often than themes associated with popular culture. Some advertisers, in the style of English Canada, appealed directly to children. Most active among this group was the Quaker Oats Company which introduced the breakfast cereal "Capitaine Crouche" as a counterpart for its English "Cap'n Crunch"; and later a cereal "Tintin", named after a famed French cartoon character. Tintin was well known to French-speaking children as Mickey Mouse and Donald Duck were to the English.

In one way or another, numerous advertisers sought ties with popular culture. Kuyper Gin called itself "le campagnon de la bonne humeur" and displayed a picture of Monsieur Bonhomme, the well-known symbol of the Quebec winter carnival. O'Keefe Beer showed a picture of a man on a go-cart with the heading "On sait s'amuser au Québec". In a television commercial for a Chinese restaurant, a Chinese man spoke French with a Chinese accent. An automobile company presented a television commercial which referred to Séraphin, a prominent miser of French-Canadian soap opera.

It would be incorrect to say that these ads with references to traditional or popular culture harked back to the status of the past. In the context of the Quiet Revolution, the French Canadians continued to use certain historic symbols, but the symbols were not defensively affirmed. They were not so much signs of subordination or isolation as they were an assertion of difference. The particular commercials cited were not nationalistic in any strict sense of the term but they did point to a distinctive French-Canadian culture and continued to set French Canadians apart from English.

Association through Persons, Anonymous and Identified. Many advertisements of national companies display pictures of people; in most cases, unidentified models. In such instances, the same pictures are likely to be used in English and French-language advertisements, sometimes appropriately, sometimes not. Less often the ads name particular people. As we might expect, if these ads are prepared by English-Canadian agencies, the people named are likely to be English Canadian. When only the words are then translated into French it is possible that the specific message is appropriate to the French-language audience but the particular persons referred to are not. Perhaps, by their names, they represent the English-Canadian world and are difficult to identify with. Perhaps they are relatively unknown and carry no prestige among French Canadians. Indeed, in the context of the Quiet Revolution, French Canadians might well resent attempts to influence them with such English-Canadian symbolism.

As we observed, some English-Canadian companies recognized this problem even before the Quiet Revolution and made appropriate substitutions in French-language ads. Thus car buyer Jim Roberts became Jacques Robin and the Bell telephone testimonial was given by "le bon employé" Jacques Langlois.[15]

Following the Quiet Revolution, the technique of substituting French for English persons became more common. An English ad for Black

---

[15] Elkin, "A Study of Advertisements".

Horse Ale tells why Cliff Egerton switched his brand of beer; the French ad tells the same story for Jean Charbonneau. A Mutual Life Insurance Company ad cites a M. Lalonde in explaining its mortgage insurance plan and the Bank of Nova Scotia shows teacher René Martin borrowing money. A Canadian government ad in 1966, explaining its new five letter name code for income tax forms, shows a taxpayer saying, "My friends call me Murph"; the French language ad, showing a different picture presumably more French Canadian in appearance, begins "Je m'appelle Thibodeau; 'thibo' pour les intimes".

Testimonials were considered especially effective in French Canada. Actor Guy Hoffman did a commercial for Maxwell House Coffee; Sports announcer Roger Baulu did one for Bell Telephone; hockey star Henri Richard gave hockey tips for a Ford Motor Company long-playing record; radio-television actor Père Gidéon helped sell O'Keefe beer; Imperial Oil for its "Hockey Night in Canada" commercials replaced English service station attendant Murray Westgate by Philippe Robert; and such well-known announcers as Henri Bergeron, Jean Desbaillets, Jean Rafa, and Pierre Nadeau gave radio commercials for Rambler Automobiles, Hygrade Products, A & P, and Pepsi Cola, respectively. Innumerable examples could be cited.

In all these instances the advertisers are trying either to forestall reactions against an alleged "anglicizing" of French Canada and/or to establish a basis for easier identification and thereby presumably greater receptivity to the intended message.

Association with Current Progress. A major theme of the Quiet Revolution was modernization. The leaders in French Canada, in and out of government, were actively seeking to make up for the many years of relative stagnation. Social reform, development, and progress were keywords of the day. This ideology served as still one further device through which English-controlled companies sought association with French Canada.

A few companies spoke of their factories in Quebec. The Moore Business Form Company displayed a large picture of a new plant and Gage Envelope Company discussed its factories in an ad headlined "Fabriqués au Québec". General Motors, when its factory opened in Quebec, showed a picture with hundreds of its French-Canadian employees and the headline, "Ils ont construit les premières Québecoises" — They built the first Quebec cars. Perhaps best illustrating this general approach were the ads of the Moore Company in which they discussed, along with pictures, the successful operations of French-Canadian owned companies, One ad, for example, included a picture of a M. Benoit Beauregard, President of La Compagnie Québec Poultry Ltée., and a story of his successful aviculture business. Another showed a M. Germain Bombardier, President of l'Auto-Neige Bombardier Ltée. and manufacturer of the Ski-doo. The ad was headlined, "Nous mettons les idées en marche" — We put ideas into action — and discussed the company's rapid and successful development, the ad ending, as we might expect, with a plug for Moore business forms. Molson's Breweries used the same device with an ad showing a M. Georges Couture whose company manufactured blades for ice skates. The accompanying headline was "Une vignette du Québec dynamique".

Pepsi Cola sought to take advantage of the dynamism accompanying the Quiet Revolution by substituting for its English "Come alive, you're in the Pepsi generation", the phrase, "Oui, ça bouge en notre génération Pepsi"; "ça bouge", meaning that things are moving, was a phrase identified with the Quiet Revolution.

Direct Appeal to Ethnic Identification. English-Canadian and American controlled companies had one major handicap in any campaign appealing to ethnic identification — they were not French Canadian. They could not therefore, adopt the strongest argument of all, the one with anti-English overtones which said, "Support your fellow French Canadians, build French-Canadian industry." This argument was closely associated with a strong *Buy Quebec* movement revived during the Quiet Revolution by the Conseil D'Expansion Economique Inc. and supported, at least in its own purchases, by the provincial government.

Some French-Canadian companies adopted this theme in their advertisements. One read: "La seule entreprise canadienne-française de machines distributrices automatiques." Another, a liquor company, advertised "l'équipe totalement canadienne-française", and "véritablement canadienne-française", and a flour milling company affirmed its French-Canadian character by naming and displaying pictures of its senior personnel. The strongest case of all was made by a company launching a new cigarette *La Quebecquoise*. Seeking a foothold in a market dominated by English companies, the directors argued that they were helping to build a French industry. Their publicity says:

> The name of the only French-Canadian cigarette has a history. It is inspired by one dominant idea, to bring together in Quebec the human and financial resources associated with tobacco.

In magazine articles, the appeal to patriotism with its anti-English overtones were expressed much more directly and strongly. Citing two such articles:

> Even though the cigarette market was saturated, the founders formed La Société des Tabacs Québec Inc. and made an agreement with the only manufacturer of French-Canadian tobacco, Tabacs Trans-Canada Ltée. Thus the team was formed — the battle begun — the little David was going to afffront the large Goliath.[16]

> Offer a Québecquoise . . . Not only from your desire to give pleasure, but also to affirm the ties that bind together the French-speaking citizens of Quebec, to assert the pride of our nationality, to dedicate a symbol, to spread everywhere a rallying sign for our common purpose of throwing off the yoke of servitude which has lasted all too long. Certainly in itself the appearance of a new brand of cigarette is an everyday affair. But the appearance of *La Québecquoise*,

[16] Pierre Marchant, "La Québecquoise: phénomène unique au Canada", *Actualité*, December 1962, p. 10.

viewed as a symbol of the liberation of an entire people, an act of defiance against an outdated suppression, takes on national significance. And it is so that we should welcome *La Québecquoise* — a banner in the breeze, every hour of every day. Long live *La Québecquoise.*[17]

For the English company, the nationalistic campaign, at least in its extreme form, had its risks. In 1963, Dow Breweries with a great to-do launched a new beer named Kébec with strong nationalist overtones. The advertising campaign spoke of the historical derivation of the name; stressed the link with Jean Talon, a famed figure of history and the first director of a brewery in New France; and displayed a new trade mark with a banner resembling the flag of Quebec. French-Canadian separatists and nationalists reacted so strongly against the advertisements, accusing Dow Breweries of scandalously exploiting the Quebec flag and insulting the Quebec population for commercial reasons, that the company was forced to withdraw the entire campaign.[18]

Our discussion of advertising themes and the Quiet Revolution would seem to have greater direct relevance to an analysis of social change than of mass media. But the discussion does help clarify certain characteristics of Canadian mass media, especially in so far as the media are part of a larger context.

Those aspects of the media which are strongly affected by the physical geography of the country and the overpowering proximity of the United States are slow to change; the problems of cost, regionalism, and Canadian identity and content persist as before. Those characteristics of the mass media however which center around English-French relationships have, especially in Quebec, been directly affected by the turmoil of the Quiet Revolution.

The mass media in French Canada played a major role in spreading the word about the Quiet Revolution and, as our study of advertising themes shows, directly reflected changes in values and orientations associated with English-French relationships. In the structure of national advertising — in newspapers, magazines, radio, and television — the French Canadians continued on the whole to serve as advisors to the English Canadians and Americans who directed the companies and the advertising agencies. Their advice was now given greater weight than ever before, but they were not rebels. They sought, in line with their own involvement in the Quiet Revolution, to achieve a higher and more appropriate level of French language advertising; but they accepted the basic orientation of the advertising ideology which justified appropriate emotional appeals. Our analysis of advertising content demonstrates that the mass media remain part and parcel of the social movements and the social structure which surround them.

[17] *La Revue Populaire*, December 1962, p. 7.
[18] For a detailed analysis of the reaction to the Kébec campaign, see F. Elkin, "Advertising Themes and Quiet Revolutions: Dilemmas in French Canada", *American Journal of Sociology*, Vol. LXXV, No. 1 (July, 1969), pp. 112-122.

Name Index

208

Subject Index

Agrarian political movements:
comparisons between France, Russia,
and U.S.A., 48-51
in Saskatchewan, 36-51, *passim*
Aklavik, Northwest Territories, 149
Ancien régime:
decline in power of, in New France,
112
in early development of Arctic,
151-56
Apartheid, as part of British colonial
policy of pluralism, 113, 125
Arctic of Canada:
culture contact in early development,
152ff
contemporary social structure in,
159-61
Hudson's Bay Company, in, 155
New Northerners, in, 161
population growth, 157
see also Native populations
Asbestos strike, as consequence of
labour unrest in Quebec, 117
Automation, 92

Basters of South Africa, compared
with Canadian Métis, 132
Black Revolt in U.S.A., 19, 22-24
Bloc Populaire, as reformist party in
Quebec, 116-17
Bolshevik revolution, 31, 48-49
British Conquest of New France
(1759), as beginning of Canadian
pluralism, 113-15
British North America Act, effect on
status of Indians, 135

Canadian independence and nationalism, 11, 16, 28-30, 43, 189
Canadian Pacific Railroad, role in western expansion, 40, 44

Capitalism:
impact on Canadian argarianism, 39,
42, 51
limited success of, in development of
northern industrial communities,
62-85
"oversuccess" of, in U.S.A., 23-24
Catholic Church:
encouragement of immobility among
French Canadian workers, 71-
72, 74-75ff
challenge to, 112, 117-18
conflicts within, 117-18
influence of, in development of northern industrial communities, 63ff
involvement with secular elites, 114,
117-18
Centennial of Canada (Expo '67), as
a turning point, 6, 30
"Chicago-School" sociologists, 56-57
Civil War, in U.S.A., analysis of
causes, 19-20
Colonization and colonial policy:
comparisons between Canada and
South Africa, 130-133
direct rule policy, as encouraging
assimilation, 113-14
indirect rule policy, as encouraging
pluralism, 113-14
settlement policies in development of
northern industrial communities,
62-64ff
Communism, 51
Confederation of Canada:
problems, 43
reasons, 43-44
threats, 36, 123
Confederation of National Trade
Unions (C.N.T.U.), as political
force in Quebec, 121-22

Imperialism:
  in Arctic development, 152
  U.S.A. policy of, 14, 21-22
Indian Act of *1867*, 127, 130, 134, 144
Indian Affairs Branch, Canada, 128,
    134-35, 144-45
Indians in Canada:
  considered as a peasant or working
    class, 137-39
  general situation of, 124ff
Treaties affecting, as coercive, 127
Industrial northern communities:
  class structure of, 66ff
  conflicts within, 68, 74-75
  development of, 55-85
  elite influences, 71-80
  French Canadian ascension to con-
    trol of, 81-85
  Quiet Revolution in, 81-84
  urban-rural contrasts within, 64-71
Industrial revolution, 91-92
Industrialization:
  Canada, 34
  occupational consequences of, 87-99
  U.S.A., 20, 21
Inuvik, Northwest Territories, 149, 160

Keynesian economic theory, applica-
    tion of in U.S.A., 22
Khoikhoi herders of South Africa,
    131-32

Labour unionism:
  in Canada's northern industrial com-
    munities, 64, 72
  in Quebec, 117, 121-22
  in Saskatchewan, 37
  in U.S.A., 14, 20

Mackenzie Delta, Northwest Territories,
    149-156
Marginality, of Canadian Indians and
    Cape-Coloureds, 141
Marxism, 18, 50
Mass media:
  biases, in research on, 166
  comparisons of Canada and U.S.A.,
    169-70, 185-91, *passim*
  development in Canada, problems of,
    185-91
  effects of, 166-67
  general discussion of, 165-205
  need for "Herald" to protect public
    against misuse of, 182-3

political manipulation of, in U.S.A.,
    170-76, *passim*
  private versus public control, merits
    of, 169-72
  Quiet Revolution in Quebec, reflected
    by, 195-205
  selective perception as communica-
    tion barrier to, 166
  theories of, 165-66
  U.S.A. influence on Canadian, 187-91
Maternalism, as policy toward Cana-
    dian Indians, 133
Melting pot, theory of, 27
Métis in Canada, 132-135, 155-56, 160
Metropolis:
  defined, 12
  discussed, 6-32, *passim*
Mexico, as potential revolutionary
    force, 31
Middle class:
  in northern industrial communities:
    English speaking, 77, 79, 82-84
    French Canadian, 76-85
  in Saskatchewan, 34, 36, 40
  in U.S.A., way of life, as general
    norm, 22-23
  see also Social class
Missionaries, relationship to native
    peoples, 153-55

National Farmers' Union, 22
Native populations:
  changes among, 124ff, 152ff
  comparisons between Canada and
    South Africa, 131-145
  consolidation among, 147, 149, 158-
    160
  contact with whites, 131ff, 152ff
  deviance among, 125, 141-43
  divisions between generations, 158-
    59
  intermediaries among, 155-56, 160
  persistent value systems of, 158
  powerlessness among, 137-140, 150-
    51, 159
Nativistic movements, social conditions
    giving rise to, 104, 144, 147,
    149, 158-60
New Economic Policy (N.E.C.), in de-
    velopment of Russia, 49-51
New France, change and conflict in
    evolution of, 109-112
New middle-class, *see* French Canadian
    population

New Northerners, in northern development and social structure, 147-48, 161
"North American Indian Today," *(1939)* Conference on, 126ff

Occupations:
and corporate structures, 89, 95-98
ethnicity and social class ramifications, 86-88, 93-99
immigration policy in relation to, 88, 93-94, 99
obsolescence of, 92-93
proliferation of, 89-91
Organizations, *see* Corporations, Occupations

Papineau rebellion *(1837-38)*, 114
Parti Québecois, le, 119-21
Paternalism, as policy toward Canadian Indians, 128-29, 133-34, 137, 151
Political oppositions:
in Canada, 24-25, 30-31
in Quebec, 10, 19, 29-30, 119-21
in Saskatchewan, 10, 33-51, *passim*
in U.S.A.:
collapse of, 20-23
examples of, 4, 20-23
see also separate listings of parties and movements
Populism, *see* Political oppositions, in Saskatchewan and U.S.A.
Post-industrial society, discussion of, 92
Pluralism:
as a Canadian characteristic, 27, 150
defined, 124, 150
destructive potential of, 124
manifested in the Arctic, 146ff

Quebec:
alternatives in future status, discussion of, 122-23
general evolution, discussion of, 103-123
independence, movements toward, 10, 19, 29-30, 119-123
mass media in, 191-205, *passim*
Quiet Revolution in, 103, 119, 195-205, *passim*
Quebec Act of *1774*, as British colonial policy of pluralism, 114-15
Quiet Revolution, *see* Quebec, Political oppositions, Industrial northern communities

Racism, in U.S.A., 16
Red Paper, by Indians, in response to White Paper, 144-45
Red power, in Canada, 125, 144
Regina Manifesto, 39, 48
Reservation systems:
as causes of ethnic group inequality, 124-25, 129, 137-143
as peasant communities, 137-39
similarities in Canada and South Africa, 132ff, 137-143
"Revolution of rising expectations", 91
Riel rebellion *(1885)*, 44
Royal Canadian Mounted Police, role in development of North, 154-55
Royal Commission on Bilingualism and Biculturalism, 106

St. Henri, lower class French Canadian community of, 121
Saskatchewan Farmers' Union, 39
Saskatchewan Wheat Pool, 36, 39
Segregation:
of French Canadian population in northern industrial communities, 66-70
of Indians, 137, 140-41
Seigniorial estate system in New France, failure of, 109-10
Separatism in Quebec, *see* Quebec, political oppositions in Quebec
Service occupations, proliferation of in post-industrial society, 91-92
Social class:
conflicts in evolution of Quebec, 103-4, 108-10, 112, 114, 116-18, 121-22
conflicts, in history of Saskatchewan, 37, 39-42
differences, in northern industrial communities, 66ff
peculiar aspects of, agrarian societies, 37-39
political aspects of, 37
theories of, 37, 87-88
variations of, in Saskatchewan, 34-35
see also Middle class, Working-class, Northern industrial communities
Social Credit Party (Alberta), formation of, as political opposition, 10, 34, 37
Social scientists, biases among, 16, 17, 104-5, 115-16

213